"Simran's teachings and writings shared ed with a depth of heart, wisdom and love. Thi u-als who desire to access their 'ultimate soul-r ill guide the reader into a deep level of self-mas

—Iyanla Vanzant, spiritual life coach a. m
Broken Pieces, Yesterday I Cried, and *The Value in the Valley*

"As a true creative visionary and transformation catalyst, Simran intimately understands that the journey to love begins with the self. We admire her so much for her honesty, vulnerability and crystal clear vision as she shares timeless principles for cultivating love from the inside out. This book illuminates the path of understanding that embracing the frequency of love is really all it takes to manifest our dreams and desires. That love is really the "secret sauce' to living a joyous and fulfilling life."

—Marcus and Sheila Gillette, authors of *The Soul Truth* and hosts of the "Ask Theo Live" radio show

"The qualities Simran brings to her work—her profession—her spiritual intelligence, and her natural respect to divine teachings make her unique in the field. She is a great treasure."

—Andrew Harvey, author of *The Hope*

"Simran is a force of nature. Her latest book *Your Journey to Love* is a joyful read. Simran will take you on a journey of bliss that you will not forget. Read this book and know that your life has purpose and meaning."

—William Gladstone, author of *The Power of Twelve, Twelve*, and *The Golden Motorcycle Gang*

"Simran is a leader and a visionary who has strong ethics down to her core values. These ethics and values guide her actions. Simran is an inspiration to those around her."

—Marianne Bickle, PhD, associate dean, University of South Carolina

"Simran is a beautiful and dedicated teacher of spiritual wisdom. Her writings and her being are full of love and motivating, empowering energy. Her work resonates because she lives what she teaches and that integration manifests outwardly. *Your Journey to Love* has the formula to create 'the Ultimate Soulmate relationship' every person is seeking, while discovering how to believe in themselves and reach new levels of awareness."

—Amy Zerner and Monte Farber, authors of *The Soulmate Path, The Enchanted Birthday Book*, and *The Enchanted Tarot*

"Simran constantly invites us into her heart, through fragments of poetry, praise, prayer, and song. She invites, invokes, and insists on the need for us to empower ourselves."

—Richard Rudd, author of *The Gene Keys*

"Simran's message is eloquently and beautifully delivered. She embodies the insight of a true Sage. Her venerability and honesty touches the reader in a profoundly moving way. This is a must read for anyone who wishes to transform and awaken more deeply."

—Aleya Dao, sound and energy healer, Light Body Sound Healing Album

"Take every book you have in your library and set it aside. This is one book everyone can read. Simran has a unique way of expressing; in this particular book, how to put people in a certain state of mind, a framework within themselves to have an introspective look. Get this book."

—Steven Hairfield, author of *Twelve Sacred Principles of Karma* and *Metaphysical Interpretation of the Bible*

"Simran writes from a place of true power, vulnerability and honesty. Her wisdom rings out through the pages of *Your Journey to Love* as her information is deep and empowering, while her stories are touching and inspiring. Simran shares from the heart, the higher knowledge that has made a difference in her life, thus awakening the same deep impact on all who read her words. You can trust Simran to steer you in the empowering direction of revealing your True Self."

—Paul Morris Segal, author of *Raising Angels* and coauthor of *How to Get the Man You Want/How to Get the Woman You Want*

"A brilliant student of the Universe, Simran draws upon her years of deep inner work and extensive direct experience to write a razor-sharp, heart-opening, and life nourishing book that promises to leave a "trail of breadcrumbs" for every reader. Simran's life is palpable proof of the magic, miracles and healing that occurs when proper rapport with the Universe is asked for, and received."

—Maureen Moss, 4-time award winning author, international teacher, and global radio host

Your Journey
to Love

Discover the Path
to Your Soul's True Mate

Simran

Foreword by Iyanla Vanzant

NEW PAGE BOOKS
A division of The Career Press, Inc.
Pompton Plains, NJ

YOUR JOURNEY TO LOVE

EDITED BY JODI BRANDON

TYPESET BY EILEEN MUNSON

Cover design by Amanda Kain

Printed in the U.S.A.

To order this title, please call toll-free 1-800-CAREER-1 (NJ and Canada: 201-848-0310) to order using VISA or MasterCard, or for further information on books from Career Press.

The Career Press, Inc.
220 West Parkway, Unit 12
Pompton Plains, NJ 07444
www.careerpress.com
www.newpagebooks.com

Library of Congress Cataloging-in-Publication Data

Simran.
  Your journey to love : discover the path to your soul's true mate / by Simran; foreword by Iyanla Vanzant.
      pages cm
  Includes index.
  Summary: "Are you ready to meet your soul's true mate? The greatest quest in life is to love and be loved. Love continually reveals everything unlike itself. Through self-discovery, real connection, and communion, the relationship that unfolds is the greatest love of all. Your Journey to Love is a guiding path along the inner road to true love, revealing how to: *Live in celebration of your magnificence as you discover you are "in the experience of Love" *Embrace living in the field of compassion and detachment as you become aware you are "of the experience of Love" *Anchor in the knowing that you are "with the experience of Love" in every moment. *Engage your complete presence as you learn to breathe, walk and express "as the experience of Love" When you discover the hidden gems within Your Journey to Love, the face of your soul's true mate will be revealed clearly"-- Provided by publisher.
  ISBN 978-1-60163-348-4 (paperback) -- ISBN 978-1-60163-413-9 (ebook) 1. Soul mates. 2. Love--Religious aspects. 3. Spiritual life. I. Title.

BF1045.I58S56 2015
177'.7--dc23

2014041687

 In Dedication To...

Simmi,

My soul's true mate,

in every place you sat,

in every emotion you have held,

in every lost moment and sacred step,

in every story you wrote,

every perception,

and belief.

I

Love you,

am eternally grateful,

incredibly honored and proud.

In awe of your strength and stamina,

perpetual persistence,

expansive expression,

and infinite

creativity.

❧ In Devotion To... ☙

The essence and experience of the Lover and BeLoved within,

In sacredness and truth...

Fully acknowledging and deeply appreciating the blessing of each
piece of the self,

in return to the peace of Oneness.

We each are individuations of the One Divine.

In Love, Of Love, With Love, As Love

Lighting and Lightening as the way, in truth and for aliveness

Always and In All Ways,

Simran

Contents

Journey of Essence
217

Foreword

Dear God, I pray that you open my heart and fill it with Love.

—Iyanla Vanzant

You want to ignore it, but you can't. You want to call it something else, but every time you get that gnawing feeling, that empty feeling in the pit of your stomach...you know. You know your behavior has gotten you into trouble...again. You've been repeating your patterns, telling your stories, doing your thing. You've been acting desperate...acting needy. You've been giving more than you had to give, settling for less than you needed or wanted. And now, you feel alone, angry...stuck and afraid...guilty and ashamed. It doesn't have to be that way. You just want to be Loved. That's what we all want: to be Loved, totally and unconditionally.

We want to be valued and honored, held and heard, understood and respected—no matter what we've done, where we've been or how we've gotten to where we are right now. We all just want to be Loved.

Our souls long to be joined, one soul to another soul for the sake of Love. The voice of Love...it's calling out to you. It's whispering gently into your heart reminding you, "I'm here for you. I Love you just as you are. Everything you need, want and desire is right here."

Love recognizes the jewel that you are, right now. Love wants to hold you...comfort you...lift you...right now. And you know what, you don't have to work to get Love. Now, it's time to work on *you*. It's time to work on your heart... your mind...your behavior...your false notions about Love that have caused the hurt...the pain...the confusion...that you blame Love for. And while you're working, Love will not leave you. Love will not dishonor you. Love will not take anything from you. Love will fill you. Love will protect you. Love reminds you that the voice of God is whispering to you from within yourself. God wants you to know he Loves you because God is Love.

In the meantime, tell Love where you hurt, why you hurt, how you got hurt, and Love will heal you. Love is speaking to you, calling to you. Is it time to listen; is it time to recognize Love's voice? How will you know? Oh, you will know! Because, the sheep always know the voice of the shepherd; and the shepherd knows how to take care of the sheep.

Love is there for you...caring for you...listening to you...wanting you to receive its gift. Just open your heart, and God will Love you, because he always has.

Simran Singh's teachings and writings shared in *Your Journey to Love* are filled with a depth of heart, wisdom, and Love. This is a *required* course for individuals who desire to access their soul's true mate. This step-by-step process will guide any reader into a deep level of self-mastery through self-Love.

Iyanla Vanzant

Spiritual Life Coach and Technician,
OWN-TV's *Iyanla Fix My Life*

Author, *Peace From Broken Pieces,*
Yesterday I Cried, and
The Value in the Valley

❧{ Journey of the Soul }❧

The Invitation

I have walked the extreme edges of what many *believe* Love to be; sadly mistaken by what was bought into. Only in willingly recognizing we have no idea what Love really is, are we able to be in devotion to the discovery of Love's heights and depths of, for, and with the Self. *True Love* is willing to be, do, and experience everything unlike itself, in the purest expression of unconditional Love for the Whole Self—The Holy Self.

This book holds a deeply buried truth, an ancient knowing held by every great Master. It is written in the language of the soul—experience, contemplation, prayer—to align with your places of heart fullness, mind fullness, will fullness—breath. It is intended to relate to where you are now, what you hold inside, and what remains that is asking to be absorbed.

This path is inviting you to gain a greater perspective of the identities you have locked yourself into and the greater space of "I-ness" that you actually are. You are multifaceted but have become entranced and beholden to only one view of your bejeweled Self.

Within the facets of your sacred incarnation, discover the perfection of each moment of your life and the beauty of every experience you have had. The face of your soul's true mate will be revealed. Through the ultimate path of devotional experience and expression, open to becoming a humanitarian for your inner world and Love catalyst in the outer world, as a sacred activator and avatar, bringing wholeness and Holiness to every circumstance, experience, and union.

I have walked the path of Self-Love consciously for the last two decades, albeit many times slowly, and not-so-lovingly. This experience of *Your Journey to Love* will integrate many pieces of the heart and wisdom. But this book is more than that; it is a living and breathing experience of each one of us, because we are the same. This ancient drumming that courses within the great heart is what links us. This writing holds the secret to truly opening the heart because it depicts the greatest Love story of all time—that which is deeply embedded in the Light and Dark of experience.

We are in the age of Kaliyuga, known in ancient Indian scripts as the darkest time in history, where there is deception, denial, and challenge. It is a time that is inviting us back into an age of Truth, but in order to go there, we must face what we have desired to turn from. This writing is an opportunity for something real, and its strength is in your vulnerability. Come in from an open-minded place of celebration for all that is Dark and Light. It will be bold, scary, and beautiful, all at the same time. It may cause discomfort. You will have sighs of relief and your breath will be taken away. The time has come to claim what has never been claimed, celebrating what society would never fathom placing in a spotlight.

You will come away embodying a deep reverence for all of life, softly smiling, standing taller, and being openly willing to be fully present to own your secrets and shadows. I write this book, first and foremost, for me. It is my catharsis, as I choose to die to whom I have been, in order to illustrate the all-ness available to each one of us. My gift to the world is in being an example of vulnerability, truth, and authenticity—one who walks her talk. And one thing I am clear of is that we have all visited the same dark rooms of thought and have available many grand terraces of Light.

I have written this book three times in the last 10 years. This third version of *Your Journey to Love* is the one that gets shared under the Light of grace, and in a perfect time, through the de-Light-Full experience of darkness. The first writing was 10 years ago, at the height of survival through the most painful experiences in my life. The second writing was a year ago, during the greatest fight of my life. Finally, this third rewrite came through the greatest surrender of my identity, with the loss of my two children in August 2014.

My life and all identities I had ever known stopped on a dime. In those moments, I could no longer be the publisher of *11:11* Magazine, or the host of 11:11 Talk Radio. I could no longer be the rebel on the road; there was nothing left within me to serve, inspire, or help anyone. I was no longer the mother I had always been. I no longer knew who I was or why I was here. None of it made sense, and I felt completely invisible. Each day, I could have fallen to ashes and been blown away by the wind, never to rise again. And yet I knew: *I*, the me I had come to know, never would. I had to face it. And, I did. I cried, I wrote, I painted, I walked, I danced—and I cried some more. It was time to bring it all down from the ethers and fully embody all that needed to be felt—all that had never been fully felt.

All that I had been could never be, any longer. It was time to pick up the fragmented pieces that lay across the ground writhing in pain from long-held oppression, suffering, physical abuse, sexual abuse, betrayal, abandonment, and great loss. It was not to put those pieces back together and survive life, but to allow them to be absorbed back into the nothingness in which I found myself. It was an opportunity to truly discover what it meant to Love oneself. It was time to discover what it meant to understand Love had always been present.

I had to let go of everything. Yet, somehow I had to embrace it. I had to let go of the need to understand the pain, deceit, and deception, or a society riddled with corruption and a legal system whose blindfold no longer seemed to serve its true purpose. I had to sink into the hopelessness and helplessness of a world that can be harsh and ugly and cruel—completely lacking of compassion—while at the same time knowing of its beauty and richness and magic. Despite all that had happened in my life, I needed, wanted, desired, and had to believe in truth, justice, and happy endings. But the happy ending, the freedom, the truth was not *out there*; I had to discover it *in here*. Once again, I was to become the student of my own teachings while continuing to walk the narrowing path Home, garnering the precious seeds along the way in order to sow hope, renewed faith, and a new harvest.

Somehow I had to embrace not understanding, not knowing the next step, not seeing which way to turn, not having what felt like my life, my heart, my family—my reason for existence.

Somehow I had to embrace me, which meant all the pain, the guilt, the shame, and the unknown "what ifs." Most of all, I was clear the only thing left to do was breathe and live the mantra I had always spoken: "In Love,

Of Love, With Love, As Love." I had to learn how to give these things to me now, when I and my life felt least deserving of it. I knew I had to Love me, Love those who had been lost, Love those who had been blind, Love those who had been cruel and violent, Love those whom had turned their back, and Love those who betrayed for their own gain.

I have walked every step I am asking you to go. Our details and stories may be different, but the heartbreak and tragedy are the same. Whether your life has been uneventful, or too eventful, pain is pain. I promise, if you're coming from a true place of listening, presence, and openness, you will find a pathway to acceptance, peace, and Self-Love that unites you with your BeLoved—and that is *you*.

This writing is not theory; it has been completely experiential. I have lived the greatest Love affair of all time. I left behind the promise of fairytale Love for the truth of sacred spiritual partnership. I have experienced myself as enemy, stranger, acquaintance, codependent being in a dysfunctional relationship, angel, god, monster, and Lover with BeLoved. We all do. I consciously chose to leave an unloving experience, a life of conformity and constraint, deep trauma, abuse, and shame.

The first step in this journey to the ultimate soul mate involves radical honesty. I am not ashamed to say how unloving or unloved I was for far too long. Will you be courageous enough to drop into the arms of your own shadows and deception? Only then will you see the open doorway of Love leading to your soul's true mate, and the real experience of communion and connection with all other beings. You see, your shadow has always had your back; it is standing behind you, after all. It has also always led the way, appearing as your mirror in everyone and everything you have met.

It can seem unimportant to face oneself, in a bauble-filled world, but it is the only way out of suffering and struggle. I am committed to this sacred experience with you so I plan to bring what we do not face, from both ends of the spectrum. I am not sure what will rise, but here is the promise: I am going to let my heart fall into the vast depths of its longing, into all the nooks and crannies that need to be filled with essence of liquid golden Light, and meander into all the cracks and crevices of my belonging. Before giving each of these identities that wabi-sabi treatment, see the cracks and crevices for the beauty that they are, knowing that they do not need filling or fixing. The Light is not here to seal them up but to bring illumination to the very depths of go(o)dness they offer. I shall take you with me, for we are One. We each have experienced the pain, challenge, and tragedy of life, resting in the *why*, the *how*, the *when*, and especially the *what now*?

These cracks were formed by perceptions, beliefs, and consciousness. Others are involved in their creation, but as "angels of the night," solicited in order to know more of the Self. This is the perfect example of the imperfect hero's journey.

We live by stories—the mythologies of ourselves. We are defined by them, becoming locked inside of them. From these, an even greater story emerges. It is time to stop believing you are your story, a victim of the past, or defined by what happened to you.

Your old story is the most sacred part of your being. It is where the ember sits, that which becomes your brilliance of Light. You have a choice: Remain as the smoldering ember, or allow it to burst forth your brilliant flame. You are a Light-illuminating essence—and when you really move into the expanse of that, only Truth will exist. In order to do so, you must be willing to face yourself: your mind, heart, will, and truth. My intention is to support you in feeling and seeing it, to finally absorb the darkness for alchemy. There is gold in that coal!

You do not have to be in the fire any longer, nor do you need to place your feet against the fire. The time has come to *be* the fire, the full blaze of Divine Glory—the Violet Flame awakened. Let the old story provide filaments that weave together a brilliant beginning. It is time to create a new world experience of aliveness. But, in order to do so, be willing to fully embrace all that is hidden, judged, and held back. In deeply connecting, a true experience of aliveness and freedom will cast ripples of change. Stories are composed of contrasts: Light and Dark, Love and Fear, heroes and villains. These opposites provide value and are in co-creation. Our opposite is the point of real attraction and the point of traction.

Do not rush through the process—the questions, integration, actions, or emotion that needs to be experienced and expressed. You are worth your own time and effort. This is a choice to unconditionally love. What you take from this DNA activation and RNA cleansing, you hold for the rest of your life, and it can never be taken from you. This will feel like work, at times, but it is the most rewarding work you will ever do. It is not for the faint of heart, and none of us are that because we keep getting up. However, we can put an end to being knocked down. You are the best investment you could ever make.

I unconditionally Love, honor, and support every step you take. I am you. As you move through this sacred walk, discover how to truly Love and BeLoved. It is time to receive that forever connection, sharing the unique and rare experience of union and communion with your soul's true mate.

I wish this soulful expression to be an opportunity for all to shed the mask of separateness and the mockery of denial, to finally be free of the illusions trap. May these experiences awaken memories within and my footprints be a guide. May any tears cleanse your wounds of debris and this text be the wrapping of unconditional Love to wed you to your soul's true mate.

I Love you as deeply as I Love myself.

I am, you are, we are the Lover and the BeLoved.

In Love, Of Love, With Love, As Love.

The Lover's Letter

Dear BeLoved,

You were conceived as a Divine possibility and this creation has been intended for you all along. A sacred contract for a moment in time, in order to experience communion. You had to reach a place where you were willing to come-to-union with me. You had to see the extremes of what you believed life and Love to be, and learn how to move through them. Now, this intimate sharing may be of meaning. Open your arms—your mind, heart, and soul for this gift of Love-making. Herein is full-hearted devotion that embraces you completely, holding space for the moments you have fallen into what you thought was Love. The company of heaven has held a sacred vigil for when you rose, time and time again. Wherever you are in experience is Divine and of great measure. Be assured, no Love has been lost.

This is in response to your call. Life may feel challenging in moments, possibly seeming as if there is no way out. This may be the greatest moment of all, where the weight of world rests heavily upon you. The pain can be uncomfortable; even tragic. This, too, is held in the Light of Love's embrace, inviting you out of the shadows of death, and into your brilliance and illumination.

Great Love is courting you, always desiring to shower blessings. This need not be hard, or a struggle. Do not make it so. Simply feel into it, allowing every tear as a sip of holy communion; every cry, a Divine call to heaven; every outburst, an announcement of being closer to Home; each moment on your knees, a bowing into the depths of your own soul; each prostration upon the earth, the soaking in of surrender; and each stand, a rising into the infinite fullness of Love never known before.

Do not rush past. Do not deny this precious moment. There is no way around or over; you must go through. Trust that you really having nothing to lose, for what is truth can never be taken. You are worth your own time and space. Your presence is enough. What you receive now, you hold always. It can never be taken from you. It shall never leave you, forever cherishing you as you are. You need be nothing else, because every piece and part of you is enough.

Do not seek the end; enjoy each step, over every pebble, rock, and boulder; into each valley, climbing every mountain and traversing the full landscape of experience; into each awareness, discovery, and recognition In Love, Of Love, With Love, As Love.

Have no regret. Be open to the wonder that you are. After this courtship, you may surprise yourself—that you would choose to relive every challenge and each obstacle, making all of the same choices to come to this point of awareness and receiving. In a deep inhale, looking back, see the beauty that you are and have been, regardless of dysfunction and chaos. In exalted exhale and embrace of every powerful moment of opening, BE the Lover. You are the BeLoved. All is Oneness.

Intertwined as Lovers in a great romance, this giving and receiving is the ring of engagement to life. Open to the great celebration inside of you and be engaged. This wedding is intimately embellished as every strand and molecule of DNA that is the soulful arranged marriage, created as the space of you, in no time and in the place of no matter.

There is no greater blessing given you than this present moment. There is no more blessed grace you may endow yourself than compassionate presence with your entire experience. My Love, you did the best you could with what you had. You have always been, and are now, whole and complete. Romance with, and in, this remembering of truth. You are a precious jewel and most Divine soul.

Sweetness, you are not in a process of awakening; you are either awake or asleep. There is no in between and no "out there." You have the choice to continue your slumber, fraught with dreams and nightmares, or awaken right now, remaining faithful to yourself for all eternity. Life is "US" as the journey—the courtship—the Love affair of all time.

Holding gratitude, lay tenderly within your sacred space of longing. You would not be who you are, nor could you have grown as you have, with any less than you have known.

*Dear One, how you have played in unfolding fields **of Love** all along. Immersed **in Love,** bringing up everything unlike itself. Know your cries have always been standing **with Love.** What has been hidden? Only you, from yourself. In each step, **as Love,** un-condition your mortal constitution and remove the veil from your sight.*

Be still and Know…

"I am here. I have always been. I never left you. In the perfect moment, you shall turn and see me. In that instant, you will discover that you have been within my embrace all along. I have held each inhale, shallow or deep. I, too, have relaxed into each exhale, regardless of its sigh, frustration, upset, or sense of relief. With every step into and out of the dark, I have walked beside and behind you, with you, leading you, carrying you, and watching over you. From the shadows, I have been fanning the ember of Light resting within. My Love is with you, my Light holds space for you, my knowing is witness to your footprints in the sand. From the lips of the Divine to the ears of the Divine, in Love's unfolding for ever more. In Love, Of Love, With Love, As Love.

I AM."

❧{ Journey of Romance }❧

⚜ 3 ⚜

"Quest I On"

Who is it that YOU have been waiting for?

What have you been YEARNING for in your life?

Where is the ONE person that will be able to love you like no other?

When will REAL love show up?

If you had all the LOVE you needed, who would you become?

What do you have to do NOW for that to show up?

How much love can you STAND?

Every individual on the planet, in this moment, is facing a variety of questions in their lives. All are on a quest for meaning, personal discovery, and life transformation, whether conscious of it or not. In a world that has become harsh, aggressive, and afraid, people seek outward for love and acceptance. Love and money rank in the top two desires for most people, with love being significantly stronger.

Every person desires to find that "ultimate soul mate." According to the U.S. census, there are 100 million active singles in the United States alone. Each one of them is seeking their true soul mate. Because of heartbreak, pain, loneliness, or a need to feel complete, even those who are in relationship wonder, from time to time, if an ultimate soul mate exists beyond their current experience.

A grand awakening is on the cusp for this planet, but cannot occur unless people wake up to themselves. There is a great need for swift and concise understanding of what is beyond the illusion of fairytale Love. In this moment, too many buy into their preoccupation of Love rather than the reality; they are the Love they seek. Regardless of where you are on your journey of Love, you have had hints of your ultimate soul mate's calling.

Are you ready?

Are you willing?

Are you listening?

How much love can YOU stand...to give your Self?

Love is neither a step, nor a process. True Love—Real Love—Unconditional Love—Lover and BeLoved Love is a path, one that goes into depths that few have been willing to travel. The kind of Love I am speaking of never hurts, and continually expands, bathes, cherishes, and holds you. We all have access to it, but few have the courage to have it. It is not black and white, or shades of gray. The essence of pure Love is color and Light, and never disappears. Most people convince themselves they know how to Love. Many may even tell you they Love who they are, but I ask you to be in the inquiry:

How much Love have you made space for?

How much Love can you allow?

Is there a limit to the capacity for giving and receiving Love?

This book is that walk, through the darkest, narrowest passage into the highest chambers of the heart where the soul beckons. Come, BeLoved. Now is the time to feel your way in. Do not be afraid to close your eyes and look inside. Shield your ears to discover the transcendent silence of the innermost parts of you. Step through the doorway and touch the skin of one who has been shrouded in opaque veils throughout time. Come with me, because there is enough Love to go around. True Love is close—closer than we all realize. But, it will require you to make space. It asks you to be big! It beckons you to open expansively to all that is there for you to behold. You carry a lot within the cells of your being. Much has been embedded over time through memories, wounds, beliefs, and patterns. These things must be awakened to so that you embody a space of innocence and reverence to receive love in its purity.

There is a place, tucked and hidden in the land of far, far away. It is in the dark, with treasure buried deeply within the kingdom. We will encounter villains and monsters, and all that has been called wicked and evil.

There may be places that are sharp and jagged, wounds that are deep and still tender. This walk has been put off for too long. As Light is brought onto this old, worn path, a new story may be created.

In a world that is wrought with abuse, deception, violence, disrespect, manipulation, adultery, slavery, oppression, and prostitution, it is easy to fall into the vast chasm of hopelessness. Ironically, that is where we must go. We each need to fall to depths, crashing upon the very rocks that we built up as our lives. And although that great fall makes us appear lifeless and broken, we must not stay there. Each of us must rise again after knowing the tragedy of our own crucifixion. It is essential to taste the nectar of such despair, to be baptized in its tears and heralded by the long-held cries brought forth generation after generation. It is in that place we let go of the illusions and the lies, especially around Love.

This moment is not to anchor into a story of blame, nor is it time to gloss over and affirm our way into a feel-good escape. It is life's long-awaited awareness and atonement of denial and held shame. It is not here to point fingers, or to judge or hurt anyone, including you. It is here—it is to hear and to heal, to see and be seen. It is spoken to uncover the blanket of shame that adorns the world in its slumber, in order to provide possibility if willing to remove the blindfold that hinders the imbalance of justice in life. It is to remove the shackles and chains boring into skin. It is time to lay down the cross you bear and finally wash off the sins that you have continued to carry, despite Christ dying for them. It is to honor the great wounds inflicted by the Self, for the Self, in the powerful romance of the soul.

Does this all sound dreary and depressing, hard and challenging? Do you want to step away, turn your head, let the mind go elsewhere, and find something else to read or do? Wasn't this supposed to be a book about Love? Well, that is exactly what I am asking of you—to truly experience and express Love.

What if you could shift how you experience what we term as dark, negative, hard, and challenging? What if that, too, could be as beautiful as Love, positive, Light, and ease? This path is the bridge of the two. It is the reconciliation point. You have within your grasp and opportunity to completely transmute and transfigure your entire experience. This is the place of alchemical change that is long-lasting and self-illuminating. This is the path to real and true Love forever more.

Most people have no connection to the flow of Love that truly exists. It is painful to look at life and the steps trodden. It hurts at times to remember what we have been through, how we have been hurt, and who deeply wounded us. It is often easy to discount the experiences we have had or emotions that have been held. It is even more difficult to look at the responsibility held in creating the very chaos that has grabbed hold.

These things layer upon one another, creating a great wall that keeps us separate and guarded from the rest of the world—both the world outside of us and the world within us. We rest somewhere in a space between that long and winding road to never-never land. We often find ourselves coming full circle, which brings us right back to the same place again and again. We are not supposed to come full circle; we are meant to go full spiral. Evolution is a spiral, both up and down at the same time. Evolution up the spiral requires involution down the spiral. This is how heaven meets earth. We have been leaping toward a heaven that seems unreachable because we have not grounded into our earthen being. Now ground, ground, ground. Dig deep and uncover the roots of your creations. Your life is a mirror of all that you hold inside.

As cracks form in the walls to the outside, the shadows on the inside become more apparent. It is within the shadows that the series of secret doors lay. These openings take us ever inward to a place far richer than any amount of money, far grander than any outer landscape, and deeper than any ocean. There is a Universe inside that only desires to bathe you in the complete ecstasy of True Love that awaits you as the treasure. Each door may be opened by the same key—that of ever increasing devotion, to the Self. You are the key!

Will you give these things to yourself? Can you be in service to you in this way? We are here to dismantle beliefs. This requires regular walks through the inner landscape. It can appear like a battlefield at times, but has the makings of an epic stroll through Lover's lane. The Love that births only grows, never disappoints, and never leaves.

I PONDER

Gentle soul from a distant time,

You take my breath,

as I slip between the sheets of my mind...

Manipulating life's coverings aligned and misaligned,

I wait and I ponder...when will it be?

I live on anticipation, adrenaline and desire...

I fall, spiraling down...my body in heat and soul on fire.

As you pull away, my heart cries out in despair,

Do you not want me? Will you push me away?

I saw you clearly, in a moment rendering my own eyes blind.

I wait and I ponder...when will it be?

I draw one last breath before I leave your gentle bosom...

Pray for grace in my surrender,

as the dark night descends...I fall into deep sleep.

Pieces of me swirl inside,

I wait and I ponder...when will it be?

I await the soft kiss of my soul's true mate...

Dancing together throughout eternity,

an affair of the mind, a matrimony of the heart,

the most soulful kind,

I wait and I ponder...when will I be?

Dark Knight

I hit bottom and had nowhere else to go. My experience of Love had been completely unloving. Becoming a weak shell of a girl, my innocence was gone, dreams had been broken, and I disappeared. The experience of Love was tainted with something sticky and gooey. It clung to me like black tar and weighed me down as if concrete blocks. I wondered if people could see beyond my masks and glassy eyes. The dark shadows of my countenance held too many secrets. My thin frame spoke of insecurity and inadequacy, disguised in the name of fashion.

The illusion was easily facilitated by wearing unique apparel. I wore clothing so cutting-edge that it distracted attention away from my face and my body. What people could not see were my beaten and bruised spirit, battered heart, and deadening soul. They did not know of the marks, cracks, or breaks. No one knew of the screams, tears, or what the silence held. Perhaps some could see that I was unhappy, but everyone ignored the frightened little girl hiding in dark and scary places, feeling incredibly alone in her own Hell.

Eventually the stress of keeping my experience self-contained would take its toll. I wanted to run as far away as I could, but my steps would be small, at a snail's pace—but in precise time, to the right and perfect place, yet never far enough away. However, there was a gift within all of it. These experiences hurt bad enough to get me seeking—searching for something, anything, everything. I had to make meaning of my painful existence; it needed to make sense to me.

When you live your life stumbling in the dark, you do not know it is darkness; you just figure out how not to stumble. Only when someone lights a match do you realize the contrast between the Light and the darkness you have been surrounded by. Initially, I was led into arms that would, at the very least, bring me back to the land of the living. Their ways would part me from my reality long enough to finally begin questioning it.

Their tenderness would resuscitate and hold me. I will be forever grateful for the space, the silence, and the service of a group of angels on earth. A God Squad, led by Iyanla Vanzant, would hold my tears and begin refilling the vast emptiness in my heart. They were guides and guardians of flesh, each having been in a similar place at a different time. They were adept in the art of midwifing, healing, and refilling "containers" that were once full but had long gone empty.

They could see me as shattered as I appeared to be, and as powerful as I really was. However, there was a deep chasm between the two. Only I would be able to cross the deep valley that was to come. There were not there to save me. Only I could do that. But they started me on my way, placing tools in my grasp and providing a safe place to remember every time the night became dark.

During a week-long intensive, in a powerful breath-work session, a young woman intensely screamed for more than an hour. I briefly opened my eyes, seeing Iyanla speaking with Renee Kizer, a brilliant breath worker and coach in her own right. Iyanla rhetorically asked, "How can that little body hold so much pain?" Renee just shook her head from side to side with the compassion of eyes that had seen this too many times before.

A couple of hours later, I discovered I was that screaming "little body" they had been speaking of. The suppressed pain I held was so intense and traumatic that I left my body while it purged. I spent the next week in bed, my physical body too weary to move from the emotional memory within the cells.

I had gotten used to pain. It was my normal. I hid it well. I lived with it. I tolerated it. I suppressed it—and I buried myself alive, encased within it. I was adept at compartmentalizing the harsh pieces of my life. I worked long and hard to pass time. I knew how to cover it, smile through it, and pretend it did not exist. I kept my head down, eyes focused, continuously multitasking so I did not have to feel—so I did not have to stop and look at anything, especially my life. Despite being in the fashion industry, I had not looked in a mirror in more than two decades. I did not even know what I looked like, nor did I want to see. I was empty, hollow, and numb, broken and deeply wounded.

That day would be the first of many moments where I found myself on my knees, curled in a fetal position or body-to-the-ground. My pain and my shame weighing so heavily on my shoulders, I could not stand. But they, the many angels dressed in white, would get me standing again. No matter what happened, just falling into the cloud-like embrace of one of the "Mamas" was enough to make it all better for a while. They made me look not only at me, but also into me. As I sat in a room with too many other women in their brokenness, holding a tiny cosmetic mirror, I saw nothing—only emptiness. It was not the wide-open kind; it was barren and dark and small.

I had not shed a tear in three decades, having been told at a young age, "If I cried, God would make me cry." So, I didn't. I already knew too much pain. I could not fathom any more than that, so I chose not to test God with any tears. Where had that gotten me? Numb. Hollow. Hard. Cold. Either way, it seemed God wanted me tortured and troubled, dying or dead.

Having to look into the eyes of a scarred face, the dam would hold no longer. As I forced myself to gaze in the mirror, the tears came. I saw how hollow and dead I really was. However, healing waters finally flowed through my portals of precipitation. My windows to the soul had spouted leaks. I realized I was not a completely numb carcass. Those tears gave me the strength to begin facing the God of my understanding who then bore two faces: One face was dark and menacing; that one I feared. That one punished, was harsh, and judged. I desperately desired to know the countenance of the gentle and truly loving one, my Father God and my Mother God, who created and cherished me with endless love.

By the time the God Squad pushed me out the door, I was standing again. I had no idea who now stared back at me from the mirror. She was a stranger, but I could see something in her eyes that looked faintly familiar. The pain was still there and I could see that—but I also saw an ember.

There was a spark that shimmered in certain angles. I had not died. A soft glimmer of Light did rest within "her" dark eyes, in the shadowy caverns of "her" face. I longed to know her. I desired to be friends with her and I had no idea how.

I returned to my facade of life, stepping back into the image of a happy, glamorous, and successful woman. It was easy enough; I had lived it for a long time. But I found the mask was heavier to carry once that I had seen something beyond it. No one knew my experiences, but I was able to move in the world again without them crippling me. My secrets were tucked away, nice and neat. I did not have to acknowledge them. I had regained enough strength to continue holding them tightly to my bosom.

However, I did want to know the woman whose ember I would catch sight of when quickly glancing in the mirror. Little did I realize that my walk back to the living would take a while longer. I had no idea how asleep I had been. The weight would eventually become too heavy to bear. At that point, I could either choose to drop it or let it pull me down. Unknowingly, I chose the latter because I did not know how to let go. I did not want to fail or disappoint. I knew I was "strong" and "tough," falsely believing these were character attributes. Little did I know that my inherent wealth and beauty lay within my vulnerability and softness, two aspects completely unknown to me.

My life certainly tells of a fairy tale, and every fairy tale holds certain elements: a time, a place, a villain, a monster, a fair maiden, Love, and a happily-ever-after. I would begin to discover all of these pieces, the most surprising to be the monster and the fair maiden— who would ultimately become the Lover and the BeLoved.

In my real life happily-ever-after, I discover the experience of True Unconditional Love that is available to everyone and anyone—even you, regardless of what you have been through. Pain is pain; don't ever discount yours. It is here to give you something far greater than you can imagine. You are just in the process of opening the gift; wait until you get inside! You will see that you have been given something beautiful and precious.

COMEDY & TRAGEDY

It seems so serious,
but it really is not.

In a twilight web,
we were believed to be caught.

In some distant place,
where there is no time,
we sit among the stars,
watching a world without reason or rhyme.

My Love,
it's so poetic,
don't you see?

Amidst mountaintops and rainbows,
existed a Love for all eternity.

Walking among the flowers,
dancing upon the shore,
Laugh and cry with me
In this Divine play of comedy and tragedy.

{5}

The Open Door

Where did your idea of Love come from?

Could there be one human being that you are to connect to?

On a planet of 6.9 billion people, is there one who loves you unconditionally?

These were the thoughts that haunted me. They ached deeply inside. No amount of work or play would distract me before the longing would begin again. No other people, amount of money, or degree of shopping—no alcohol, medication, or addiction—no adventure, experience, or achievement would satisfy the hunger of wanting to be completely, utterly loved and cherished. The mind rumbled these themes as my broken heart lay quietly wounded, hoping one day my true soul mate would come.

I grew up hearing fairy tales of love. I was not focused on them; I just remember hearing them. It was enough to imprint my mind with a template for life and romance. Many people subconsciously hope for and seek a prince charming or the beautiful princess. From the time we are young children, we are told fairy tales of love and believe in them, not realizing we are also buying into the story of loneliness, pain, the need to be rescued, and one true love somewhere out there. In the search for the "ultimate soul mate," the fairy tale is re-created in life, again and again.

Like so many others, I continued the cycle of handing down cultural stories. When my first son was born, I bought the complete *Grimm's Fairy Tales* collection. I wanted him to have memories of being read these time-honored stories. What better way for us to bond than fairy tales? I wanted him to believe in happily-ever-after. *I* wanted to believe in happily-ever-after.

I would imagine the name "Grimm" should have been a clue. The stories are grim, to say the least. They do end in a happily-ever-after, but at what cost? The Grimm brothers were projecting, and processing, emotions and thoughts through the fairy tales we have grown to love.

Their own lives and the love modeled to them were anything but a fairy tale, completely lacking of a happy ending. Although the collections of stories published by the Grimms were gathered folklore from various sources, they likely chose ones that resonated with them in some conscious or unconscious way.

Growing up in a household with a successful, busy father and a caring, melancholy mother, they witnessed disconnection and loneliness. Having three siblings who died at birth, a father who died at a young age, the loss of financial security—and witnessing their mother, single with six children and struggling to support the family—leaves an indelible desire for happy endings. They died struggling financially and filled with a sense of the injustice in the world. The fairy tales were their way of coping with outer life, by experiencing an ending they would have happen.

We have done the same thing. Cultural stories, thoughts, and beliefs have been adopted and integrated. We have had proof by watching the relationships around us. After all, they bought into these stories as well. We witness how people treat themselves in relation to life, love, and experience. We see how people treat others, those whom they supposedly love. It is apparent why we have heartbreak, pain, and dysfunction. We just follow the blueprint handed down generation after generation.

The question that lingers in the minds of mass consciousness is *Will I ever Love again*? This typically happens after our first heartbreak, while picking up some baggage on the way out the door. *Will I ever find my ultimate soul mate*? follows, ready to carry that baggage right into someone else's life, someone who has his or her own mismatched set. The problem is that the baggage we have been carrying from the time we were children will affect every relationship we are to have. This continuous accumulation leaves us asking the same questions while piling on more baggage.

In reality, the ultimate soul mate does exist for every individual on the planet. That ultimate soul mate is already here for each person, waiting for the awareness, the recognition, and the acceptance to appear. It requires the removing of the all baggage, which happens to rest deeply inside.

To meet your ultimate soul mate, the ultimate courtship must take place. The Lover and the BeLoved are a union of this world and beyond. In dismantling beliefs, a journey through the inner landscape reveals the intricate beauty of all that is truly natural. Through integration and inspiration beyond all limited or traditional thought, an active courtship is possible where the true soul mate is ultimately revealed. This love that births will only grow, will never disappoint, and will never leave.

Self-Love is the key to the abundance, happiness, and the oneness everyone wishes for. This is an intentional, integrative approach that consciously supports the journey to real love with the ultimate soul mate. Would you be willing to do anything to meet yours? Are you ready? Are you able to accept all the Love that is available to you?

The ultimate soul mate has been with you all along. This soul mate has been with you daily, waiting for your recognition. Your soul mate stares back at you each and every day from the mirror. This one has been loyal and unconditional in its loving. Have you? Will you minimize this connection?

Close your eyes and imagine the type of relationship you wish you could have. Imagine being with that person and how that makes you feel. Imagine being held, caressed, kissed, and communicated with. Envision yourself making Love, laughing, playing together, and being fully present with one another. In your mind's eyes, see the small and large things you would like to do for your partner and for your partner to do for you. Sense, feel, and imagine what being in love looks and feels like.

How do your face, your body language, and your approach appear to the world? What is your attitude and how open do you feel? Imagine the face in front of you begins to change. As you gaze more intently, blinking your eyes, the face becomes clearer and you see your own.

What happens? Are you able to hold the same state, or does it change? For you to have the Love you most desire, you must first give it completely to yourself. You are your true Ultimate Soul Mate. You attract to you relationships and experiences equal to the degree you Love yourself. If you are not completely there, then let's dive in and discover the hidden doorways to your bliss.

Love's Kiss

Are you truly ready? Are you truly willing?

Are you ready to dive into a true experience of Self-Love?

Can you spend minutes, days, hours, and months with you?

Do you feel a soul mate presence waiting for you to notice?

Can you be comfortable in the silence together?

Will you allow a conversation to take place?

Are you going to discount this love?

Can you release past baggage?

Will you ever love again?

The choice is yours.

YOU

are the

union and communion you seek.

The one and only.

YOU.

I.

Fairy Tales

I grew up hearing fairy tales and happily-ever-after enough to imprint my mind with a template for life and romance. We all do. Stories, like all mythology and sacred writing, are holographic representations of the templates for life we choose, simply repeating throughout each of our lives. Every encounter and relationship is this same holography, splitting and expanding until awareness dissolves it back into nothing. Life as art; art becomes life.

Like most little girls, I wanted a prince charming. I wanted to believe in happily-ever-after. From the time we are young children, we romanticize fairy tales and the Love they hold, not realizing we are also buying into their themes of loneliness, challenge, villains, the need to be rescued, and a perceived happily-ever-after. In the search for the Ultimate Soul Mate, the fairy tale is re-created in life, again and again. But, the story is not just a fairy tale; it becomes the tumultuous journey of Love being sought externally. Once entered, we don't know how to get out of the story.

I look at what we have been exposed to through fairy tales and subsequently modeled by the lives of parents, caregivers, friends, television, and movies... In fact, those stories are first embedded within us at very young ages. As children, these become the dreams we hold in our hearts and minds. It is not a wonder the journey to Love is a bumpy ride. Nor is there a question why so many people have issues with communication, trust, connection, and feeling. It is no surprise that we are preconditioned to view men and women in certain ways. What fairy tales do you recall being your favorites from childhood? Now look at your Love relationships. Are they similar in theme?

Somewhere inside, we believe certain elements are necessary to deserve being swept off our feet and carried into the sunset by the Love of our lives. We have bought into the images of the white picket fence, two and a half kids, and a dog running in with the newspaper. Surrounded by images and sounds of heartbreak, in our homes and neighborhoods and on the news, everything outside of us merely depicts the cracks and crevices within us. Even reality television illustrates the grand expanse of illusion that has been bought into. And we support it and watch it, enjoying the "drama." But, we are not Grimm stories any more than a Norman Rockwell painting—and yet we are.

The beautiful truth is that we are perfectly imperfect. The ugly lie is the imperfection of our perfection. These are two sides of the same golden coin. One side faces down into the dark ground; the other is face up glistening in the Light of the sun. One part is denied, while the other is valued. We are always seeking "heads" while denouncing "tails," when it is our very roots that create the wealth of experience and eventual understanding. Our best thinking got us exactly where we are. We must drop out of our heads for true Love to have a chance. It's time to explore the roots that experiences of challenge and heartbreak have grown from.

Aside from the stories we are told as children, we witness our greatest story of all by watching the world that surrounds us. The family story creates an "umbrella" imprint on the psyche. Every decision and experience fall beneath this covering of consciousness until a choice is made to step out into the rain. Only when fully willing to embrace the storm surging within will the sun shine in. Choices, behaviors, and beliefs about love and life are influenced completely by what parents, caregivers, relatives, and siblings show us. Although what they say carries weight, how they live is the real teaching. Reactions and responses, equally illustrated in how they treat themselves and others, are the real teachers of what life and Love become identified as. From these lesser gods we learn how to do Love, life, relationship, and connection.

My mother's childhood was a version of Rapunzel in the castle, as was my dad's—as is my sister's, my brother's, and my own. We are all, including you, imprisoned by the bricks of past belief and conditioning that extends far beyond what any of us know or remember. Cast high into the towers of consciousness, each individual remains in isolation, spinning stories with the yarns of time. In not extending the Self, we do not know ourselves, nor does any other. Remaining isolated and at a distance, the depths of our longing and the heights of our dreams remain in places far, far away.

In letting the hair down, we drop all that is held in the strings and strands of the mind for others to see, grab hold of, and climb aboard. This manner of victim and victimizer, being one in the same, is the greatest illusion of all. We project inherited versions of Love onto all that is outside. This legacy of wounding has been the crown handed down from generation to generation. There is no villain. There is no victim. There is only amazing richness, depth, and beauty in each individual creating their fairy tale Love story of a lifetime.

We are all Sleeping Beauties. In our hearts, we are Peter Pan and Robin Hood, while the wicked sorcerer and band of lost boys live within the mind. All the while, the beast is hiding within the shadows. We are all of it and none of it. These archetypes are costumes adorned as we step across many set designs. I believe we are missing the greatest story of all, the plot twist hidden within each one. It reveals that the wicked and the beastly we fear and want to turn from, actually Loves us enough to be the villain for a story to unfold. It is a Love that is unconditional. This epic saga has the ingredients to be the awakening to true, fulfilling, sustained, and loyal Love.

I was greatly influenced by the fairy tales I had been told, unknowingly passing on the same to my children. Television and movies reinforce them. Our lives are not for entertainment—and they are. But, the story deserves acknowledgment: its beauty, richness and creativity. And, at the same time, we give personal life stories too much weight, getting caught up in them so much that the identity becomes defined and the character is locked in an endless replay. For many it is paralyzing, creating inertia and stuck-ness that feels like moving through quicksand. However, we choose to dive feet-first into that. No one puts us there, although it is easier to believe the contrary because that helps prolong the story.

There are situations and circumstances that happen, in all kinds of beautiful and damaging ways. But in the end, we choose the experience with what is believed and in holding onto stories that are painful. We have the ability to make our own happiness and create our lives. Standing upon the mountaintop, with the forces of nature whipping all around, we are the wizards of Disney's *Fantasia*, casting forth the magic of our sound, light, and color magically manifesting forms upon forms. From nothing we create something. An idea, creative inspiration, feeling, and desire; sparks fly, the music crescendos, and forms are created in our own image. We become gods of our own destiny, knowingly or unknowingly, through the sheer force of will and inspiration.

There is always an opportunity to create a new story. Life is beckoning for one that is more consciously aware and completely present. The new story cannot have the old you. And, you are not supposed to know the new you. That is the surprise—the magic—the unknown Divine willing itself to become known. Every good story has these elements of creation: exposition (intent), conflict (disharmony), and resolution (harmony). Earth is the land of opposites, creating the experience.

Witness the greatest story of all by watching the world. We are one organism, working it all out. Every decision and experience fall beneath this covering of consciousness, which is replicated among the collective. The focus of consciousness is awareness of all of itself. The world may appear as chaos but in actuality it is a beautiful structure constantly organizing itself. It is nature; the seasons depicting birth, rest, harvest, and death—only to allow rebirth and endless cycles upon cycles.

Life is not about winning or achievement. Ultimately, neither is the story. Life purpose lay within the full remembering and embrace of every piece and part of the Self. We are meant to be singing in the rain and dancing in the moonlight. Every step occurs so that we discover how to dive into the puddles and walk on clouds. Each mountain appears so that we know how to leap over canyons and fly without having wings.

Stories are rich in experience and opportunity. When we learn to be so fully present to experience experiencing itself, the stories will become obsolete due to the attainment of being.

We lose out on life when reliving and rereading the same scene over and over again. Additional harm is caused when all other stories are not perceived as sacred, regardless of their appearance.

You are the common denominator in every life situation, regardless of whether you are a participant or witness. There is no place for blaming, shaming, judging, or complaining any longer, because you are the recurrent element in every experience, especially those that appear to have nothing to do with you. There is no one else here, only you and God in the room. How do you treat the aspect of God in front of you—in your family, your community, or the experience you now witness?

No matter where you go from this moment forward, can you see God in the room, showing up in different places with different faces, but always as you talking to you, showing you a side of yourself you have not seen? Source Presence will show you who you are, and who you are not. God will let you see what needs to be reviewed and what needs to be revealed, what is deeply Loved and what is terribly un-Loved. This mighty and creative Source will continue to speak as the people, the challenges, and the chatter until there is no sound or reflection.

Will you sit in embrace of all the ways you show up, regardless of what appears, until only the highest frequency of Love remains? Won't you see that all of our conversations are the same? Only the details of the story change. Once-upon-a-time has finally come. Life is not about being positive; it is about being real. You are not to wait for a happily-ever-after; it is the attitude that you choose to embody regardless of what is happening. This is how we create "heaven on earth"; otherwise hell's fires will blaze brightly around every corner, on every news station, and through every projection. The miracle is not in the just resolution of what happened to you, but in how you handle it in words, thoughts, and actions coming through you.

The *Maiden Without Hands* is the story of a miller who lost everything except his family, home, and an apple tree. On a walk home one day, an old man offered him tremendous lifelong wealth if he could have what rested behind his home. Thinking he was only losing an apple tree, the miller excitedly agreed and rushed home to tell his wife. She cried out in horror because their daughter spent the day behind the house.

The day came when the old man, who was actually the devil in disguise, came to collect the young girl. However, he could not take her because she was too clean and pious. He asked the father to keep her from bathing several days. The devil returned, but this time the girl had wept so much that her hands became clean. Once again, the devil could not take her. He demanded that her hands be cut off. The miller asked how he was to do that to his own child. The devil threatened to take him instead. The miller chose to chop off his daughter's hands rather than go with the devil. She cried so much that her tears cleansed her stumps and arms. The devil left, angry that he had not gotten his promise fulfilled.

Of course, the girl could no longer remain in her home. She had been betrayed deeply. She went out into the forest, after gathering her belongings and tying her arms behind her back. She wandered for days, becoming very hungry. Finally, the young girl came upon a castle with an orchard. An angel in the night appeared and helped her cross over the gate to take some fruit.

The next morning, the king wondered who had been in his orchard. The night servant recanted the story of an angel and the handless woman. The king wanted to see her. He watched for her the next night and fell in love with her beauty upon first sight. They married and he had two silver hands fashioned to replace the ones she had lost. They lived happily for quite a while.

The new queen was expecting a child when the king had to go off to war. While he was away, the queen gave birth to a son and a message was sent. The messenger stopped to nap by a stream. The devil, who still desired the young woman, replaced the letter. The new correspondence said the queen had given birth to a changeling. The king wrote back a compassionate response to care for the queen. Once again, the devil switched the letter with one that ordered both the queen and baby be killed. It requested their tongues and ears be saved as proof. The king's mother could not follow the instructions. She had two doe killed instead, saving the ears and tongue. Then, she told the young queen to run away. She tied the baby on the queen's back and sent them into the forest.

When the king returned, he was told that the queen and child had been killed as ordered. Having been shown the ears and tongue, he cried out in grief. Seeing his genuine heartbreak, the king's mother told him they were alive. He set out to find them.

The young queen had traveled for many days until one evening the angel reappeared. They were guided to a refuge, where she and her son lived the next few years. After seven years of wandering, the king came across the refuge and found the queen and their son, Sorrowfulness. The Lord had allowed the queens hands to re-grow because of her piety. The king and queen had a second wedding and lived happily ever after.

Did you notice any themes in this story? The young girl feels extreme betrayal, abuse, and pain from those who love her. This tells us those close to us will hurt us. She finds herself alone and deformed. Although a king takes her in and loves her, she finds herself experiencing the same heartbreak, turmoil, and loneliness again. This story implies that men are violent and not to be trusted. It illustrates that women are to beware and run. She names her child with the emotion that she feels: Sorrowful. Generationally the lineages are now imprinted with this named sadness.

Metaphysically the hands represent power. Having no hands meant having no power. Being replaced with silver hands has to do with value. Silver represented a monetary value. Her father had betrayed her, over wealth, in the beginning. There is a great deal of symbolism regarding value. Metaphysically, money and wealth are directly related to relationship experience, the most important of which is the relationship to Self.

Have you ever noticed how your money dries up when your relationships dry up?

Ask your wounded heart what part of you feels broken, missing, or lacking?

A beast had been hiding within a high remote castle, far away above the forest, having been victim of an evil sorceress's spell. He was large, scary looking and horribly gruff in personality.

One day, a merchant travelled through the forest on the way home to his children and lost his way. Seeing the light of a castle atop a mountain, he ventured up. It appeared vacant. He was hungry and tired, so he helped himself to food and lodging.

The next morning, he left, but not before taking a rose from the garden. His youngest daughter, Beauty, had requested a rose from his travels. As he pulled the rose, a large Beast came forward, enraged that the man would steal his rose after having been treated so hospitably. He demanded that the man's daughter be given to him in seven days for the trespass.

The man returned home. He gave the rose to his daughter. After seven days, the man asked of his daughter, "Do you love your father, Bella? If you do, you will do something for me." She loved her father more than anything, so, of course she said yes. The merchant told Bella of her new fate with the ghastly beast.

Beauty (Bella) was held captive and terrified of the Beast at first. She was treated well and given anything she wanted. Over time, they began to have long conversations. They would spend time in the garden near the rose bush that her rose had been plucked from.

One day, Beast asked Bella, 'If you could have anything in the world, what would it be?' Bella replied that she would go home to her father. The Beast's heart was broken because he had grown to love her. He decided to let her go, feeling deeply she would be lost forever. He knew that once she left, she would never return.

Bella went home to her father, fully intending to return to the Beast. When she got back to the castle, she found the Beast very still in the garden. His body was curled up under the rose bush. She began to weep over him. "Beast, I am sorry to have left you." Realizing he was close to death, she spoke from her heart, "I have grown to love you. I came back to be with you and live out my days by your side." In that instant, the fur covering of the Beast separated. A handsome prince emerged. He had been cursed with the appearance of a Beast until a fair maiden could love him for who he was. The two were married and lived happily ever after.

How many people view themselves in a harsh way? How often are games played to see if a person will be loved for the right reasons? How often do you test people to see if you are really loved? How often are you putting yourself to the test of love and loving? We have learned to challenge loyalty, love, kindness, and friendship, fearing they may not be real.

In what way have you forced people to engage in things they may not want? How many things have you felt forced into, in the name of Love?

This fairy tale implants thoughts that men betray us, abandon us, and think of themselves first. Love means doing anything for the other person, even if to our detriment. This illustrates that women are under the command of the male figure. Women are to be held captive. We must give ourselves up. Women must be given lavish material items and comforts to gain love. Men are beasts. One must nearly die to hear words of Love. In this case, the beast has to die before hearing words of Love. Women are shown that the handsome prince is under underneath the gruff beast, the ugliness and harshness. Love is conditional. Love is based on appearances and actions. Love leaves. Let your heart reveal what it believes to be your deficiency.

Where are your beastliness and your beauty?

When have you controlled, held captive, or left someone behind?

What have you traded off in the name of love?

LOVE'S PRESENT

Through the light of my awakened thought,
Through the heat of my heart,
Through the force of my pure intention,
With my sincerity and understanding,
I call upon "You"nion as the Lover,
I call upon "You" nion as the BeLoved,
I humbly stand before the door of devotion.
Establish your dwelling in my breadth.
My heart, my life and my deeds await you...
Awaken me with your sweet kiss,
your gentle touch,
your fond memory,
that my dream be self-realized.
I long and belong to you
In Love, Of Love, With Love, As Love,
Forever and more.

Date With Destiny

Destiny is a word that elicits powerful images of some far-off time and place that an individual reaches. It is the endpoint, hopefully a zenith. And yet it is also this thing that seems somewhat out of one's control. It is at the top of the mountain or the end of the road. It is often portrayed as the height of success or a level of measurable greatness. But there is something about destiny that many do not realize, and in large part why it appears unreachable. *Destiny* is made up of *des* and *tiny*. *Des* is defined as "data encryption standard," and *tiny* means "extremely small." Individual greatness is connected to how we become encrypted with data that lead us to believing we are smaller than everything else. We are led to believe a small self rests within the greater self. We tend to believe once we discover that greater self, we will also discover our destiny. But, what if the greater self and destiny are actually resting within the small self, the hidden self, the shadow self. Perhaps your date with destiny actually has you going in, rather than going out?

As I wrote the first version of this book several years ago, I had done much inner reflection. Yet, as I look back, that book was written from the part of me that was in process. I had made it through the chaos and was looking back. I was really living the same patterns, just a different version of them. I had traded in "the box of the broken one" for "the box of the one who could be broken and survive," one who was strong enough to have made it through the rain and was still standing. But, I was simply witnessing it all from a very surface level. I had felt a lot, but in no way had stopped long enough to dive into the deepest, encrypted, tiny part of me.

The second time I wrote this book, I had just come through another period of challenge. I was in a new box, unknowingly so. My new box was "the spiritual one who had done her work and could handle anything." I not only had witnessed it, I had the courage to talk about it. I even allowed myself to take risks—what felt like leaps and bounds.

It was a journey of Love, courage, and commitment. It was very real and quite profound. There was a sense of needing to honor my story and all that I had been through. This was a place of no longer telling the story of what happened to me, but in proving what it had brought through me—again, an experience on outer levels of creation. It took me deeper inside as well, but I had still not touched that tiny self. This new place was one of celebration for all that had occurred and whom I had been at each stage.

This third version of the book is different as well. There no longer is an outer destination. I am really not interested in whether or not I achieve or attain anything. I write for the pure sense of creative expression, inhaling and exhaling so that I fill and empty. In the breath, beyond the sound, past all thought is the tiny—and that which is larger than I could ever imagine.

This is a place of true intimacy and devotion to the Self. I have a real desire to know Love—my own. I also know it is the place of the Wild Divine, that part of me that can truly live in both the "smallness" and "bigness" of myself. And this time it is not about becoming. Neither is it about witnessing. The observer is just another identity. This is truly the place of being, amid the large and small, dark and Light, Love and fear, masculine and feminine. It is the merging of all opposites—Oneness.

I want to truly know the smallest ember of myself, that birthplace of Light that I am. If the entire Universe began from a spark of Light and evolved into All That Is, where is that in me? I am my own Universe, merely a cell in the body of earth, which is but an organ in the vast body of the cosmos. It means going deep, to my very core; and it's very dark down there.

Some part of me has a knowing that everything has beauty and value, especially all that has been branded as "bad," "ugly," "wrong," and "evil." I ask how the highest essence of Love would hold things such as these.

The answer I receive is EVE: *e*mbrace—*v*enerate—*e*mbody. I contemplate this and I think of the creation story, the myths, the legends, the psychology, and imprinting. What had Eve done? What had she become? What was she really? She was woman, as am I, but she represented more than that—as do I. She was the feminine aspect, anima. This inner self, not the personality, represents the soul, both the individual and the collective.

As I looked at her name and the sign it represented for me, I saw that Eve equated to 'night, the dark... the time when all Light is shadowed'. And yet, the words I intuit about her represent intimacy, receiving, reverence depth and grounding. Eve is the rawness and realness of earth. She is all that is in the shadows. Eve signifies that dark space of rest, where something can hibernate and wait. There is no question that she, being woman, also depicts immense power and magic. The darkness is where birth spontaneously happens from nothing. The spark suddenly appears without anything else having to be done.

This magic of infinite space is where the black hole and the white Light marry. In this way, she is also the EVEning, beginning as an ember. This Divine spark, illuminated in the dark, must gestate for a period to grow and be nurtured. It is fed and receives from outside itself to gain strength and thrive. However, it is connected in Oneness with that outside experience until it gets cut off from it.

Long before that separation, a journey outward begets a new experience, again and again and again. This is evolution (Eve-volution), *Eve* being the dark and Light, *volition* being a spiral turn. Eve brings us full spiral rather than full circle. She guides and leads the way with ancient sage wisdom. This place within Eve that we all travel to numerous times in our lives is a womb space. It is the cauldron and the fire. There is water and ether and air. You are the elemental substance that alchemizes into Divinity. This sacred dwelling within an earthen mother swells and fills with the molten essence and lava/Lover's purest form. Every beginning moves through a fallopian (fall open) tube. As Light grows, sounds can be heard from within and the energy expands. There is movement; a dance is happening. Possibility is resting in a place that cannot yet be seen but does exist.

When it does empty, everything releases. The water breaks; the heat rises. It is raw and messy. It feels as if the insides are going to be torn apart. The pain can be intense, and the only way through is to breathe. This birthing from the dark is often down a very narrow canal that no other can fit. It is traveled alone, as the walls contract all around. In these moments, we are pushed forward, sometimes stopping and at times, stepping back, before receiving another push. The moment of grace occurs when the pain stops and Light surrounds. In the right moment, at a perfect time, that which is unknown becomes known. And, we find ourselves in a whole new world, not able to talk or walk. In release of the struggle is the miracle of new life. And this, too, is Eve. Born as the innocent child, it is endowed with the gift of knowing it is upheld in all ways. In this way, a child trusts and takes the whole world in with wonder.

However, within this experience is a memory. That memory is beyond the mind. It is cellular and global, cosmic and "galax-ial." It is the knowing of being separate and Oneness. It is the re-memory of being finite and infinite at the same time. It is the knowing of being a part and the whole. It is the moment of separation. This, too, is who we are. It is the ever-increasing expansion of creative essence to its most infinite point, and back. Imagine turning the wheel of a kaleidoscope. Color, crystal, and form expand and contract, creating beauty and then merging back into nothingness for more beauty to create. Yet, no one considers that the pieces inside are broken glass, tiny pebbles, or seen through the use of distorted lenses. This juxtaposition creates something from all the parts. What is uniquely individual becomes a magnificent part of a whole. Is separation really the problem we face today?

The earliest point of human separation may be considered as the moment the umbilical cord is cut. However, division occurred in our cells long before. The egg divided into two, and then two, and then two, and so forth—creativity continuously birthing creation. And before that, we were star dust, the big bang, the cosmos continually expanding—appearing minuscule in the grand scheme of things, tiny but huge. We are not apart from any of it. Perhaps duality, in itself, is an illusion. Instead, judgment creates the illusion of duality when it is all Oneness.

In light of this, all things simultaneously exist and are all good. If judgment were removed, would separation return to Oneness? In the name of consciousness and evolution, it is purported that ultimate separation is from the opposing forces of fear and Love. We are constantly asked to choose fear or Love. However, what if they are not opposing? What if they are actually allies? What if they exist within one another, each required for creation's continual experience of itself? Perhaps the sin, or missing of the mark, is not fear but what we do with it by judging and reacting.

We can no more face Love than we are willing to face fear. That provides reason as to the degrees of Love and fear on the planet. They are actually balanced. In looking at Love from the universal and Divine perspective, there is no fear. It is all Love. Nature provides the landscapes, experiences, and means to balance out all that Love currently encompasses. The big question in either case is: Of that which we call "Love," what degree is unconditional Love versus conditional Love?

It is time to heal the deepest schism of all—between dark and Light, fear and Love. Can I be unconditional in loving every fear that possibly exists? In doing so, will it cast Light on all that is distorted in my mind, heart, and being? Shall I walk into the garden of good and evil, extending my heart and opening my arms to embrace—venerate—embody (EVE) everything in the land of opposites?

The Land of Opposites

Chaos and peace.

Action and stillness.

Naked and complete.

Empty and full.

Failure and success.

Loneliness and communion.

Insecurity and security.

Sickness and health.

The black hole and the white Light.

Nothing and everything.

Slavery and freedom.

Poverty and wealth.

Demon and God.

Death and life.

Fear and Love.

I am ready to dive into the midst of the dark and decrepit, this ever-maddening ecstasy of the shadow and its band of fears. For much of my life, these opposing forces dueled in the confines of my mind. I long to know them. I desire to speak their language so they may finally be honored upon center stage. I sense they are angry and tired of being behind the curtain. They have no care or judgment of feeling such things. They know the truth. In this moment of destiny, they come with one simple request: "Let us be seen, felt, and heard. We are not as bad as you believe. We are allies. We lead you to the places you desire to go. Without us, you would not travel. In fact, you are unknowingly enamored with us, so much so, that you cling with an iron-clad grip—no matter how we push you and test you, scare you, and tease you. Do you not see you are already in Love? However, you do not unconditionally Love us, or yourself." Well, who could pass up that invitation?

So, I have a date with death, loneliness, rejection, misery, pain, disappointment, ridicule, imprisonment, and the unknown. Rather than continue flirting with them, I am going to take a deep dive into relationship with them. And you shall come with me. Fear not. We will meet up with this band of fears, encompassing all that deals with commitment, intimacy, imperfection, sickness, and failure, and have the time of our lives. They, too, only seek to be Loved.

Let your heart be seduced by the ramblings of fear gone wild. Get to know each other better and, by the end, you may find yourself in rapturous ecstasy, rolling around in the dark shadows of your own countenance, which also is Divine. When one is truly in Love, the ugly is not seen as ugly, the bad not experienced as bad, the wrong can do no wrong, and even the devil becomes a god.

As I anticipated how I might become intimate in these places of my being, I realized these parts have been oppressed and suppressed, which is why depression occurs. I have always known depression as a cry for creativity. Now that knowing had a whole new meaning. If one held in a baby, both could die. If a child is oppressed, it dies spiritually. When depressed, we are the walking dead.

If Eve represents shadow—creativity—birth—connection, and it has been treated this way, then the collective feminine aspect has been treated this way. Within anima/animus, the masculine exists unconsciously. Women only became masculine because it was within them. Men hold the feminine inside as an unconscious part.

Women suppressed their femininity by allowing masculine parts to become more dominant. I knew this place. I had lived most of my life using masculine energy: doing, toiling, hunting, and gathering. I never knew how to receive. Many of my physical and creative births could not survive, because I could not receive and rest and allow. Why? How did the feminine move from a place of rest and allowing creation to that of action—initiating creation? I could feel it so clearly inside. People, regardless of gender, became active creators rather than the essence of creation. The distinction was as fine as a hair, while being the hairline fracture that began a Divine drama.

Words echoed in the air: "the journey outward begets a new experience." The word *begets* means "to father." But if all of creation began from an initial birth and continuous births, then all began from a great Divinely feminine presence. Where is the masculine in that? It did not exist, except as an undercurrent of energy once the creation process began. The masculine aspect was where consciousness placed its attention within the new creation, instead of maintaining presence within itself. Is that not what we do as human beings?

For example, a child is born and it becomes the center of one's world. We do everything for the child, molding it in our image, based on our beliefs, teaching it to see from our perspectives. We never consider receiving what the child brings: innocence, openness, laughter, enthusiasm, play. Instead of realizing the child's entire experience as the gift, the parent establishes control and interference that only serves to replicate a program. Is this not the same as infection. Focus and doing are masculine energies. Receiving and awareness are feminine energies. Our masculine natures have taken over. The child is born to balance out the feminine.

Another example would be the experience of life as chaos draws one's attention. Rather than reeving and allowing it to play out which wild be feminine, we engage and seek to control the outer and the other. The balance lay in the centering of the truth for the original space of boundless timeless creation to reemerge. Chaos is actually feminine. Control and interference are masculine. Change is the balancing. The origin of all things is feminine. Birth of anything new is messy and the feminine knows to hold a space of power and presence, and change will arise. Eve held that space.

There is a need to examine the creation stories because at the very mythology of each of our lives, these stories are embedded in our cells to play out with our own unique details. The archetypes radiate from these stories of time, most of all those of biblical significance. These stories are the basis of our suffering, martyrdom, darkness as well as our triumph, resurrection, Light.

"For God so loved the world, that he gave his only 'begotten' Son, that whosoever believeth in him should not perish, but have everlasting life." (John 3:16)

Any son that is born has to come from the feminine as the original primal force of creation. In the case of the world, the feminine "fathered"; it begot. The Divine feminine is both mother and father, one in the same— Oneness—undivided—Whole. Many would say this is blasphemy, because of how woman, feminine, vulnerability are still viewed in the world. The masculine is control and does not want to release control. Once again, I am not speaking of man woman, but of masculine and feminine which is within every man and woman.

Jesus was not a spontaneous creation. He was a 'chosen one'. The creation story was intentional. It was interference, a controlled action of the Universe. Jesus was specifically created for a purpose. This was conscious attention with the intention of Divine free will. This action was masculine in its doing. The 'animus energy' (masculine) within the Divine feminine created a being that would be made in the image and likeness whose unconscious piece was anima, feminine. 'As within, so without.' Jesus held and portrayed the essence of the Divine Feminine through his openness, heart, deeds, and words. His miracles, spontaneous healing touch, loaves of bread, and baskets of fish were the gifts of Love's Divine feminine presence of allowing, grace and receiving.

"It is Christ, the light of truth, who says, 'See,' and it is through him that we are able to see ["I am the way, the truth, and the life"], for he is the light of the Father, without which there is no light in heaven or on earth."

—Jan Ruusbroec

In being "the Light of the father," he is "active". The dark womb of the mother is ' native", in other words at rest. It is the space of the void where nothing becomes something. We can create anything we want. Shall we create what is g(o)od or what is highest in our G(o)od.

"I am the way, the truth, and the life." Jesus speaks of "the way" of the feminine, the original Divine Mother Creator that allows the spontaneous spark from nothing to something. "I am the truth"—the combined aspects of creator and creation, Mother and Father, anima and animus—all that is. "I am the life." He was creation personified. Jesus was a free will creation fashioned from Divine will.

"Without which there is no Light in heaven or on earth." Jesus personifies and purports Love's presence guiding the Universe. Through the inner coming out and the outer going in, we have created the sacred stories of life. Within each one of us is a swinging pendulum of masculine and feminine polarity. In this weaving together, creation continually births itself in a juxtaposition of signs, symbols, synchronicity within the chaos, experience, and challenge all organically self-organizing. Pandora's box symbolized the free will creation of mankind—Adam, animus: accept—desire—act (Act-I-on)—master.

"So God created man in his own image, in the image of God he created him; male and female he created them." (Genesis 1:26–27 NIV)

This most profound statement—"his own image"—now has new meaning. This is the face of Divine will and free will created as one form. It is not the literal human, male or female. The image of God is 'creation' itself. Whether we appear as male or female is irrelevant, it is simply a form that is a sign of what is missing that must be embodied. As we balance out these two forces, we shall see the emergence of a new being that is both and neither.

"Male and female he created them" echoes this first section. Additionally, men and women embody both masculine and feminine power. We have been blinded by the physical form, rather than seeing the essence beneath the skin.

We live in a world immersed in evil ("Eve"-l), while disrespecting and denying it/her. By not honoring the shadowy parts, time created more of the same in increasing degrees. The masculine became dominant and the balance of the world moved into force rather than the pure essence of power. The shadow only shows us where nature has become skewed, while inviting us back into the dark space where the body goes to the ground until ready to rise again surrendered, renewed, and reborn.

Because women have been disrespected and diminished, Jesus would have to have been created as a man, but one whose wisdom was ancient and demeanor gentle. Jesus represented that. He was the picture of man, but his heart and soul were the "Embrace—Venerate—Embody" of the feminine. At the same time he illustrated a sense of stillness in how to Accept—Desire—Act-I-on—Master. Jesus was the example of embodied union of Christ Light. Even through crucifixion, the harmonious attributes of masculine and feminine energies were illustrated. His resurrection was a spontaneous, miraculous moment of Divine Feminine birth, that which is the true creator force of the Universe.

There could only be one begotten son, because the world had become so masculine in both men and women. Birth can only happen through mother. The universal soul is Divine ancient feminine, and, to balance all of the masculinity, a son had to be fathered that would bring the feminine nature of love back into balance by embracing that which was dark.

The true mother is unconditional in her loving. She is forgiving and nurturing, whole and complete. Jesus clearly exemplified all of these things. In a time when women were prostituting and had no power, a time when men were in their animal and barbaric behavior, Jesus—as did others in different places and times—radiated the Christ Light and Christ Consciousness.

All is in equal balance and indeed everything is our mirror. If Eve is the symbol of creation, creator, shadow, and Light, then Adam, too, had to be the same or hold such within himself. The feminine had to be the unconscious aspect within him. The masculine had to exist within the feminine, and the feminine within the masculine. It is the only way we as a society could have gone out of balance or know how to return.

We are being asked to do that in our lives. Most have become anchored in masculine energy, whether male or female. We are being asked to birth anew. Rebalancing happens by interweaving and dancing between the veils as a new world is co-parented in Oneness.

Life does not have to be hard, or painful. It is intended for you to experience your richness, your depths and heights. You are a beautiful, bejeweled tapestry that embodies creation, contrast, and texture.

Embrace—venerate—embody the italicized dialogues listed in each Heart Fullness section of future chapters and continue journaling with your own words.

Contemplate the Mind Fullness sections, revealing your inner wisdom awaiting the invitation to Accept—Desire—Act (Act-I-on)—Master.

Build your Will Fullness through exercising your inner strength.

Step into Truth Fullness by always staying in the inquiry.

CELEBRATE YOU, ALL THAT, and MORE!

LOVE'S GIFT

Wishes begged of heaven...
Gifts born of time,
Illusory dreams become reality...
yet, we still miss the forest for the trees.
Heaven sent packages...
eyes to cherish as precious gemstones,
a melodic heart in song for new life,
yet, we still miss the forest for the trees.
Listen to my cry
Teach me all of your infinite wisdom.
Show me great Love so I may know how.
Hold my hand tightly until you have to go.
Through you I shall see the forest...
I shall touch each tree...
And I will remain open.
When the time comes...
I shall hold your hand...
My lap will cradle your head...
My heart will cherish your memory,
for you will have taught me to see,
not only the forest...
but also, every tree.

❦{ Journey of Time }❧

8

Love and BeLoved

Heart Fullness

Is there someone I can fall madly in love with, one who can support me, love me unconditionally, listen to me, and cherish me? Is there someone who could have a sense of the pain that I have encountered, be compassionate toward my weaknesses, be understanding of my messes, and be gentle, even when I venture to the dark side of myself?

Do I have an ultimate soul mate that could fully comprehend my deepest desires, be genuinely happy for my accomplishments, and cheer me on when I have all but given up? Is it too much to ask to have just one person on this planet that loves me for me, exactly as I am, does not need me to do something, is not requiring me to change, does not need to control me, or have an agenda?

Can that one person do their best to not hurt me—not abandon me, dishonor me, speak harshly toward me, act with disregard for me, or break my heart? Can they be committed to me, honoring of me, and devoted to my well-being? Will this one person be my lover, my confidant, my best friend, my twin soul—and I be their BeLoved? Is it too much to ask? Is it too much to hold out for? Holy Father, Holy Mother, is it too much to pray for?

Continue this dialogue, using your feelings and words. Journal your thoughts before moving to Mind Fullness. If words do not come, draw. If you cannot draw, doodle. Breathe. Feel. Allow. Receive.

Mind Fullness

Do you silently and secretly keep waiting for your love? Who does not dream of Loving and being Loved by their one true mate? And the rest, those in relationships, often feel as lonely as, if not more alone than, many singles. Because of heartbreak, pain, loneliness, or the need to feel complete, most wonder if an "ultimate soul mate" exists at some point within the relationship.

> Could there be *one* being that you are to connect to deeply and unconditionally?

> Could this be an integral part of the soul journey for every human being?

> Through this experience of real Love, can you fully recognize and embrace all others?

We live in a world filled with guarded hearts that have been broken. One hand reaches out looking for Love, while the other remains curled up tightly against the stomach to temper the questions rumbling inside. The greatest desire every human being has is to be Loved deeply and unconditionally by just one other being. The other commonality is that no one wants to hurt or feel pain. Somehow, the game of life is set up so that Love first attracts everything unlike itself, in order to rid from within us everything unlike the essence of Love that we really are. We will attract relationships that anchor into the very beliefs we consciously and unconsciously hold, until choosing to shed light on them.

We have been taught, and have believed, that Love and pain are one in the same. Continuing to flaunt, fantasize, flirt, and fight, we never really commit to, or are, Loving to the other. Instead, Love becomes a battle-field and barter-ground, walked upon casually, and resulting in many trade-offs and casualties. We never confronted those who never Loved us, nor have we faced how we resent ourselves for not being more Loving. The war silently wages on in the depths of being. In the meantime, renegade thoughts deploy reconnaissance missions from the subconscious caverns of the mind to keep denied fires of longing burning. We create hardened shells upon the wounds of the heart, slowly crumbling on the outside until there is nothing left to stand.

Why do we buy into Love being a struggle or relationships needing to be work? Is it true? Or is it possible that we have never been modeled, or even experienced, real Love? Did caregivers know how? They were also wounded, dysfunctional, baggage-carrying gypsies of time, compounding this plague of pain, generation after generation.

Can you be transparent?

Will you open to vulnerability?

Are you ready to trust true intimacy?

What are you willing to discover so that you can be in romance with the unknown?

We have become a society of scar tissue that needs to be tended to, but instead we have bandaged ourselves, continually tightening the bands into a "mummified" existence until we stop loving, stop living, and stop breathing.

At best, Love is watered down into an intellectual concept, as a tool of manipulation and a drug for those unworthy and un-Loved. Perhaps the closest thing to Love anyone of us has truly experienced are random acts of kindness and moments of tolerance. This is a bold statement, likely to trigger the deepest spaces of insecurity and fear. Must we face that this is the way of the world at this time? Yes, because truth is our only way "in." No more hiding, pretending, justifying, or conforming. No more excuses. Be the change.

Codependence runs rampant in the world. We make sense in the mind but can only make Love in the heart. Intellectualization has us "heading" into places where unconditional Love has no ground to seed. We are operating from sensibility instead of sense ability.

We have been shown that Love is a familial and socictal legacy of code-pendent conformity, rather than cooperative and compassionate honoring. Is this too dramatic? Or, is it triggering what you have been too afraid to see, feel, and speak? Love awakens its opposite beliefs, thoughts, and actions through triggers, upset, chaos, discomfort, and struggle. These forms are the blocks to Love, Loving, and being Loved.

On a planet with more than seven billion people, there must be one person who could fit each ones mold. How do you find the one created specifically for you? This quest is not gender-specific; it speaks to the emptiness and disconnection we each feel for far too long. It is the true place of separation, replicated throughout collective consciousness—the grandest illusion of all, passed through generations, throughout time. Could you step beyond superficial Love? Can you release being distracted by the outside to touch what is real and long-lasting?

This courtship invites you to commune with the unknown—all that was unkind, unloving, or betraying, *and* that which is unconditional Love, honor, and loyalty. This engagement asks you to "care-frontationally" embrace the abuser, abuse, harshness, and pain, while meeting your BeLoved. It implores you marry shame to honor, abandonment to communion, and betrayal to loyalty. This path will wed your most wounded, battered, abused, and wrong self to the present moment of your brilliance, radiance, and essence. Can you maintain communication with your self-imposed adultery, bullying, and enslavement? This is not about therapy, healing, shedding, or closing doors. We are not going to discard, burn away, or let go of anything. This is a new way, a loving, compassionate way of holding, allowing, and being—in fact, absorbing.

This special Love will lay you down softly, gently holding the most wounded, damaged parts of you as he/she guides you toward true intimacy, vulnerability, and transparency. The oncoming romance escorts you down the 13-inch path from the multi-chambered mansion of the mind to the elegantly simple Divine and sacred cathedral of the most-high heart of your union.

Layer upon layer, begin inviting into your conscious awareness all that blocks you from the highest experience of Love that is your birthright. Completely surrender the denial, enmeshment, codependence, and invisibility held. "Tear"-ing of the veils reveals what has been hidden: tears of remembrance. Tears of recognition. Tears of separation. Tears of reconnection. And from tears, rivers of Light form to heal your world. Every memory is a "peace" heaven sent to receive the piece lost. Every moment returns the promise of all Being brought to Light. And so it is, as orphans of Love return home.

> Will you rise into being Lover and BeLoved in Divine romance and sacred partnership?

> Will your human self let go so your soul may have the romance it desires and deserves?

Truth Fullness

> » Do you trust life? Do you trust the world? Do you trust Yourself?

> » What are the thoughts you currently have about Love, Loving, and being Loved?

> » How do you feel about signing a vow of devotion to Love yourself above all else?

Will Fullness

The Vow of Self-Love to Love Self

I commit to Loving and being Loved. I willingly walk this path at a pace that feels gentle, disciplined, and compassionate. I shall be unconditional in my acceptance and forgiving when I cannot be. I am open to discovering a new way to Love, be Loved, and live as Love. To truly Love others and be Loved by others in the way I deserve, I choose myself with honor and loyalty, and in communion always, in all ways. I decree and declare this to all parts that I AM.

May I know you in full brilliance; you are orphans no more. I shall honor you and keep you. Come to me; I turn away no longer. Come into my eyes, my ears, my arms, and heart. Come sadness, anger, grief. Come apathy, longing, need. Come joy, bliss and ecstasy.

Let me hold you dear, guilty one, precious shameful one, deeply denied one. Let me know all of you, rejected, repressed, and separate. I am here, fully present to receive you. When and where shall I meet you? Take me to the moments that rise in this sacred space of Love; I am ready to see me now. I will be with me. See me. Cherish me. Love me. Let my eyes meet yours. Let this life be my liberation. I am here to be still, and to know. I hear my call. I am peace and parts of the same, aligning myself in everlasting devotion. I vow to give myself fully and completely to this courtship, engaging the sacred marriage of soul and spirit, human being and Divine Being, Lover and BeLoved.

_____ (Signature)

Fear or Be Feared

Heart Fullness

I don't know who I am. I don't know why I am here. I don't know what my purpose is on the planet. I have so much to say, yet it is as if something chokes the words in my throat and does not let me speak. There is a pounding in my gut. I want to scream at times. There is so much inside of me that wants to be heard, to be seen, to be shared—to serve.

But who am I? I am not like other people. I don't have what it takes. I am not smart enough. I don't look like them. And, what do I have to say, anyway? Why on earth would I be so special? I wish I knew how to be strong. I wish I were not afraid to leap. I might take a wrong step or make a mistake! How do I know if I am doing the right thing?

I become paralyzed inside myself, unable to move. And the world just passes me by. I feel so small at times. I just want to hide and escape. I am even afraid people can see that about me. What if I fail? What if I am laughed at, or embarrassed? I am afraid. What about my secrets? What am I thinking? I can't be anything more than I am. Most of all, I just don't know how.

Continue this dialogue, using your feelings and words. Journal your thoughts before moving to Mind Fullness. If words do not come, draw. If you cannot draw, doodle. Breathe. Feel. Allow. Receive.

Mind Fullness

We know as much about fear as we do about Love, really not knowing either because we never address them head on. We talk about them. But when have we faced them, held them, or become truly intimate with them?

When have we stood with them? When have we gotten to know them—really listened to them? They are casual acquaintances that we turn our backs on. They remain under the surface as relationships we pretend not to have, until we choose to know them better so they may be given what they most need: attention and Love. They are "calls for Love."

Most individuals think they Love themselves. They hope they do. They want to believe they are doing so. But is it true? Our actions, our lives, and, most importantly, our words betray us. Just listen to how you think or speak about yourself, your body, and your life. These very words and thoughts are actually the voices of deeper fears that are carried.

You are unwilling to allow the heights of Love to the same degree you cannot face and embrace your fears. Just as many are in Love with the "idea of Love," never really surrendering to the full-bodied experience of it; most live in fear of the "concept of fear," never really taking the time to dive in to see what is there —if it is actually real or simply perceived. You will likely discover you have already created most of your worst fears, or you are on your way there if not taking the time to dive inward. When you dig really deep, you will discover all that remains is simply the concept of fear, clamoring in the bottom of a container lacking of evidence.

Do you know what Love Is?

Do you Love yourself?

Can you Love better?

Do you fear yourself?

Does fear run your life?

Does fear rule your choices?

Is fear the security blanket you use to not have Love?

These questions will stop you in your tracks, and leave you speechless. Are you afraid of yourself? The quick response would likely be *no*. Check the internal response. You may discover a silent, quivering *yes*. Most of the world is. Just look at the degree of violence and war present today. We project it outwardly, suppressing the self: in fear of seeing it, feeling it, recognizing it, owning it. We do not want to face it. What is "it"? It is the dark resting inside.

We are afraid of the dark. There is a monster in there. Even worse, we might discover that the monster is the same face being reflected back from the mirror. In looking too deep, we may even discover a degree of hatred—self-hatred—we never wanted to know. If there is an uneasiness wriggling inside, you may have stirred it within your "sleep" and bump into it fleetingly on a daily basis through your experiences.

Fear typically gets packaged in a nice, neat, little compartment, way back in mindless storage, where it only needs to be looked upon once in a while, if at all. You might discover it is hiding with the Love that you also lock away. Unless you do a thorough inventory, you will never account for it. Yet, somewhere inside, we do keep checks and balances of all actions, words, and thoughts. Upon that moment of reconciliation, an audit takes place that clearly illustrates whether we have richly banked each moment or reached the point of emotional and spiritual bankruptcy. Completely unaware of the reserves that lay hidden deeply within the well, deposits are tucked and sealed away in the body vault. In every account, the interest accumulated will be the savings of a lifetime that return what was meant for you all along.

Even if you have done much inner work, there are pieces and parts of your life, of yourself, you are too afraid to look at. Fear stands in front of Love because it protects. It stands guard at the door, knowing it has to lead the way. It is the bridge between you and your Love. What lay between you and fear? A walk in the dark, as dark as night, utilizing everything outside of you, for as long as you choose. These things will tug at you, pull at you, agitate you, and ask you to let go of them, especially those you most cherish. Fear will taunt and tease the mind with chatter around the past and the future, leaving you questioning how to save, fix, or heal the situation. You will react in ways that activate your masculine sense of doing, believing enough action will make the change. However, only one simple step actually creates the miracle: you opening to feel. You must *be* the change. Everything about you must change from a place of mindset and heart-set. Love is bringing up everything unlike itself for the sake of being known. What lay between you and Love? Only your self-created veils of resistance, warrior-ship, and pride. They begin appearing in increasing degrees until you surrender what you Love and what you fear.

We want to be at peace, prosperous, and abundant, and find Love. We want to be whole, discovering the breadth of our Light and the depths of the soul, but we do not know how. We seek to find the way, the truth, and the life, but we keep seeking outwardly, instead of hearing the sacred spoken message to "go inside." The way is on the inside. The truth is on the inside. The life we outwardly keep searching for lay on the inside.

We desire to be with the Divine, immersing ourselves in all that is holy and venturing into lands of ecstatic trance. We seek to be timeless, boundless, and expansive, but unwilling to recognize inherent qualities of omniscience, omnipotence, and Godliness.

What holds human beings back from what is most desired? The answer is distraction from the truth path of longing and Belonging, where Lover meets BeLoved. Uniting within the shadows of the night and ever-expanding horizons of Light, emergence happens when merging takes precedence.

Most turn away from the past. Everyone wants the grass that is greener on the other side. Their own is brown and dead, only because they have not been tending to it. In a world of humans being, humans doing, and the dead walking, what has been lost? Our humanity—mistakenly referenced outwardly as seven-billion-plus people.

Each one of us has lost varying levels of personal humanity. Not as elevated as animals, nor as authentic as beasts. Not as enlightened as the mythical beings, or ascended as the great Masters. We are fallen angels trying to rise above ourselves after having clipped our own wings. Upon the surface, we bow down to others who have also fallen, wearing the most intricate of masks in a great ball called Earth.

> Does the ball have to come to an end for all masks to fall and angels to rise, or can you create heaven on earth by bringing Light to all that is in the shadows and darkness?

> Can you invite onto life's grand stage the fallen, the weak, the derelict, and the homeless?

Can you bring forth the insanity, giving it the spotlight to be seen?

Can you ask the beaten, the bruised, the imprisoned, and the molested to stand with you in the bubbling fountains of used and abused, as the waters of re-memory bathe you back into your mellifluence?

These cleansing waters will heal all the his-tory and her-story that has compiled over time. They will wash through the great divide between masculine and feminine forces, creating a unified Divine river that nourishes all back to their righteous place in the kingdom of heaven. The water flows nearby, within our grasp right here, right now. It begins with a baptism upon all that is separate. A blessed communion bathes each one of us in the Light of Christ Consciousness, being the Light of unconditional Love, acceptance, and compassion. The problem is not the sin we believe we have committed. It is that we have become gluttons for punishment and intoxicated by our own stories.

We want to forgive them. They want to forgive us. But how and who and when and why should we? Forgiveness is necessary, but celebration is liberation for one and all. Celebration of what happened, how it happened, why it happened, and to whom it happened is the calibration that moves us from a victim's story into the sacredness of the whole Divine text.

We are each a sacred text walking, filled with wisdom, a plethora of story—and a whole lot of made-up stuff. Because we are good at making stuff up! But sacred, nonetheless! And yet, we are scared at the same time, mostly of the stuff we made up. This scare-city we call earth will only come into its whole-fullness when we are real with one another: open, honest, vulnerable, and transparent.

We have been determined to be God-fearing; it is time to be God-loving. Who do you think God is, anyway? Just look around and you will see God, in everyone and everything—animate and inanimate. If you cannot see God in all, then you cannot see God at all. The world is in a state of fear because we are seeing All That Is from a displaced perception. Instead, become gods walking that are "all seeing gods."

We have come here to do what we have come to do—in Oneness, in pieces, and parts—in fragmentation and unification, through the beauty of story and for play. Let yourself be open to the idea that all of your life has not been Love, but instead, a call for Love; two halves of a whole in beautiful harmony, the comedy and tragedy, yin and yang—the absolute beginning courtship of a romance of Lover and BeLoved. In this union, a call for Love brings on relationship; an idea of life that offers opportunities for greater connection and aliveness.

It is time to open your heart, tearing down the walls built around it to keep everyone and everything at arm's length. It is what life shows each one of us about us.

How do you keep people at a distance?

How do you test them?

How have you prejudged every relationship experience?

What is your life revealing to you, about you?

Imagine you can see beneath the surface of the physical body, it may look hardened, fractured, or decayed. Your heart will show you the texture, even though the mind may convince you otherwise. Beneath this calcified landscape lay the authentic you. Chipping away at what is hardened need not be work. It requires presence, a commodity that is a rare treasure. Take stock of everything that has led you to this point and build bonds that will grow exponentially.

It's time to know the truth, hear the truth, and tell the truth. In attention and present intention, open to receive more Love while also realizing that it is all a call for Love. Judgment day has come. This is the day of reckoning. Will you judge or be judged? Will you set yourself free? Speak now or forever hold your "piece"? We are made up of many fragmented pieces that are to be reclaimed, reunited, and recognized. When we find each one, we also find peace.

Who is the one calling for Love?

Who is the one to BeLoved?

From where and when, why, and from how far back?

Telling the truth is not for the current self, for there is nothing to fix. Heal your history, creating a new legacy for being. Unwrap your bandages placed over time, revealing a face beneath that was the one to fall, and is to rise, into Love. You will know this familiar countenance by the eyes, forced smile, and remunerations of the heart. Wisdom rests upon the wrinkles of time, slumping shoulders, and tired footsteps. The ongoing story sits upon a strong will of human spirit, evident even in the weak embrace, endless yawns, and ever-present demeanor of doubt. There is an ember—a smoldering light—that continually survives. It holds the space for another day.

This is the part of you that has been waiting for permission to thrive. It is not the you of now; it is the you of then. It is not the dreams you think you have; it is all the dreams that have been cast aside over the years. There is a part of you that is the long-forgotten innocence who has watched an entire journey unfold from the sidelines. We each hold a story, a mythology. Within this epic tale are the seeds of greatness and the passionate blaze of Light that we become, as the ember becomes the fire. Now that part of you awaits its true story, a courtship and Love story that you have desired your entire life.

What of our children and future generations? By revealing what I have kept hidden, even from myself, would I damage my children? Would they walk away? Or, would it set them free? If I am willing to stand in my story, honoring it fully, would I actually give them permission—permission to mess up, permission to fail, permission to go against the grain, most of all permission to not have to be like their parents, by traveling their own paths? Is it possible children already know, feel, and see everything on some level? Does it impact their bodies, their choices, and their lives? How can it not? How many stand in fear of their children discovering something, anything—everything? Stand in the truth. Everything else falls like a house of cards. When that happens, the only thing left standing is that one—in their truth.

The highest essence of Divine Love is presence. Your presence is enough; it is the miracle inside of you ready to happen. In freeing yourself of identity and the masks you believe yourself to be, you will see that fear has been the excitement of your own wings unfurling. The cocoon is the environment that has you trapped in specific beliefs and thoughts. Pushing beyond fear and allowing the wings to unfurl is an experience of Love that creates flight. Identifying yourself as a butterfly that birthed merely gives you the experience of the butterfly. That is where the limitation sets in again.

Who and what keeps you limited in life and in Love?

Can you continuously surpass the limits that you and others buy into?

How often are you willing to die to feel more into your aliveness?

How deeply will you dive into your heartbreak to know real Love?

If you choose to believe life was to birth, to live, and to die, then that is what you will have. You may crawl, you may sit, you may stop, you may fly. And, all is good. It is what you are choosing to create based on what you believe about your environment and its limitations. What if the butterfly chose to believe it was an eagle? It would not know any better than to fly higher—and it would, because it believed it could. Even that would be a story with its own limits.

Truth Fullness

»   What are your greatest fears?

»   Are you already living out those fears?

»   What are you most afraid of losing?

»   What are you most afraid of gaining?

»   What do you fear most about truly being loved?

Will Fullness

Close your eyes. Place your left hand flat against your chest. Feel the beat of your heart pulse into the center of your palm. Breathe into that pulse as if you are controlling its strength. As you experience this moment, notice: Someone is drumming a sacred rhythm from inside of you. In the midst of this quiet space is movement, the serenade of the heart. Stillness is both quiet and movement. Witness from a neutral position—no judgment or thought, just the present. Notice "both" of You.

As you hear this inner rhythm, take the first three fingers of your right hand and tap upon your heart in the same beat. Find your rhythm. If you feel like, tap another beat in harmony to what you are hearing. Keep your eyes closed and be present to the one who is knocking from inside, the one knocking on the outside, and the space between.

Meet at this door, at least three times a day, for a minimum of three minutes for 33 days. Every time you lose sight of yourself, move into anxiety, depression, worry, or upset, rest your hand upon your heart. Breathe, listen, and feel for the beat of the inner witness who holds a sacred drumming vigil in your honor 24/7. This BeLoved One is always near and will respond at your beck and call. Here sits your inner grace, your place for giving you back to you.

❧{ 10 }❧

Body of Work

Heart Fullness

I wish I looked different. I don't want this body. Why can't I lose this weight? I wish I had different clothes. Why couldn't I have been more attractive? I just won't eat. Why are some people so beautiful? And sexy? I must have missed that line when God handed out parts! I'll just wear black. It covers up everything. And I will stand in the corner. No one is going to notice me, anyway. It's not fair!

I hate my hair! Look at this belly, these hips. What's the use? I'll just eat what I want. It's no use. I can't compare to them, anyway. My body will never look like that. I don't have the genes or the willpower. Maybe I can have surgery. Then, I might feel better about myself.

It doesn't matter; I'll just fake it. Who cares, anyway? I just need to stop looking in the mirror. Ugh! It's pathetic. How do those people on TV look like that?

Continue this dialogue, using your feelings and words. Journal your thoughts before moving to Mind Fullness. If words do not come, draw. If you cannot draw, doodle. Breathe. Feel. Allow. Receive.

Mind Fullness

Self-Love is the key to the abundance, freedom, peace, and oneness every person desires. This "attentional" approach consciously supports the journey to Love. The first radical change is in living with attention, instead of pursuing life and Love from just setting intentions.

Intention is external, related to the mind and repetition, instead of the knowing in the moment. Entrenched in ritual for outcomes and agendas from fearful minds, who are desperate and wanting, once again we have created a "doing" out of a "being." We attempt to trick the heart, using the mind, and it is not that gullible. The heart is not interested in distant results, it resides here and now. Your true Self is in the heart and will not fall for deceptive ego-ic attempts that keep you in tension, if not supporting a present moment experience.

Attention is internal. It is presence in the now. Attention takes you inside, bringing you intimately closer to the Self. You have gotten distracted, by following others in how to do things, how to look, how to act, and especially how to Love. You bought into mindless ritual rather than mindful experience through conscious and present breathing. See how you scurry, multitask, and strategize. This is the way of machines doing, not of Spirit being.

Bring your attention to the heart of the matter, grounding "Self" realization as Love at the center. Anything desired must first be rooted deeply in the core of one's belly through the acceptance of what is. Only then will you be able to project those things outwardly and attract more of the same back toward you. It must be embodied and breathed in fully. Ideas, emotions, and experiences must be embraced by the heart and held in the gut until ready for release. You will know the feeling of the space being empty again.

Your attention to live and Love in this way will give rise to a higher resonance experience that perpetually exists. Embodiment, in this way, requires a lifestyle change. It will beckon simplicity and rest. It will go against the grain of what society views as normal but will lead you deeply into your core and its true desires. And there, you shall be upheld. The soul knows its truth. The body is imprinted with its design. Your cells are here to celebrate in that creation of Love's essence.

There comes a moment when we decide to be the Light on the horizon. The past feels like the past and hope of a new life is held. The desire is to swiftly move forward, detaching from everything that has happened. The mind wants to run quickly past any latent residue, lingering thoughts or feelings clamoring for attention. The ego pushes to believe in positive thoughts, state affirmations, and move on. This will not sustain a new experience, nor bring the heart's deepest longing. Sit in everything that rises. Take it from the mind into the heart. Then breathe it from the heart into the gut and let it sit there until digested. The body shall know what to keep and what to release as waste.

This is the point that has been worth the journey thus far, the sweet drink at the end of a long and winding road. This is the moment of truly being able to set oneself free. But it requires turning back, rather than forward. In doing so, the discovery is that the only way out truly is by going in. We must consume ourselves, becoming entirely self-absorbed. Our shadows, darkness, beliefs, behaviors, and patterns must be absorbed into completion for real Light to emerge from all that was nothing.

People survive by doing the best they can, even if that means hiding, changing, or running. However, those fragments, the orphans of wounds past, are still caught in their time zones in a composite of layers upon layers of experience. Looping continuously, unresolved moments filled with pain are trapped fragments of the self continuously reliving their pain. Each moment is a bubble of time that still occurs unless met with the sweet embrace of recognition and compassion.

The moment experience freely rises without threat of emotions or actions being controlled by story or judgment, drama and trauma no longer reign in the kingdom. This does not mean every incident of life must be remembered, but the presence to clear any discordant residue is required for freedom of these aspects of the self. Revisit those moments, extending a hand and a hug to whoever internally desires your attention.

Celebrate life in all the glory the movie has been and will become. Take every part of it with you to enjoy the ride, leaving no piece or peace behind. Experiences will reveal themselves as remembering; all those things that are "relative" with whom you lost touch, will begin coming home.

The Divine is knocking, desiring to be in relationship with you, within you, and between you—longing for your longing, needing your needing, yearning your yearning. In that meeting place is every withheld desire and lost dream. In full sensory perception, allow the memory of stagnant emotion to shift, so that energy may again be in motion.

Emotion is a mouthwatering fruit that drips down the chin. It's messy and juicy. When truly imbibed, it leaves one wanting just a little more but yet often full so that no more can be taken at the time. Allow each emotion to drench you with its full and expansive flavor, whether agony or ecstasy. Can you sink in deeply enough to satisfy the unquenchable thirst that keeps you searching? Will you invite it, begging more of it, to find all you have stored away as aging fine wine? Immerse in the feeling, soaking within it, bathing, marinating, completely savoring its flavor, from a place of experience not attachment. Within the depths of your longing, you will find your belonging. And that which is all so Divine will bring you to bended knee, laying you down upon the earth in order to raise you to heights of cosmic bliss. In the moments between the dark night and early dawn, the courtship begins as Lover and BeLoved find a-muse-meant for all eternity. Succumb to it; allow it; detach and engage.

Detachment is not letting go of emotion or turning it off, nor is it separating oneself from human experience, spiritual arrogance, or emotional apathy. Detachment is allowing of emotion, without being attached to the story that created it or the outcomes. It is not the feeling and expression of emotion we need to detach from; it is the need to have something to resent or project onto the emotion, person, or experience involved. We must detach from the need to fix whatever is in front of us and just let it be felt. True spirituality is fully being within all experience, permitting the self to be flooded with the power of emotion. Through the flood, all is washed away and cleansed for a new beginning to occur. In doing so, the expansiveness of being human is known—and the opportunities of creation as essence are awakened.

The voice of the spirit reminds us that every situation is always in the highest good. There is a knowing that a big picture holds all possibility and the place of miracles. The soul's sounds echo from the depths of humanity, which have been buried beneath layers of life. It's song resounds as meanderings of the heart flowing from the crown, allowing access to inspiration, Love, truth, and deservedness. But, the heart is also veiled in resistance, negative self-talk, and disempowering core values from perceptions chosen over time. Emotion rises to dissolve the curtains that stand between you and your truth. Your body holds those buried criticisms and judgments.

To hear, only be open, listening attentively and disciplined in your believing. Environment provides the setting and perceptions that create each story, the *where* and the *when*. Belief brings forth the energy of creation, allowing for the *what* and the *who*. These things at a distance, yet so close, are the experiences of separation and oneness at the same time. Elements juxtapose to create patterns that support the *how* in manifesting. Beyond and within the same space is the unknown, that which people define as destiny, fate, karma, and Divine. Here is the question—and the "quest-I-on." In seeking answers, it truly is the "quest I AM on" that wields both mystery and Mastery, bringing the extraordinary out of the ordinary to ultimately uncover who the *one* is. Although chaos is experienced as noise, the chorus of voices is simply a way to "a choir" (acquire) the greater symphony a soul has come for. Within the noise is silence; within the sound of silence is *one* voice that is heard above all else.

Truth Fullness

> » What are the stories, fables, and fairy tales you bought into?

> » How are these ideas confirmed by people around you?

> » Have you created fairytale elements in your life story?

> » Is it possible for you to let these stories go?

> » Are you ready to walk the path of Self-Love?

Will Fullness

Sit in front of a full-length or large mirror. What do you think about yourself? Look at yourself. How do you feel? Look deeply into the eyes. What are they saying to you? Speak to this person out loud. Introduce yourself. Speak about the things you Love, what you dislike, your greatest desires, your hopes and dreams, your failures, your deepest pain. Maintain focus directly into the eyes. What are you willing to reveal? How real will you be? Be aware of any discomfort, or the desire to rush or stop. Can you be with you?

Tell yourself how you hurt. Reveal why you hurt and how you got hurt. Be aware of your feelings, the need to look away, and the thoughts that go through your mind. Allow emotion to rise. From time to time, close your eyes and imagine what your reflection is saying back to you. Open to this being the first of many conversations.

After doing this several times in the coming weeks, move to another level of realness, intimacy, and transparency. Remove your clothing so that you are bare naked. Reveal your thoughts about your body. Feel any discomfort that arises, listening to chatter in the mind. Can you find beauty and compassion for every crease, wrinkle, bump, lump, pocket of cellulite, misshapen bone, bruise, or intricacy of your body vehicle? This is the "sacred space" suit you have been gifted for this lifetime.

Be aware of your need to fix or change any part of something that was created in Divine perfection. Can you Love and accept yourself as you are? Your body is an altar to your very being.

Every extra pound is the body's way of emotionally protecting you from the actions and words of yourself, especially those you project back onto yourself from others. If overweight, how have you eaten each heavy emotion, every criticism, painful experience, and abusive encounter? If underweight, how have you starved yourself of Love and life?

Look at how has this body Loves and serves you, despite yourself. This battle-worn body has fought and served internally and externally for you all of your life. How can you nurse it and recover it? This sacred space suit is the only one you have. How have you served it? Can you like it, Love it, and cherish it?

Be gentle. This practice may take time. Meet yourself as often as you would a Lover. Spend time with you. This is likely to be the first real and honest relationship you ever have. It requires conscious conversation, radical honesty, and tender presence. It is the first step toward creating new choices.

Solid Foundations

Heart Fullness

My mind constantly goes. At times, I can't sleep at night. And then, throughout the day the stories spin in my head. It's like I cannot get away from the negativity around me. And when I do, it seems to show up in my head. Why do all my sentences have "no" or "can't" in them?

No one helps me, either. They are always consumed with other things. It just seems everyone is always in chaos and they infect my world. It's exhausting. And now my head hurts. And, my back is killing me. I am so sick of it all. At times, I don't want to get back up.

How do I get rid of what I feel when all of my experiences continue to make me feel this way? These feelings bring the negative thoughts because the negativity surrounding me is overwhelming. Do I have a choice? Do I really? It does not feel like I do. This one pushes me this direction. That one shoves me in that direction. I am repressed, oppressed, and depressed.

Are we really free? This does not feel like freedom. Is there really good in the world? My life does not look very good right now. How do I find the goodness when everything in my world reflects the opposite? Where is God in any of this?

Sorry, God. My faith is wavering right now. I want to believe. I really do. But if I am honest with myself, I am not sure I ever really have. I am not sure I really trust you—or anything, for that matter. Show me. Show me, God. I need to know that life, my life, has meaning. I need to know that all of the obstacles, challenges, and pain have happened for a reason—a really good reason. Show me. Is anyone out there?

Continue this dialogue, using your feelings and words. Journal your thoughts before moving to Mind Fullness. If words do not come, draw. If you cannot draw, doodle. Breathe. Feel. Allow. Receive.

Mind Fullness

When knocked to the ground, you may think you need to get back up. Instead, stay there a while and be supported by the ground you lay on. See the foundation you are facing. What grounding of beliefs and limitations made you stumble and fall? After adjusting, stand up and create a more solid, supportive foundation. Ground into that. Life will throw you curve balls; not to have you miss but to let you know a new way to bend, turn, catch, and land. Just enjoy the game.

Your state of mind is the place you live, work, play, and raise your children (creations). What state do you come from? What state do you live in? What state would you like to move to? Can you really complain about your "environment" if you choose to live there? The environment may look like what is outside of you, but that is merely a reflection. Your true environment is your mind. How is your mind set?

Where do you sit? Are you in the stands watching? Waiting on the sidelines? In the game? Have you left the building? What are you sitting on? Your laurels? Your bum attitude? Your soft intentions, or a strong vision?

Where you sit determines the game you see, the perspective you have, the excitement you experience, and the paradigm you play in. The passion and pleasure, the abundance and prosperity, the enthusiasm and excitement all rest in the inquiry. The world is waiting.

Prejudice is judging something without really even knowing what it is. We can only be prejudiced to others because we are such strangers to ourselves. We do not know who we are, nor do we take the time to get to intimately know ourselves. Instead, the prejudiced mind is driven by fear and insecurity, worthlessness and inadequacy. In an attempt to act and appear better than, one denies their fear of being less than what appears before them. Force, arrogance, anger, and bullying projects this self-hatred outwardly, as one tries to be master over another.

Your world is at a critical point. You can turn a blind eye and deaf ear. You can wait on someone else to take the lead. You can pretend things will be fine. You can even eat, drink, shop, medicate, or chant your way into believing that all will be well, but will it?

The paradox: Everything appears to need fixing, yet it really is perfection. It is perfect in that you are being given everything necessary to create something new, while remembering something ancient and eternal. We live in the land of opposites, until we realize it is sameness, and Oneness.

The things you judge most in the world, those you run from and ignore, and those too terrible to consider are the reflections of the inner mind of humanity—your humanity. You hold these issues in the psyche. If it is showing up around you, it lives in your inner world. Where are these expressions of the world within you? Where is poverty? Where is pollution? Where are you at war? What parts of you are homeless? Where are you diseased or dying? How does the violence express, and with whom?

In order to create a dramatic shift in your world, an evolutionary leap is required within your life—within you. You cannot change the paradigms of the planet unless you actively and consciously contemplate these dynamics within your own unique experience. There is no longer room for blame, apathy, or mindless seeking; nor is this the time to escape to the mountain, isolated within the semantics of how you will hold space for others.

Life has lost meaning because words have lost meaning. "In the beginning was the word...." That was the beginning point of creation. Words create through speech, mind, and heart, albeit good, bad, or misinformed. We use them as tools of empowerment and weapons of massive destruction. The moment a person is ready to redefine limiting mental and verbal constructs, they begin a completely different life journey. Speaking words with new meaningfulness creates experience. Wisdom and feeling bring lives of greater definition. Allowing language that is more fluid impacts, engages, and touches the heart in a profound multidimensional way. When we create something meaningful, we drink in the elixir of ever evolving thought forms. This is socializing in the truest sense.

Every birthing idea brings about new questions that expand internal revelations and external conversations. If allowing, words provide opportunities for expanded views, those that involve individuals to greater witnessing, inquiry, and contemplation of the self. Then, people evolve beyond inhibitions, familial constraints, limiting experiences, and egocentric goals. Herein, each soul may journey from limited constructs to unlimited construction.

Language is used to communicate and understand. But when remaining only on the surface level, unwilling to dive deeply, meaningless conversations occur. There is no heart, leaving each other wanting and yearning for a communion we each know is possible. With surface contact, we miss out on communication and understanding of and with the real self. You are to become intimate because you need it, not because the other does. This is service and spreads to the other in the process.

Conversation is the way we get to know ourselves. It is the only time we are able to speak what we need to hear, discover how we feel, and place in front of ourselves what we think. Everything that happens outside of us is for us. Isolation is deprivation of the self to know itself. We either have to communicate with the one on the outside or make a concerted effort to speak with the one on the inside.

Miscommunication and misunderstanding are the birthplace for addiction, which is an activity of escape from connection, conversation, and communion. Ironically, we endeavor in addiction because we deeply feel something missing. In engaging with the substance of our addiction, we do not realize we are the missing piece. We are not being in relationship; we are escaping it.

At some point, we begin to discover that things have meaning because we are in relationship with what is around us. The story "as-signs" how we define ourselves. In finding connection, the environment as-signs expansive and meaning full lives when present to everything. Ultimately, meaning loses any necessity, because we are so connected to everything around us that we finally begin listening rather than talking. What once was perceived as evil, bad, and wrong becomes understood for what it truly represents: a courtship for greater communion of the self, with itself. Through it all, the soul witnesses and experiences itself so that it may birth again...and again...and again. What you have believed has been smoke and mirrors, an illusion to take you into what is real.

We never realized we made it all up: the story, the meaning, the lies, and our versions of truth. This is what the mind does, while the heart awaits our surrender. Experience the fullness that is speaking in, as, and through you. Listen—really listen. When all story is recognized for what it is, truth is revealed. And then, story is no longer necessary.

Truth Fullness

Where do you stand? Are you at the doorway? Waiting to knock? Have you turned your back on the door? Have you placed yourself in a box on the doorstep, waiting to be picked up? What is required for you to stand differently? What will move you through the doorway of your own consciousness? What touches your soul so deeply that every part of you breaks open? Can you make this human existence a humane experience?

Will Fullness

Select a word each day that you want to discover within your experience. Write this on a small sticky note and wear it on your heart. Notice the words you back away from or are triggered by. These hold the deepest reconciliation for you.

Each moment that word reveals itself by name, experience, or action, place your hand on your heart and tap three times. Breathe in the new understanding. Be "meaning-full."

Set up a chart (see pages 94–95) with the headings you see in bold. Define and give meaning to the words on the list. Journal through these words or any others that you have need of discerning.

Word List (Keep adding to this list.)

The Word	The Definition	My Definition	The Experience
Joy			
Mother			
Life			
Knowledge			
Health			
Father			
Death			
Wisdom			
Abundance			
Friend			
Illness			
Truth			
Wealth			
Enemy			
Poverty			
Energy			
Prosperity			
God			
Dying			
Growth			
Happiness			
Devil			
Prison			
Earth			
Freedom			
Love			

Word List (continued)

The Word	The Definition	My Definition	The Experience
Sadness			
Universe			
Power			
Human			
Anger			
All			
Force			
Spirit			
Jealousy			
Nothing			
Blame			
Shame			
Denial			
Prejudice			
Guilt			
Genocide			
Rape			
Human Trafficking			
Starvation			
Murder			
Sex			
Enlightenment			
Spiritual			
Religious			
Law			
Crime			

Inhale I: Attention to See Me

My presence is enough. I do not have to know *how*. I need not know *why*. There is nothing to do. I am simply to be with all of me. I have nothing to prove. I am enough. Every part of me is enough. As I unwrap the surprise that I AM, I awaken to the beauty that I have always been; in every place, at every time, in each action, in every circumstance, through every experience, with every fall, and in each rising. Today is a new day. Each memory is a new dawning. Every step is Lightening. There is no other in the room. I only see me.

On this day, my attention and intention is to:

1. Hold you close.

2. Accept you.

3. Feel into you.

4. Inspire you.

5. Care for you.

6. Honor you.

7. Listen to you.

8. Cherish you.

9. Laugh with you.

10. Love you.

11. Be devoted to you.

Exhale I: Communion of Presence

Dearest Ultimate Soul Mate,

I open my eyes to see you. I wait silently to hear you. I sit that you may touch me deeply. I am here. I am open. I willingly lose all barricades that block you from me. I am ready. I am willing. I am able to be Loved. Show me how. Help me recognize you. Reveal to me the depth of my being. Awaken me to the core of my true self. Share with me all of your truth. I will fully meet "you" where you are, in every place, at every time. Expand my heart beyond measure. I am in devotional service to you now, here to bond with you. I am here to marry all separation. Come union; may all space between us be filled.

I call forth my angels, guardians, guides, body devas, nature spirits, cellular structure, dimensional selves, parallel selves, Highest Self, Future Self, Holy Self, Ascended Masters, and Light Beings, in all places and at all times, to fully support this journey of Love, Loving, and being Loved by attuning my frequencies to the highest available now. I ask for healing holograms and sacred geometric forms to be placed around me, supporting the highest recognition and recalibration in remembrance of the Love I AM.

As these heartfelt words are spoken, I know them to be activated and charged with the energy of fulfillment and completion in the most profound and nurturing way. I find union with the greatest, most expansive expression I AM. I decree and declare this, from the great Divine soul central to my being, for US. So be it…And so it is!

Forever and in All Ways,

Yours In Love, Of Love, With Love, As Love,

The Lover's BeLoved

Self-Inflicted Nonsense (S-I-N)

Heart Fullness

I feel disconnected from everyone and everything. It is as if the world is passing me by and people are all doing what they need to do. I do not want to be left behind. I want to feel like I am part of everything, but I do not know how. People do not understand me. They do not know what my experiences have been. There is always a wall that stands between others and me. I never fully engage.

I guess I am afraid. I do not know if I can trust people. I have been hurt so many times. People make promises but they do not keep them. I meet friends but they are surface relationships. I want to experience deep connection but am different from everyone else. I feel like such a misfit. My family does not even get me?

I need space. If only I had time to get to know me again. Could I become my own friend? I need to reconnect to who I once was. I had dreams once. I had a voice. I believed in Love, passion, and goodness. Where has it all gone? How did I forget who I was—what I wanted? Will I ever find it again? Will anyone ever love me? I do not know if I even love myself. I certainly do not treat me that way.

Everything that I knew is now gone: hope, love, dreams. I keep standing up and find myself on the ground again. I have been hurt again. I have been betrayed again. I am here again. I feel lost and there is no one to reach out to. There is no one to hold me, to comfort me, to tell me that it really will be okay. What if it never is? What if this is as good as it gets?

Continue this dialogue, using your feelings and words. Journal your thoughts before moving to Mind Fullness. If words do not come, draw. If you cannot draw, doodle. Breathe. Feel. Allow. Receive.

Mind Fullness

We are all children of the Source. In the infinite wisdom of the Universe, we are all sons and daughters. However, we forget our Divine inheritance early on. People are quickly brainwashed by those who have been brainwashed, culture upon culture, generation after generation, family within family, creating the legacy of the human condition. Every person drinks the Kool-Aid upon birth and blindly follows those whom we make our Gods, from parents and church heads to teachers and politicians; and through money to man's law. Individuals conform; we learn to fit in; we become conditioned.

As energy beings, we also tap into ancestral memory that matches those frequencies existing in the body as a dormant possibility. Those encountered merely resonated so deeply with the frequency, it had to be felt and awakened inside. Any level of codependent feeling would also be a reflection of something that was within. No one can ever truly do anything to us. We are simply available for something within us to come to awareness either through self-realization or experience.

Children are sponges, sucking all experience into the body on cellular levels, emotional levels, and as energy. They subconsciously carry generational secrets, until the same experiences have to be lived out—all from the burden of holding stuff that was not theirs to begin with. Details and expression may change, but the essence of the secret remains. Betrayal, abandonment, abuse, scandal, and so forth—all breeding more of the same. It is all energy, changing form and changing hands.

From zero to 7 years old, we experience in the body, embedding encounters as memory within the cells. We do not have the language or emotional capacity to comprehend what is happening with the "big" people, much less understand issues like stress, anxiety, depression, apathy, abuse, codependence, adultery, divorce, alcoholism, betrayal, or abandonment that swirl around us. It is taken into the physiology. The open nature of the child soaks up the world womb surrounding them. This new womb is a melting pot of energies. This is what we all marinate in, what those before us marinated in and became a part of. Over time, we each add our own unique ingredients to simmer within a cream-of-soul-split-being soup!

What do we take in through respective environments from ages 0 to 7? Anger, sadness, jealousy, shame, guilt, depression, hate, apathy. It is not to say there was no joy, happiness, or pleasure. We are born in the highest vibrations of the spectrum, so they are inherent when we come in. However, heavy, denser emotions settle in, trapping lighter emotions beneath. It is not a wonder most people numb out or leave the body at a certain point.

Between ages 7 and 14, we move into the emotional body. Here we begin to get a "feel" for what is happening around us. We still do not comprehend it, but sensation strongly increases. All of us are empathic, soaking up the density that hangs in the air. Herein begins the experience of reaction, acting out, or repression. Emotions kick in, or out. An unconscious choice is made to be introverted or extroverted, passive or aggressive—or no choice, becoming both. The emotional body is compromised as we compromise ourselves by becoming people pleasers.

Age 11, a marker of Mastery, is the moment that each one of us experiences a life-changing scenario that either keeps us in the power of our Light, or sends us on the scenic route, also known as the dark night of the soul. This is where we begin our sleeplike state, waiting for true Love's kiss to fully awaken us. Until then, we may convince ourselves of awakening, but it is merely another stage of sleep. You are either awake or asleep; there is no in between.

The are many types of experiences at age 11 that can send an individual off course: a move, a death, a birth, a change of circumstance, a major event, trauma or drama, a health issue, a divorce, a marriage, and so on. Look back and you will see it. If you inquire deeply enough, you will see the pattern of reincarnation. In addition, you will see opportunities for stepping back upon the soul path at every double digit Mastery age to follow (22, 33, 44, 55, 66, 77, 88, etc.).

From ages 14 to 21, we try to make sense of what we have felt. Cognitively, we sort out the chaos, moving away from having to fully feel it. We begin thinking our way out. The level of mental control is directly in line with the degree of feeling that has been suppressed. The mind takes experience and weaves its own perceptions, possibilities, and stories. Thoughts produce action, reaction, and response in equal measure to accumulated physical and emotional pressure within. Once we begin to ignore the feeling brain, the mind computes a story by processing from the data entered from the environment.

As children, we do not always have words or explanations; we have feelings that guide us. Belief systems create our lives. Every experience in life is simply the reincarnation of a prior experience brought forward to reconcile the positive and the negative, so that we ultimately move to the "neutral" mind.

In many cases, beliefs are based on perceptions that are totally untrue or falsely taught. But, we create every experience in our lives from that filter, until we reclaim empowerment and Divine nature, by letting go of the story, identity, and ideology. We will create countless opportunities to unlearn the lie and remember truth.

Beyond filters and perceptions, the chasm occurs because of two common unconscious intentions:

I want to be just like everybody else, so I fit in.

I want to be special, like no one else, so I stand out.

This two-faced intention means that we create both. The funny thing is, we do end up like everybody else, and no one else, in our self-created chaos and dysfunction. There is more of an average quality to success than there is to the story that got us there. However, there is average-ness in that every person creates dysfunction, addiction, abuse, betrayal, adultery, and the like. We all have skeletons in the closet, those we hope no one ever finds. We try to fill in deep holes of shame with external gratification or by giving up the rest of ourselves.

We also make ourselves equally special and unique in the details of the story, both the downfall and the rising. By believing we outdo everyone in our expression of chaos, victimhood, obstacles, and challenge, it becomes a ping-pong rally of whose pain is bigger. *Her sin was bigger than his. He is more messed up than she is. My story is really bad compared to that.* We are competitive!

Although most of us do not want to face the past, we have no problem carrying it around with us. As much as we want our pain gone, we do not know who we are without it. Equally so, we do not realize who we are truly being in it. The irony is we have not discovered this secret to life—one that opens gates and keys within our DNA, and avails us of the power that births gods.

We are beautifully individual in how we create the comedy and trag-edy of life. We Love success because of the story it is born out of, not so much because of lavishness. Many believe it is about the vast materialism or fame, but it is really the celebration of someone who "made it through the rain." The hero's journey is why we came! We are always protected, guided, and held. The signs and symbols show up, especially when hit-ting bottom. At that point, we are able to surrender enough to be more aware of a living world surrounding us, one that has been breathing life into everything animate and inanimate purely to support the awareness of our deeply magical nature. We create both—the average and special—being exactly like everyone else and, yet, uniquely individual.

At that point, we finally begin to discover what real success is, one by one, opening our eyes to the value of time, presence, Love, community, and service. Money, cars, homes, drugs, alcohol, and sex are not enough to fill anyone, or make them feel whole. There will be something missing, and it happens to be the most sacred and beautiful part of your life—that which sits in the shadows, hides in the dark, and waits for you to see how fully devoted it has been to you. This side of you recognizes and expresses true unconditional Love. Yet, it is an enigma because we perceive it com-pletely opposite of its purpose.

This part of you is the complete package you have boxed yourself in. With strings attached, you have allowed yourself to become caught in ties that bind, lies that linger, and garbage that piles up. You live out story after story, while being cast in a spell of enchantment. This is your Mastery, and it is your mystery/"my-story."

Truth Fullness

>> What did you buy into?

>> What did you give up in order to conform?

>> What are you doing that you really don't want to do?

>> What are you saying *yes* to when you really want to say *no*?

>> Who are you allowing in your life that you really wish were not?

Will Fullness

For a period of time, tell the people in your life that you are unable to take on any additional responsibilities. Give back the things you have been doing for others that you do not like. For every other request over the next 40 days, say *no*. Be conscious of the discomfort you feel in saying *no*. Upset could arise within or from others. Their upset is not your business; yours is your work.

Take off your watch if you wear one. Remove all lists from your life. Do not keep lists on paper or in your mind. In order to discover your ebb and flow between doing and being, test the limits of time by doing things in the moment as they come to mind. The ability to trust and know that time is on your side is necessary. You will begin to discover that following your heart, and choosing what you truly desire, provides its own space. Time will create more of itself. It is also a lesson in understanding that the important things will come to mind when the clutter of the past, and of other people, has been cast aside.

Extreme relationships may need a stronger form of discipline. You have taught people how to treat you, allowing it to happen. They do not realize they are harming you. Take the time and space to shift extreme relationships that are completely unloving: friends, family, parents, substances, experiences. Quit these completely until you feel ready to gently step back into connection. Until you know how to maintain loving interactions, place strong boundaries. Lovingly let people know you are stepping away and do not wish to be contacted. Relay that you are taking time to work on yourself and your life.

This period of silence allows both sides an opportunity to reflect, and time to miss one another, so that future interactions hold more respect. Restate boundaries when lines have been crossed, so that you and they are re-taught what you are willing to allow and what you are not.

Learn to live for yourself, moment by moment. With each breath, do what comes to mind. Follow through with action. Then, sit back and take another breath. Continue this practice for at least one month. You will be surprised how fulfilled you feel. You will accomplish more, and have time for you. You will begin interacting with those people who help create supportive and meaningful experiences instead of just settling for what is there. Be aware of how stress decreases when presence increases. When we help ourselves, the Universe gets the signal to give us more of the same.

❧ 13 ❧

Heal Your "Elationship"

Heart Fullness

I feel so alone. No one understands me. I feel like an outcast in my family—the black sheep. I can't do anything right. I walk alone on this path of life. I do not even feel as if I know myself. My greatest fear is to be lonely and alone. What if it is like this my whole life? What if there really is no one I can love or who will love me? What if there is no one or nothing I can trust? It feels as if I walk in the shadows. The thoughts of my mind haunt me and keep me isolated. I want so much to live the dream and yet it feels like a nightmare at times. I wish someone would find me. I wish I could find myself.

Is there anyone out there? God, do you hear me? Send me a sign that I am not alone. Where is the Light? Where is the Light in me? Help me. Help me.

I want to be cherished by someone. If just one person could love me for me, I would feel complete. I know that my soul mate is out there somewhere but I have no idea where to find them. I feel lonely but I do not want to settle so it is better to hold back until my soul mate shows up.

I just need to fill my time with something. But, I'm bored. I'll try a vision board. I will write a letter or create a description so the Universe is very clear. Maybe I will just watch some TV.

I should get out and do something, maybe even have some fun. I know I need to exercise, but I will start tomorrow. I need to eat healthier and a few more hours of rest would help, but I have other things I need to do. I will travel everywhere when I have someone to go with. I will feel like exercising and eating better because I will have someone to do it with. It is just a matter of time.

Continue this dialogue, using your feelings and words. Journal your thoughts before moving to Mind Fullness. If words do not come, draw. If you cannot draw, doodle. Breathe. Feel. Allow. Receive.

Mind Fullness

Every challenge in your life boils down to one longing: communion as relationship. First we seek it in the outside world through things and other people. Eventually we evolve, discovering it lay completely within the self. Then, it transforms all on the outside as well.

Each person brings forth a story of tragedy and triumph—Love and pain—success and failure. However, it is the story that keeps us separate. Even the stories of bonding keep us separate from other groups that are different in some way. Stories require at least two sides to exist. What if the story is dropped? What's left? What remains? Nothingness. No "relationship," because there would be nothing to relate to. It would all be connected—"elationship."

However, the path to elationship is not in avoiding or cutting off relationships any more than it is buying into beliefs that connection can be solely through energy or electromagnetic fields. You came to experience a body and a full field of possibility. You came to be human, in order to experience your humanity. We are not here to float into the ethers. Nor are we to be sucked under by our own circumstances, but we are to feel. We are here to be in the world, but not of it.

When relationships do not seem to work, or ghosts of the past rear up, there is nowhere to look but in. Rather than react, re-in-act. Go inside and ask:

Where has this happened before?

What way are you to act now that is different from how you have in the past?

What experience of me is asking to be revealed?

Every encounter is only a holographic representation of a prior projection. It is time to put the ghosts of the past to rest, once and for all. Your relationship to others, or non-relationship, is simply the magnified version of your relationship to your self.

Non-forgiveness creates dis-ease in the body—your body and the collective body. Take time to heal by finding forgiveness for those who you believe have hurt you. Take time to forgive yourself for all you have and have not done. Free your body. Free your mind. Free your soul. Forgiveness appears as if it is for the other person, but it is for you. Forgiveness, a miraculous healing elixir, is for-giving you back to you.

See every experience with Love, in whatever way or degree you know how. Hold compassion for the individuals involved. What you give to them, you amplify for yourself. See them in their power, truth, and wholeness, especially when they cannot. In that moment, they are stumbling in the dark, just like you.

But do not be mistaken: Although you need to revisit your past, this is not about the past; it's about the present. And, it's not about what's wrong. It's about what's right. It has nothing to do with "out there." It is always for recognition of what's "in here"—to gain clarity around what you are presently co-creating with. Co-creation involves the manifestations derived by both the conscious and unconscious selves. Be clear: It is all you.

You will only find peace outside when you discover the pieces inside that are calling out to you. That piece/peace will be found when you truly admit your deepest fear. That vulnerable opening is the reconciliation of your greatest lie, as you step into greater truth. Peace of mind equates with "piece of Mind." We are also here to know the whole self through experience, the full spectrum of dark to Light. This is a great lesson in trust and greater lessons to be determined. The negative experiences that appear are not the issue. What we do with them, how we hold onto them, and what we attribute to them is the issue.

Trusting oneself to take all appropriate steps is important. Trusting is key. Most importantly, allowing healing in whatever manner it appears is true surrender. At times this can appear as crisis, chaos, and breakdown, but healing is still happening. There are many instances where life obstacles create a payoff. Growth requires moving beyond the immediate singular gain toward a sustained collaborative reward.

Healing can occur in an instant, if blocks are removed. This is possible because we are, in actuality, already whole. The obstacle is that we deny and repress one end of the spectrum within wholeness. All that is required is the choice to acknowledge oneself with and in the full spectrum. This will occur where open and honest communication with the self exists.

Healing should not be approached because you are trying to rid yourself of something. Healing occurs because you are willing to experience yourself through the full course of that dis-ease, obstacle, or challenge. In embracing all aspects of the healing process fully, the initial discomfort is a gateway that allows transformation.

Life is a journey of opposites with continual opportunities for discovery. Within each one, birth happens. Every experience is for moving through, not holding onto. Every step is meant to have a beginning and an end. By willingly diving into a process of death at each stage, empowered births into the unknown are realized. This is awakening. Far grander than knowing, it is unknowing.

The dark is Light. It is sacred. This is why it should be remembered, celebrated, and acknowledged—not hidden, denied, or forgotten. Your Divinity, your wholeness of being, is all of you, and what you have been through. Darkness, the dark night of the soul, is one Divine half of that wholeness. It creates the full brilliance of light that finally shines through you as the other half of your Divine wholeness. From total darkness the Source created Light. So, why would we not sit in our own darkness, and dark night, to reach the Light?

Your divinity is "in you" as the dark shadows and secrets you hold hidden. Your divinity is expressed in the way you fight or take flight, survive and thrive, fall and rise. Your Divinity comes "through you" in the steps you walk to reach the heavenly gates of your own understanding, heaven being the higher mind. This is how the Divine expresses in, as, and through you. You deny the Divine when you deny any part of yourself.

There is nothing out there. It all exists as the matrix of *you* so that *you* choose what inspires *you* and do what helps *you*, fixes *you*, changes *you*, saves *you*! It has all been created for *you*—to know yourself and all of your creative capacity and expansiveness. Let go of what you think you are doing. Dive into the Essence and activation of your whole Being!

Truth Fullness

> » Who or what have you duped yourself into believing you are here to inspire?

> » To help?

> » To fix?

> » To change?

> » To save?

> » Who are you really here for?

Will Fullness

Look at the relationships in your life, your most challenged ones. They are re-creations of relationships and experiences from childhood. Who do those individuals represent? What wounds are you re-creating and reincarnating as experience? What behaviors of yours have allowed the same relationship to happen again? Contemplate how the relationship would be had you entered into the relationship differently than your way of seeing, hearing, behaving, and reacting. What experience of you in personality—creativity—expression—behavior is asking to now rise?

It is time to learn to become still. Deepen your stillness practice beyond what you have. If you still have none, begin one. Take some time and be quiet for contemplation.

❦{ 14 }❦

Shhh-a-Me

Heart Fullness

I feel overwhelmed. There is not enough time and so much to do. I am filled with stress and anxiety. I never feel as if I have a moment for me. The projects continuously pile up: work, family, bills—the obligations. I am exhausted. I wish time would stop for a while. I cannot figure out how to balance it all. How do other people do it? Why can't I? I cannot seem to be the right parent, partner, friend, or employee. I feel so average, and at times it just feels like I am failing at everything.

I don't feel as if I know who I am anymore. I may never have known who I am. I don't even feel a part of life. Everything feels so scattered. I move through each day so quickly that I am not remembering most of what happens. I cannot even remember half the people I saw. I am not sure if time is speeding up or I am checking out.

I feel pulled in every direction. My feet feel unbalanced as if they will not fully support me. My beliefs, morals, and values have been buried in a pile across the room. At times I remember them; other moments I do well just to get myself and my family where they need to be.

I wish I could feel safe and grounded. I want to be supported. I want a real sense of who I am, who I came to be—not the lost wanderer I feel I have become. Will I last? Will there be enough time? I have lost faith—in people, in life, in myself. I feel like such a failure.

I don't care. I don't care about anything or anyone anymore. I'm numb. I do not feel. I pretend I care, but I don't. I am sick of how things are. I am tired and fed up with always taking care of everyone else. What about me? What about what I want? What about what I need? Who is there for me? What about my pain? When is my lucky break? I'm angry. I'm angry, God! Why me? Why my life? Why this?

I wish I had drive and desire. It's all been sucked out of me. I want to do things but do not have any energy left to do them. Life is an endless loop of work, bills, sleep, and to-do lists. I do not have any fun. I do not have any freedom. All of my passion is gone. I do not really enjoy being here. I am not sure I want to be here. I think I have all but given up.

I do things for others to try to feel good about myself but I do not feel any better—just more exhausted. I'm done. I'm done!

Continue this dialogue, using your feelings and words. Journal your thoughts before moving to Mind Fullness. If words do not come, draw. If you cannot draw, doodle. Breathe. Feel. Allow. Receive.

Mind Fullness

You can fool yourself into believing you are all grown up. But you're just playing dress-up. You are always and will always be the child. The question is: In every moment forward, are you being childish or childlike? One is reactionary, tantrums, triggered, and in the shadow. The other is engaged, present, and available to the gifts. Mind yourself, now. Either way, most of us grew up too quickly, being handed responsibilities and emotions that were not ours in the first place. This is the birthplace of two parts where one begins to live a dual life. The duality is in living life from two eyes. One eye/I sees through the perceptions of the shadow, also known as the beast, monster, or devil self. The other eye/I sees from the perspective of the angel, hero, or god self.

Choices in life allow you to be the beast and angel, but never exclusively either one. Life is spent being one and then the other, escaping this one or that, desperately wanting the experiences of both, and unable to claim either one fully. Only when willing to succumb to the beast within will you fully engage the angelic presence that lay dormant in the very heart of the monster you don't want to see. This monster unconditionally Loved you enough to be your wounding. That part of you is simply awaiting your unconditional Love in response.

Anxiety and depression are opposite ends of denied shame. Anxiety says, "I fear the future where I will fail." Depression looks at the past, seeing "where *I* have failed" failed. Depression is a cry for creativity. Anxiety is a call for presence.

The "present"—the gift of oneself—can only be found in the moment one is willing to embrace the shame of the shadows. This is the phantom of the opera: The one who wears the mask of both light and dark is being beckoned by the music of the night, while in the midst of an angel of innocence and purity, adrift with Light.

Guilt arises from crossing boundaries, breaking rules, or some type of violation. Shame arises from being unable to meet the mark, failure, and falling short—in fact, a belief in the wrongness of being. However, guilt and shame rarely present themselves separately. The one who is embedded in shame uses guilt to reinforce the shame. Guilt focuses on the *things that have been done*; shame identifies with *I*, the *doer*.

There is a misconception that we are made to feel ashamed by others. However, shame can only be given to the self, by the self. It is quiet and hides. We become embarrassed once our shame is seen. But in both cases, shame is held like a rare gem, because it allows the person to stay small inside his or her mind. It is the grandest and most subtle form of narcissism. We all have it, but few are willing to own it, much less reveal it. Holding shame is feeling bad about oneself to the point of being unable to fit. These are the statements we say within the quiet spaces of our own being:

Guilt	Shame
"How could I have *done that*?"	"How could *I* have done that?"
"What have I *done*?"	"*I* am a failure."
"What a terrible *thing* to do?"	"What a *fool*!"
"I hurt *them* so badly."	"How terrible and worthless *I* am."

Our deepest need is confrontation with the shame that has been held. It is the greatest block to Love, where we become our own worst enemy. The enemy is "in-a-me." No one wants to claim their shame. That in itself seems shameful. Surprisingly, however, the sense of shame is actually a good thing. It is to be cherished and valued.

Guilt's opposite is to be guiltless, meaning innocent and blameless—reasons to feel good about the self. Shame's opposite is to be shameless, which requires an even greater disrespect and insensitivity toward the self. Shame is actually the precious gift that gives real insight into the human condition and patterns we create in life. In addition, it provides the most evidence for an individual's power as a reality creator, thus also providing impetus to change and create new paradigms. If the Law of Attraction is not working for you in the way you desire, look again. Could you be attracting your deeply denied shame and all the beliefs about yourself? Universal laws can't not work.

Shame gives rise to the paradox of being human, allowing us to see the limits and limitlessness we each possess. The irony is that where there is wholeness, there is limitation. In being human, we experience the tension and intention of always being pulled in opposite directions. This is the angst of being more than, and less than, human. The central point between devilish and godlike is human being. To uncover and face individual shame is to walk hand-in-hand with personal demons and the god of personal understanding, having touched the far reaches of both heaven and hell.

When we think of recovery, we think of the addict. This is an individual returning to a more whole being than he or she was before. It is defined as one who habituates or abandons oneself to something compulsively or obsessively. Addiction is a synonym for human being. We are all addicted to varying degrees. We have habits and patterns that keep us in obsessed states of mind.

The greatest addictions lay in withheld guilt and shame. These become expressions of denial, repression, separation, and rejection. This is the human condition—the perceptions and stories that feel very real, but are the illusion that is habitually created. In this place, we continually abandon the self.

This is also the meaning of psychosis: the minds delusions or hallucinations that indicate impaired contact with reality—in other words, perception. Psychosis is the state one is in if experiencing any degree of pain, because we are in addiction. If you choose to reject, repress, deny, or separate from this idea, go back and again read from the beginning of the Mind Fullness section of this chapter.

The greatest gift of freedom lay in holding these parts of ourselves with tenderness and understanding. They require deep listening and space. Every event in life that has offered up additional pain is a call for Love from these very parts of us.

Each aspect is a flower that has been cut from your garden of Eden. It offers itself in the beauty it holds, but has been cut nonetheless. Give it water through your tears, and fertilize it with nutrients of acknowledgment, space, and time. The warmth of your sight is the sunlight that lets it remain lifted up, or you give it nothing allowing that part to wither and die in a 3-D reality: dry, desolate, darkness.

You are Love personified in its fullness, that which is addicted—the drug, the drugged, and the rehabilitation. It is a sobering walk, but an intoxicating one at that. As you drink of yourself, you will enjoy the drunken stupor, one that does not hang over you heavily, but keeps you on the high in your heart. There is no need to search outside for someone or something to fill you. Your flask is already full with communion. You need only sip your "whine" and be nourished by your "breadth," as you raise your hands to the sky, in the celebration of your spirit.

To fully realize the god within, embrace the devil. To fully stand with the devil, let your idea of the god die, understanding they are one in the same. A true devil can authentically own his deeds before other gods. A real god can stand in his own devilish creation, with reverence for all other devils. In the sacred symbol of Namaste, gazing deeply into one's own eyes, the hidden secret to life is found. Look carefully. Within the pupil lay the fire and brimstone of one who is willing to be the chaos and insanity, meeting another pupil who is willing to be the pilgrimage to higher ground. All the while the "third eye/I" sees and knows all is, simply, a comedy of tragedy. This is the great cosmic joke of Love; dreaming it is unLoved, in order to awaken to the Unconditional Love it has always been again and again and again.

Truth Fullness

> » Where in your body do you hold your guilt?
>
> » Where in your body do you hold your shame?
>
> » What did you give up by taking on shame and guilt?
>
> » Have you really lost that?
>
> » What is the voice of your devilish self, the one that rests within the shadows?
>
> » What is the song that echoes in the night from the angelic self?

Will Fullness

Write out the dialogue of one story. Write a Love letter, poem, song, comedy, or tragedy, or paint a picture in honor of both the angel and the devil within. Next, find a person or people who feel safe and can hold the space for you to share intimately your story, especially the details of your guilt and shame.

If you do not have anyone, find a coach or counselor. Whomever you use, a friend or professional, let them know you are not seeking any assistance or need anything fixed, you are just looking to share and be heard so that you may honor your own story.

Experience Experiencing

Heart Fullness

Feeling broken, but I am holding on. I am barely holding on. But I know there is something strong inside of me. I am down. But I know I can get up again. I have been brought down to my knees. I have been pushed to my breaking point. I'll get back up. I'll get back up. One day, I will stand again. Today is not that day.

After a while, this will pass. There will come a time when it won't hurt. One year from now, this moment won't matter. I am stuck between if and when. But, there will come a moment where I will understand. And then it won't hurt; then it won't hurt like it does now. I have the scars, but they will heal. There will be a day that the pain ends. There will be a day I am whole again. I won't stay broken. I won't give them that pleasure. This, too, shall pass. Right now, I'll just lay here. Right now, I will feel what I can feel. Right now, I am where I am.

Continue this dialogue, using your feelings and words. Journal your thoughts before moving to Mind Fullness. If words do not come, draw. If you cannot draw, doodle. Breathe. Feel. Allow. Receive.

Mind Fullness

Every experience helps us prove the rightness of beliefs looping within the mind. They are what we are looking for, so they appear. Each statement and action are given as a pathway for choice: a loving path or the unloving one, leading either to the empowered self or the wounded one. Actually, our goodness and our wrongness are both acceptable. They are both experience. Whether we choose the dark side or the Light, it is all Light reflecting—and all roads lead back home. Our work is in accepting both, especially our wrongness.

God—the Universe—Source is an unbiased, non-judging energy that desires to fulfill our beliefs, whatever they are. Regardless of where belief systems stand, every person has the opportunity to choose again. We are here to continually let go. They are merely garments to be worn and discarded. In this vast Universe, the one constant is change, and his fraternal twin is creation.

We are made in the image and likeness of our Creator—that face that is constant creation or creativity, and its resulting experience of itself. We are creative capacity and have the pure possibility of any manifested creation. The body is an experiential vessel to house the creative force, and our greatest ally. Thoughts in combination with feeling, expectation, and will create beginnings and endings with infinite expansion into growth and transformation.

Right thought, right feeling, and right action allow for a right resulting manifestation. If thought, feeling, and action are not in congruence, a misaligned manifestation occurs as course correction. This is not punishment, because the Universe does not judge. This is a self-determined autocorrection, so that we calibrate toward full alignment with the true self. How long it takes is inconsequential because we are timeless, boundless beings that continuously transform.

Everything creates an emotional response. If something does not turn out as desired, it is because embedded guilt, shame, or unworthiness has produced mirroring results as course correction. This offers an opportunity to look at whether or not our thoughts match the words we speak and the actions we take. Opportunities will continue appearing, giving the chance to have what we truly want.

Experiences are passing waves. Old experiences are not for getting swept up in or drowning in. We are to stand in the waves, strong and solid, allowing ourselves to feel them come and go. As guardians of our own ocean of experiences, we witness life. This is what it means to be in the world, but not of it. We stand in the ocean, feeling and experiencing every wave as it washes forward and retreats. We have the choice to turn away and have it catch us from behind, often knocking us down. We have a choice to let it crash into us or to face it by walking gently into the wave. We also have the choice to stand strong, or get pulled into it by the undertow of attachment. Regardless of how, all are ways to experience and be one with the ocean.

Source Energy experiences each of us, in full Love with presence, but not getting caught up in our nonsense. Finding itself in each piece, as each piece, expressing through each piece, experience experiences itself. True creation has no positive or negative, only neutral. If you go to the beach, you do not get caught up in a single drop of water, do you? You will miss out on the entire ocean. In the same way, will you withhold the rest of life based on one incident?

You make the choice to feel pain. You choose to have it in your life. No one is punishing you. No one is branding or cursing you. It is all you. This is not said for you to punish yourself even more. This is to know how powerfully you have created, and that you can create again and again.

Judgment is the method used to continue pain or karma. Pain is actually the signal that beliefs held are not right or true. It is the indication that you are not living in the now, but lost in something past or future. Pain results as course correction for you to reevaluate where your mind, heart, and body have gone. Bring them back to the present moment and you will see there is no problem.

Truth Fullness

- » How have you been judged?
- » How do you judge?
- » How have you gossiped about others?
- » How have you been gossiped about?
- » How are your thoughts serving you now?
- » Are there any thoughts that would feel better?
- » Any behaviors?
- » Any words?
- » New friends?
- » New choices?

Will Fullness

On a sheet of paper, list all of the beliefs about yourself that have created your current experience. Allow a brain dump so that you can see the construction materials of your life. These were the foundation of the hero's journey. Honor them; cherish them. They are why you will create a brilliant new story.

Get a package of sticky notes. Go through each statement on the list, and create a "new beginning" statement: On each sticky note, place an affirmative new beginning belief. Go through the list until there is a new concept for every old one. Make copies of each sticky note. Place the copies everywhere: in the kitchen, your closet, the bathroom, your office, your desk, the mirror, the car—anywhere you spend any time. Each time you read one, take a deep breath, as if inhaling and anchoring it inside of your body. Plant the new belief within the fertile soil of your mind. Carry it down from crown into the earth. Inhale back up, bringing it up around the body and sending it into the Universe.

When repeating these affirmations, say them aloud in the beginning, in order to hear your voice, or move your body in some way to have an experience. Be witness to your new claim on life. If ever any thought or feeling arises that doubts these new beliefs, acknowledge the negative thought and repeat the new affirming belief again. Breathe in and out deeply during the process.

Each morning in your prayers, ask that the new beliefs be proven to you. Expect them. Look for them. Know they are there. When something occurs that mirrors the new belief, acknowledge yourself and your Higher Power for creating that in your life. Sit in the gratitude. Express gratitude. Gratitude breeds more to be grateful for. If an experience arises from the old belief, take this opportunity hold the new one.

Allow new beginnings to unfold in your life. As you continue this practice, seek expansive, more powerful, and supportive beliefs. We are infinite in our ability to grow and expand. The human self sets ceilings. A proactive effort of conscious allowing raises ceilings to new levels, while releasing old belief systems.

Inhale II: Attention to Mind

Right thought is the realignment and recalibration to a neutral stance of witness, honoring everything surrounding me and encompassing the ability to hold myself evenly—despite external appearances. Right thought is not doing or being, but the integrity of both presence and absence. I open to the full experience of authenticity, beginning by righting my mind.

It is in my loving Attention to bring right thought to:

1. Creating conscious choices in every arena of my life.

2. Visioning with creativity.

3. Embracing change as an experience of Self.

4. Viewing every event and circumstance as a success.

5. Committing with courage in everything I do.

6. Celebrating life's gifts through the eyes of innocence, the gentle touch of wonder, and an open heart of gratitude.

7. Breathing in every moment with the excitement and enthusiasm.

8. Embodying the lead role in my life.

9. Stepping softly and calmly with reverence.

10. Inspiring my world by living in and as infinite possibility.

11. Uniting in Oneness through bridging my being-ness and doing-ness.

Exhale II: Communion in Right Thought

Dearest Ultimate Soul Mate,

I lovingly commit to being present to US. I welcome consistent right mind fullness for US. I am willing to walk my talk, in alignment with my highest expression. I am willing to understand and allow all experiences that engage a deeper awareness of my mind and life. I ask now that we engage in righting and rewriting the conditions of the story. I ask for US to rise into the highest possible state of self-respect and self-value.

I ask that I see my darkness and my Light, recognizing easily where I am misaligned and aligned. I now move from seeking to seeing, from hearing to listening and from clouded thought to clear thought fullness. I initiate a new neural net, charged and activated into the rightness of being, in its highest possibility.

I ask for the assistance of my angels, guardians, guides, body devas, nature spirits, cellular structure, dimensional selves, Highest Self, Holy Self, Ascended Masters, and Light Beings, in all places and at all times, to fully support this journey of loving consistently, placing US firmly upon the Divine scale of balanced living, being and knowing the truth that I AM.

As these heartfelt words are spoken, I know them to be activated and charged with the energy of fulfillment in the highest state of unconditional Love. So be it...And so it is!

Forever Yours,

The Lover's BeLoved

❧{ 16 }❧

Dropping Masks

Heart Fullness

I don't know how to tell them no. They will be angry with me and might stop speaking to me.

She triggers me so badly. I can't stand when I get angry. I am more evolved than that. The last thing I want is for anyone to see me get riled up. I just can't give my power away like that. I have to control my emotions in front of people. It is not good to let them see me cry or get upset.

I want to be popular. I want everyone to like me and think I am a good person. Good people are not angry or mean or bitchy. But how do other people get away with it? Where is their karma? When do they get theirs? I have come across some pretty interesting people. You would not believe what they do or how they act!

The worst is when I feel jealous about others. It just makes me want to talk about them. There is nothing wrong with that, is there? Everybody does it. Who knows what is true or not, and I am sure they are talking about me anyway.

Continue this dialogue, using your feelings and words. Journal your thoughts before moving to Mind Fullness. If words do not come, draw. If you cannot draw, doodle. Breathe. Feel. Allow. Receive.

Mind Fullness

We live in "civilized" cultures that thrive on gossip, tabloid stories, news headlines, controversial television, and a viral internet. Addiction to our human condition is only superseded in how enamored we are of the interplay of functional and dysfunctional conditions of other human beings. Are these not the ones we make our martyrs, villains, and celebrities, casting spotlights upon them? In our cliques, social circles, broadcasts, and reality shows, everything is based on conformity, ratings, and dramatic appeal.

We Love bad girls and devilish boys. We glorify them and then tear them down, while unconsciously playing out our own soap operas and dramas. Many yearn for fame and fortune, with long lists of followers to laud and applaud. Then, a controversial moment arises in which they are lynched by those who loyally idolized them at one time. Celebrities, politicians, and religious figures are the best scandals to our sink teeth into. We are not much different from a hungry pack of laughing hyenas, sheepishly moving about as scavengers, ready for the kill.

People will do what they do: point the finger, blame, shame, project—simply because they do not want to witness their own erring. It is easier to project onto another's foibles. This is the true expression of one who is wounded, keeping one's own things hidden, until they are not. Transparency is salvation. Authenticity is freedom.

A new drug—hypnotic heroine, injected via "the tube"—produces virtual highs as society mindlessly escapes into what they perceive as drama and trauma beyond their own. Each exposure deadens the senses a little more. These "make-believe" ideas drive desires deeper, resulting in addictions of wanting—reinforcing fantasy, chaos, force, and results. By programming ideas into the mind, we unconsciously create from these perspectives. What is watched on television will tell-a-vision of what is to happen in our own lives, a technological version of psychic prediction, because it places those very seeds within the psyche. Science fiction foretold of computers taking over humans. Has it come true? Through video games, children are trained to kill; why are we so shocked when it happens in real life? Is this not a form of brainwashing—the very thing we condemn terrorists, cults, and religions for? Are we being conscious stewards of life or unconsciously facilitating death? Haven't our distorted brains, the computer processors of the body, run away with us? They compute every worst-case scenario, identifying with fear and projection.

External gratification, the consort of the mind, tempts people away from what really matters. These truths rest quietly within the heart and gut as voices that have gone unheard. Emptiness and lack of purpose and need are the mind's groupies, filled with chatter and superficiality. Instead of choosing to find the real self, multiple identities express as dis-eased outcroppings of the embedded pieces we think are being escaped.

There is no way to escape the false self, or the real Self. Eventually both will appear, the former coming into the room first. The false self anchors deeply, finding the ways to get comfortable in an uncomfortable world, being convinced that all that is wrong with the world has nothing to do with them. After all, the false self is a Master of *con*formity, *con*viction, and *con*volution—in other words a "con" artist. It is all the Self, merely shadow and Light. These forms are not false at all, but fallen.

Most individuals become what everyone else wants: people-pleasers, people-fixers, people-savers. Seeing ourselves as others see us, we replicate those we have come from, despite any determination not to. We chase footprints to live up to being who they have been, but not more than. We are really here to be ourselves. How many have followed family footsteps into businesses, relationships, addictions, and wounding? What we don't realize: Their stories become the thorn-laden crown passed down as rulership, their dis-ease—the ailment carried as the cross to bear, their unfulfilled dreams—the torch held against the feet, and their fallen self— beaten, battered, bruised, and left to die.

Self-crucifixion keeps us searching for peace, happiness, and worthiness. Continuously dying for their S-I-N (self-inflicted nonsense), we place these real or imagined burdens onto others in line, and we call that Love. A moment will come where it hurts bad enough that we cast aside the briars, lay down the burdens, and step away from the fire. In this place, we find the power in our pain as the ember within is fanned with the strength of the human spirit. The "call for Love" will be to recognize, to hear and hold, and to honor and see what has not been. Who is that "One" with the capacity to be devoted, fully and completely?

Truth Fullness

> » How many places in your life are you people-pleasing?

> » Does always adjusting, conforming, and giving yourself away create any tiredness or anger?

> » Do you let others do things for you?

> » Do you ever do things to please yourself? What? When?

Will Fullness

Lay in a comfortable position with eyes closed. Open your mouth wide and breathe, keeping it open the whole time. Breathe in deeply, exhaling with a "H-A-A-A-A-A," never letting the mouth close. Take the breath deeply into the body, imagining it traveling into every crevice. Breathe in an even rhythm, a circular breath, with each one beginning as one is ending. Make sure the mouth remains wide open while breathing.

After a few minutes, you may begin to feel a tingling sensation in the body or feel slightly light-headed as emotion rises up. Notice the energy. Where is it tingling, feeling trapped or stagnant? What is rising up? Just continue to breathe into these spaces. Stay with the breath, regardless of what begins to rise. Allow the feelings to express. Breathe through the discomfort. Let emotion come. Your breakthrough is beyond that moment where you feel you can no longer continue.

Bring the right hand to any place on your body perceived as broken, ugly, or uncomfortable in some way. As you breathe into that space, see white healing light extending from your palm. Breathe.

Transform this area by feeling into it, being in conversation with it, and by caressing it in a circular motion with unconditional loving light and energy. Tell your body how you feel about it. Let it speak back to you, informing you of how it feels about you. Let it divulge the kind of host you have been. Notice the emotion held. Listen. Feel. Listen. Feel. Listen. Breathe.

Comfort this area of the body as you would a child or soldier that has been wounded. Speak the words of Love and forgiveness that you need to hear. Be held in that way, spoken to, nurtured, and Loved. Breathe.

Visualize the body healing, transmuting, and transforming with the healing light energy emanating from your palm. Continue until you only see pure white Light and/or feel peace. When complete, place your right palm upon your heart, over the heartbeat. Put your left hand over your right. Let your left hand and the pulse in your body recharge the right hand. Feel gratitude. Breathe.

Continue this practice until you have connected to all areas perceived as broken. Do not rush through these processes. You are learning how to really Love for the very first time. Love is not mental. Love is a full sensory experience. Initially, it may feel as if you are thinking into Love rather than feeling into it, because it is what you have known. Be gentle as you discover how to really feel. You have identified with a story—with what people have told you about you. The identity is the encasement—the coffin; the real you is trapped inside.

Note: If you have trouble sending loving and forgiving thoughts, imagine you are working with a small child or see yourself as a younger child version of you that believes they are broken or has been severely abused.

Pain in the Neck

Heart Fullness

I keep having this pain in my neck. It is interesting that it shows up at certain times or particular places. You know, it happens every time I get around [insert name(s)]. I am always helping them. I spend my time, my money, and my energy. I do not even get a thank you. At the very least they could say, "Thank you." They really should do more than that. I needed help moving. Do you think anyone showed up to help? All of a sudden, everyone was too busy. It is always about them, what they need, and how I can help. I am tired of playing this game. Friends do not do that to friends. Even my friend! She had the gall to resent me, after all that I have done for her. She needs to take a good look at what I did on her behalf. If anything she owes me.

Continue this dialogue, using your feelings and words. Journal your thoughts before moving to Mind Fullness. If words do not come, draw. If you cannot draw, doodle. Breathe. Feel. Allow. Receive.

Mind Fullness

All dis-ease and discomfort on the physical level stems from emotional suppression. Blockage of emotion, non-awareness of feeling, and masking of pain create physiological changes within the body. In addition, we are subjected to psychic, emotional, and thought pattern grids, handed down from parents and ancestors. This causes a reenactment of patterns, behaviors, and projections until awareness or clearing occurs. Dis-ease serves a purpose. It is a road sign set up to stop us in our tracks.

Reoccurrence of dis-ease is related to the degree of attachment to generational wounding, misaligned actions, curses, and suppression of emotion. We are constantly given opportunities to review the mental and emotional landscape. It is a chance to reconcile and recollect what was lost. When we heal past pain of this lifetime, or a prior generation, we clear it for future generations. Diseases are linked to specific emotional and mental maps deeply ingrained within cellular structure.

Individuals often feel as if their circumstances, problems, and negative occurrences are tied to them, following wherever they tread. Yet, we do not realize we are the ones who tie them to our ankles, dragging them with us. We get used to the noise and weight they have, believing they let us feel. In some twisted way, we use them to bring relevance to our lives—to ourselves. We wear badges of honor to prove we were strong enough to survive. Challenge is used as a distraction from living powerfully. We fabricate external longing to avoid the grave depths of internal longing. Each apparent outward "near-death experience" creates the illusion of belonging.

Acts of survival are versions of thriving. We are given every resource on the inside to create even that. These are all points on the spectrum of experience. Consciousness is not the act of rising above them. That is hierarchy, no different from perceiving slave and Master. Instead, true consciousness is just being with them, without the need to change anything. This "living" of life is "being" fully immersed in the bodily sensations as Kali—"knowing" all endings and beginnings as acts of sacred creation. Embrace each new birthing. Be willing to palpably be with every arising death. In doing so, presence to each cycle integrates you into your true power. The infinite possibility within is what activates the infinite possibility without—without restraint, angst, trauma, heartache, struggle, or pain, because you already walked through it.

Will you accept that as your truth, or are you still allowing an old tape to loop in your mind? Where is the B-U-T (belief-under-transition) that needs to be worked with? Is there a conversation running in your head, telling you all the reasons why *your* life cannot be different? Do you perceive the people in your experience as obstacles to your expansive life? Or, are you the obstacle to your expansiveness by what you hold onto?

This is the error in perception: the birthing of thought through the ideas of others taken on as your own. Be willing to move from perception to inception. Birth a new paradigm—*now*. Do the inner work to realize every second when your mindset and heart are not in alignment with your greatest desires. Mindfully monitor your thoughts. Wherever there is discomfort in life, residue of the past exists. When the body holds tiredness and sickness, pieces of you still reside elsewhere calling to be reclaimed. If there is too much body weight or too little, beliefs have taken residence—either eating you up with resentment, or having you eat away at yourself. Energy will continue to express unless transformed.

All spaces hold energy. They attract you and you attract them by the Law of Harmony: Like attracts like. There is a method to all things in the Universe. It is a rhythm that moves naturally with its own intelligence. It needs no controlling factor or guidance, as it is perfectly calibrated to be the continuous creation of itself. Energy only remains as energy, however it transforms, always evolving towards higher level and understanding of itself. Sometimes, due to the resistance it encounters, evolution appears as "evil-ution," devolving in the pursuit of the highest state. Energy grows as we grow. It expands as we expand. It moves when we move. And even that which we desire to term "evil" has its place in the process. And, it, too, is good.

We believe the ego has power over us. However, the ego is a small child in pain. It is the child that has been bullied and now bullies. It hides its weakness through control. What it seeks and desires is to experience Love and compassion, just as each one of us. The ego is the self who protects the dense childhood energy embedded within a person's body. It is simply being a soldier, fighting your battles in the only way it knows how.

It is this young one that reacts in defensiveness, cries out in harsh language, and lashes out in violence. That ego—the one that wants to argue or not let something go—is the small, wounded child. When two are engaged in conflict, it is not two adults; it is from the age stages of their greatest wounding that are duking it out. Countries at war are being ruled by little boys on the playground. Nations in peace are being guided by one disciplined hand calming and protecting the child, while the other wisely steers the adult.

Do not condemn the ego for creating a safe haven when you were unable. It is the homeless part of you, surviving in a cardboard box of the garbage it has had to contend with. See the ego not as an enemy, but as a small, orphaned child, cowering in the corner.

See that young one peeking out through two palms, silently begging, "I'm afraid. Please Love me. Don't leave me"? All the while every situation is a version of the parent it desires Love from. The ego stood up to defend in the best way it could devise. But, it never was more than a child playing dress up within Mommy and Daddy's closet. It waits for a Loving embrace to say, "It's okay, little one. I am here. I will Love and protect you. You are safe."

Belief systems and patterns energetically stand as a surrogate for embedded emotional disturbance. This is merely survival mode. The POW or veteran needs support from childhood post-traumatic stress disorder. They have only taken on behaviors necessary to survive.

This is why children often repeat the lives of their parents or why some places have a consistent experience. It is all energy, repetition, and memory. Everything has an energetic DNA structure that holds a form until it is brought to evolution through healing and new life. These things cannot let go of us until we are willing to let go of them.

Oftentimes, we do not realize the attachment we have to being in pain, discomfort, or dis-ease. We make it our Lover, because it at least grabs hold of us in the most intimate of ways. It seems loyal. It may be the only way we know to find a way into someone's—anyone's—arms. Sometimes, it is the only way to get attention—to get those around us to pay attention.

You have the gift of free will. There is no right or wrong choice. It is simply what you choose to allow and experience. You always have the opportunity to move out of any experience. You are an infinite being with infinite possibility. If you are living a limited existence, it is because there is a payoff attached. But when it finally does feel bad enough, a decision to change will arise. Have *more* and *better* right now. Question your attachments. Look at your experiences and discern if who you are and where you are, are what you want. You are the creator of your reality, and it is time to stop believing a hand has been dealt to you. Instead, charge yourself with the responsibility of creating your hand.

You are All That Is. Call it in. Receive it. Ask for it to be alive in support of your highest need, desire, and creation. Open to receiving the miraculous birth within it. Allow yourself to open to your greatest calibration, most attuned note of harmonic resonance, and an experience of light-sound-color that radiates in service, truth, and unconditional Love. At the very least, that is what you deserve. The angels told me so.

Truth Fullness

» What are you most attached to in your life?

» What people are you most attached to?

» What beliefs are you most attached to?

» What if you had to experience life without those things?

» Who would you be if you were not attached to your thoughts of lack and limitation or smallness?

» Who would you be if given permission to live beyond those around you?

Will Fullness

To what degree do you need to give yourself the very things you are giving to others? Use the following steps to help you move out of numbness and disassociation. Be gentle, as you unfold and unfurl from the experiences that have you knotted and curled up inside the deep crevices of your broken-heartedness.

Close your eyes in a place that is safe and quiet. In this moment, it is not about forgiving anyone or understanding why things have happened. This time is for you to gift yourself the ear, witness, and compassion for what you have endured. Breathe. Don't push, force, or traumatize. Breathe and invite and allow.

Position your hands in a way that cradles the heart. Imagine your heart in its fractured, broken state, in need of care and healing. Visualize what you believe it to look like: hardened, fragmented, cracked, blistered, shrunken, or hollow. Wrap your hands around it.

Ask your mind to show you the incident blocking you from healing and feeling. Go back to whatever time rises up in your mind. Stand back and watch the movie that plays out in front of you. See it and feel it, knowing that you are safe. Allow emotion to surface so that the cracks, crevices, and hardened sections of the heart have the opportunity to soften, rise, and change. Be with it until you have squeezed every bit of juice it holds, quenching your thirst in whatever you need to receive. Your tears and reactions will be the salve that lets you move to the next step in your journey. When you re-experience and absorb this, something in you will shift for the better.

Tell the Truth

Heart Fullness

I know what I would wish for if I could really have it. I guess I do not believe it is possible. To have what I truly desire is asking too much. Who am I to have all of that? What have I done to deserve even half of that? I should just be content with what is here. But when I see others living the life I wish were mine, it makes me feel jealous and angry. Why do they have it? It is not that I want it taken from them, I am just sad for myself. Why did I end up with my circumstances? Why am I being punished? What did I do wrong? What did I do to deserve this?

I deserve to have more. I am tired of living according to everyone else. I am going to take what I want. It does not matter who gets hurt, because I have been hurt. No one listens to me so I am not going to listen. No one cares about me so I am not going to care. It's going to be all about me now!

Continue this dialogue, using your feelings and words. Journal your thoughts before moving to Mind Fullness. If words do not come, draw. If you cannot draw, doodle. Breathe. Feel. Allow. Receive.

Mind Fullness

Life always leads to our initial, ultimate, and most powerful intention to connect with what asks from deeply within. Every challenge, pain, and heartbreak will lead you back there, which is why you feel it in your heart and core. Everything that seemingly kills you holds within it the seeds of aliveness. If you are willing to dive into your depths, you shall awaken that power of creation again.

Whatever you are focused on, particularly what you keep tossing around and around in your head, consciously or unconsciously, is your psychosis. When you take radical responsibility for your behavior, you will be ruler of your kingdom. Until then, you are merely "subject" to all that is outside, having to "soldier" many struggles and conflicts.

When you tell one lie, you must make up a dozen more to keep that one appearing as truth. The same goes for the lies that we tell ourselves about ourselves. The most dangerous thing in life is the lie that is believed. It wanders and winds like a vine, choking the life out of all that is in its path. These are the pieces hiding in the dark that must be found. Otherwise, they destroy everything in their wake—actually, until their wake.

This is perception, always uniquely individual and original. How we see things is not the truth. It is a *con*version of the truth. Perceptions are distortions, colored by the filters of upbringing. It does not mean things have not happened to us. However, each experience asks us to be conscious and responsible for what we have created, how we have created, and what we do with it. As we share perceptions with others, they flow like a virus infecting, affecting, and effecting the world. Take your perceptions inside rather than spraying them outwardly. Inquiry and contemplation will reveal what you hide from yourself. In doing so, you will be witness to the inception of truth.

Until you are willing to speak the absolute truth, in radical honesty to and for yourself, it will block the view of the path you are to walk and the vision that is to unfold, even if it's a pretty pink elephant. These are the veils that keep you from your truth, power, purpose, and peace.

It's time to take down your self-defeating masks—the bully, villain, abuser, and manipulator in your life. It may appear these are people outside of you. Do not be mistaken; they are merely reflections of you. We never see our own shadow. These parts form because you do not say what you need to say. Instead, you beat up on yourself. Sitting within your depths, holding your secrets, hiding your statements and feeding your lies—parts of you have been brooding and creating things to get your attention. They even enlisted those outside of you to help.

It is time to tell the truth. Open your arms to that part of you—the part of you that needs to tell where you hurt, why you hurt, and how you hurt. It is not so others recognize it; it's so you finally do. Speak your truth so you can hear it, even if others cannot. The first one you must teach to Love you is you.

We have tamed ourselves, keeping dreams caged and feelings restrained. What will it take for you to release your self-imposed shackles and chains? Do you not know you are the Wild Divine? Feelings are designed for personal experience. They are to be felt and brought deeply inside for greater knowing of self. They are to be responded to internally, but never internalized. In order to do so, you must stop and rest. Get still.

If you wonder why you are not treated well by others, look at how you have been treating yourself. Others only treat you the way you have taught them to. They cannot read your mind anymore than you can read theirs. No one wishes to be invisible in the world, but we remain invisible to ourselves. We desire to be seen and heard, yet we have not taken the time to sit and listen. So, why should anyone else? Silence speaks loudly. Stillness holds great presence. Rest creates sacred space. Quiet moments provide the opportunity to meet the "possible self."

Our freedoms are given when we are born. We are to feel the entire emotion spectrum, from pain to joy equally. Then, let them go. When willingly sacrificing freedom, you martyr yourself.

Something inside watches, knowing another will one day see. It waits to catch the sight of you. Stillness rests at the base of your soul, with the ability to look in all directions, allowing any outcome that presents itself. This deep part of you knows there is no need to do anything other than watch and contemplate, wait and wisen.

When in lower frequencies, signs appear as the chaos, obstacle, and challenge. Deeply within your being knows to use chaotic dynamics to get your attention. It sees you have lost sight and vision and attempts to bring all to focus by swinging you so far out that you have to come back in.

The human need to control has not only created the complete opposite of what is desired, but also forcibly engages cause and effect, so actions and results ricochet off one another. This manner of active manhandling creates internal dysfunction and external chaos. Need only results after chaos has been created. This is in direct opposition to Source and supply. In believing erupting chaos needs to be fixed, we presume incorrectly. However, interference with that chaos creates further chaos. If allowed to play itself out, chaos will dissolve on its own. It need only run its course. Chaos, in itself, is Divine intervention—righting places that are inharmonious and discordant. Chaos is a time to be still.

Stillness honors who you are, where you are, without need—providing the space where change can happen. Creation unfolds organically, keeping all things in flow. It lets the body rest, even if the mind is restless. In this "manor," there is no tampering, allowing natural laws to move everything in harmony and balance. This field of neutrality is what brings awareness to signs, coincidence, synchronicity—"God-incidences." Universal intelligence knows us better than we know ourselves. As awareness strengthens, signs appear through the chaos in playful ways to help us lighten up. At some point, we begin to realize ourselves as harmonic resonance within Universal intelligence. This is mana; you are mana.

REST (Rightfully Expressing Source Truth) is an inherent gift but can only be given to the self, by the self. Rest is necessary to respect the wholeness of being that exists, regardless of the illusion created. It allows us to hear what we have not heard through the many words exchanged. It opens us to feel what we have repressed. Most importantly, it opens us to dream about what our spirits are truly calling for.

The birthplace of self-value, self-worth, and self-Love occur when the "eye/I" of the wounded catches the "eye/I" of its holy counterpart, bowing in recognition and honor. Namaste. When the gaze connects, romance sparks and there is interest to deeply know the "other." Courtship may be fast or slow, but true commitment brings healing and growth.

Self-value is the moment of encounter and willingness, believing the relationship is deserved. Self-worth is the moment between the desire to kiss and the kiss, where the space is open for anything and everything to be experienced. Self-Love begins when an intimate relationship within the dark does. This trinity is the cusp of a new self-perception. The art of romance encourages the new self-view.

If you want to see the end of something, take a good, hard look at the beginning. Everything is a cycle—wheels within wheels. You once Loved yourself; the spiral is coming back around. You will Love yourself again, and it can only be in greater degree than before. Imagine the degree of Love that existed at conception, the moment you birthed in the mind and heart of God. This infinitely outweighs any degree of Love in human conception.

There come many moments where life comes full circle. It won't be exactly the same place, but it will feel reminiscent. This circle is a spiral, ever rising, ever deepening; you can never go back, only in and out—involution and evolution. These spirals take you to the farthest reaches of yourself. The Infinite has no beginning or ending, just a continuous series of such—in you, of you, with you, as you. What will you allow?

Truth Fullness

»   What is the elephant in the room?

»   How long will you continue to ignore it?

»   Can you afford to remain in denial?

»   Where else in your life is this happening?

Will Fullness

Sit in a quiet space. Close the eyes. Request each part of your body to come to rest, one by one. After each asking, take a deep breath. For example, "I ask my toes to rest. I ask my feet to rest. I request my legs to rest." Be attentive with each body part.

Deepen these breaths into an even rhythm once you have gone through each part of the body. Imagine a line of Light beginning at the tailbone and rising along the front of the spinal column. Breathe into this line, so that it continues to extend high into the Universe. Anchor it there, drawing energy from above. Extend the line of Light downward from the tailbone point, deep into the earth, allowing it to anchor into the molten center.

Imagine the Light energy looping back up through the body, to the high point and down to the deep point, and looping back through. This looping stream of Light creates the symbol of infinity along the spine as it weaves in and out. Imagine yourself as a generating, and regenerating, system of the Universe.

Continue to breathe into this line of Light, making it brighter and brighter. With each inhalation, magnify the intensity of Light. With each exhalation, expand the Light to become a widening column. Let this cylinder fully encompass you, your family, and your life. Rest within this column of Light regularly to receive boosts of energy, inspiration, and clarity. You are connected to Source Energy, which continuously holds this flow of energy. In unison with all other "experience," you are part of the field. Be at REST (Rightfully Expressing Source Truth).

Conscious Living

Heart Fullness

Explain it to me, God. Show me. I need to understand why this world does not feel good. Why do I seem out of place? Why do I feel so different from everyone else? I have never felt included, or accepted. Is it true? Or is it just what I have come to believe?

I let you get close enough to hurt me again. I gave it my all and you stabbed me in the heart. You kicked me in the gut. You pushed me to the ground. How could this happen again? I won't let you close enough to hurt me again. No one will ever do this to me again. I will never let anyone in.

I do not want to be hurt again. I deny my own pain by seeing the heartbreak of others. I see so many in pain, taken over by illness, life challenges, heartbreak, and having hard times. Life has so many obstacles. Why must it be this way?

If I could heal, I would help so many. Why do bad things have to happen? Why must there be pain and discomfort in the world? I see it all around me and I know that so many are worse off than I, but in this moment... Please, will you help me? Why do I have to feel pain? What did I do wrong?

I feel the angst in my life. There is so much discomfort in my body. I know what deep hurt is and I do not want it anymore. Take the pain that is in my heart: the sadness, the shame—the unworthiness. Take the anger from my mind. Remove the loneliness from my experience. I ask for a miracle.

I am tired of my own story. It hurts bad enough now. I am ready to change. I am ready to be the change. Help me know how.

Continue this dialogue, using your feelings and words. Journal your thoughts before moving to Mind Fullness. If words do not come, draw. If you cannot draw, doodle. Breathe. Feel. Allow. Receive.

Mind Fullness

When we finally become conscious to the power inside, which plays a hand in creating experiences, we start to notice the correlation between our deepest desires and the things that appear around us. This awareness usually arrives after going through various darker stages of the soul's journey. We all have our skeletons in the closet, the experiences we hope no one ever knows about. In a sense, experiencing these stages is unavoidable. When we are willing to set them free, we set ourselves free. And in looking back, a beautiful beginning occurs.

The soul sets the program we are to experience as life. The choices do not matter, because the soul sets up many channels of experience, providing various outcomes for soul reality to "tell-a-vision" to come. The illusion is that any of it really matters. In actuality, there is no good, no bad—only experience. We can judge it. We can allow ourselves to be affected by the judgment of others, who have their own skeletons equal to or worse hiding away. We can be in denial. Or, we can live out the divinity of all of it by being in the experience, fully present.

Early life experiences provide the foundation for the program to play out, always aiming toward the awareness of inner power. We come in knowing, only to forget what we know. In forgetting what we know, we take on the beliefs of others. Pieces of who we are fragment off. In a sense, we are all split personalities in an insane world. In the journey of forgetting, we engage remembering. In fragmenting, we open to the endeavor of recollecting. The soul then seeks to "re-member" and "re-collect" itself.

The script organically unfolds through living by default, unconsciously and consciously, but does not require the individual to pass through all three stages. Loving choices and a commitment to self-awareness move a person through.

Some people live by default, meaning they live what is dealt them. They do not make choices because they take the choice that presents itself.

Career choices often result in this manner. A person in the medical field will have children that go into healthcare. Entrepreneurs breed entrepreneurs. Those in show business have children who follow suit. A plumber's son becomes a plumber or equivalent profession. Other areas subject to default living can be religion, language, health, reaction, addiction, or any form of conditioning.

Unconscious living involves making choices from the ego, desperation, and need, without acknowledging inner pain, conflict, and heart desires. During this period, one chooses to place blinders and deaf ears upon thoughts and feelings that require inner reflection. This is the time of the act out—the need to satisfy the ego self. Those outside outweigh honoring the true self. Ego needs result in choices to seek rapid satisfaction and fulfillment, despite anything or anyone else. Decisions are made from a place of pain and will result in pain. Numbing agents assist in the avoidance process (excess in food, smoking, alcohol, drugs, sex, shopping, etc.). Unconscious living is the beginning of the end, inviting the "dark night of the soul." Unconscious choices lead to further dysfunction and chaos, ultimately unraveling the fabric of one's existence. Unfortunately, for some, that means complete annihilation. When things finally hurt badly enough, steps toward living consciously are taken.

Conscious living occurs when we are tired of ourselves, of living a robotic existence, and of the stories. We want more and better. We begin to realize that to have better, we must do better. A greater awareness begins to unfold, resulting in the understanding that "out of control" and "in control" are both unnecessary. Instead, the use of mindfulness is conscious control. This is the power of conscious choice. The new guiding question becomes: Who am I? And, if truly willing to know, the pieces begin to reveal.

In order to have more of a life than you have, something has to fall. Your life requires your death. Travel your dark caverns, eventually meeting within the same sacred chamber of knowing—that place that rests in the deep dark spaces Most High, that which weaves and winds its way into the depths of longing and in the wide-open terraces of belonging. Feel the sting of sharp thorns of the past that help rip away the binding skin of the false, where the knotty roots rise above the surface as painful missteps. Falling of the angelic self reveals the body being Light, emerging through every cell, as the seeding of stars laying within the vast Universe of Union—the bliss of Oneness.

Truth Fullness

» Are you living by default, consciously or unconsciously?

» Where are you guarded?

» At what point do you push people away?

» What has to happen for them to get past your walls?

» What has to happen for you to get past your walls?

» Do you really want to create that?

Will Fullness

Breathe. Just breathe. Sometimes, all you can do is take a breath. Be with what is happening and breathe. It is the best thing you can do in the moment of utter chaos. In one of those breaths, something will open. Something will release.

And when you can't breathe, find a sacred space and scream. Just scream. Let out sound at the top of your lungs to move the energy around you.

And when you cannot scream, stomp your feet. Stomp hard. Put on music and move your body, grounding yourself into the earth. Move the energy in your body as you take a stand for your life.

And when you need to fall, fall. Melt to the ground and sob. Let the tears flow. Let the anguish and pain conquer you until there is no sound left, no scream, no movement. And breathe; just breathe. And rest; just rest. And be; just be.

The moment you are to rise, you will know. But wait for it. Trust yourself and do not leave this sacred space a moment before you feel it in every cell of your being.

Inhale III: Attention to Creation

Mastery engages my ability to allow *all* experiences with a calm heart, quiet understanding, and sacred surrender. Mastery allies with my Higher Self and my Holy Self, standing on either side of my Human Self with palms clasped. In front walks my Intuitive Self. In back walks my Wise Self. I Am a Master at my core. I awaken to Mastery in each moment, as I walk through each protrusion arising in my path.

In becoming, remembering and uniting with the Master I AM.

1. I ACCEPT where I am, fully and completely.

2. I RECOGNIZE that 'how' I handle the issue is more important than the issue itself.

3. I HONOR the circumstances I have created.

4. I CELEBRATE the challenging and painful events that appear as places of growth and wisdom.

5. I IDENTIFY every past step as doing the best I could with the knowledge I had.

6. I allow myself the opportunity to be Divine as I re-DISCOVER my humanity.

7. I SEEK healthy environments, nourishing food, loving relationships, and nurturance for the body!

8. I COMMIT to a daily spiritual and study practice that fulfills my mental strength, emotional response system, and sacred body temple.

9. I CLEANSE my words and thoughts.

10. I allow time to consciously BREATHE, be still, and know myself.

11. I acknowledge every experience as written in SACRED contract.

Exhale III: Communion as Compassionate Embrace

Dearest Ultimate Soul Mate,

I compassionately embrace my human experience, my soul experience, and my Divine experience. I acknowledge these as layers within one another for the sake of uniting US. I face the dark and shadowy places of my being with loving kindness. I invite healthy boundaries in reference to others for the sake of creating a sacred space for US. I willingly witness the various levels that surround and support US in completely unfolding into an embrace. I am willing to wrap my hands, arms, and head around how I do what I do, and why I do it, so that I may remove the veils standing between US. I will use compassion within my experience as I allow the highest possible creative expression in life and Love.

Help me remember what I have lost. Remind me of my innocence so I see the truth once again. The shadows I see in front of me seem to be others, yet they are my own. Forgive me for casting those roles. Forgive me for creating a story where I needed you to be that. I Love you for loving me enough to do so. Thank you for the sacrifices you have made for my experience.

I ask for the assistance of my angels, guardians, guides, body devas, nature spirits, cellular structure, dimensional selves, parallel selves, Highest Self, Holy Self, Ascended Masters, and Light Beings, in all places and at all times, to fully support this journey of loving consistently placing US firmly upon the Divine scale of compassionate embrace for the highest degree of living, being, and knowing the truth that I AM.

I ask for healing holograms and sacred geometric forms to support the highest recognition and recalibration in remembrance of the Love that I AM.

As these heartfelt words are spoken, I know them to be activated and charged with the energy of fulfillment and completion on all levels, at all points in time, in the highest state of unconditional Love and in the most profound nurturing way. So be it...And so it is!

Forever Yours,

The Lover of the BeLoved

❦{ 20 }❧

Self-Help

Heart Fullness

Maybe people won't notice I am insecure and shy. I will just act busy and seem as if I am on the phone. I know people can see through me. I have to act a certain way with these people. I will behave differently at work, though. If people only knew who I was when at home.

If I smile, people will not see my pain. I'll make everything look good. She has a fancy new car. I would never have known they were in financial trouble. He comes across so nice, who would have guessed he could be so cruel. I wonder if people can see through the things I do.

She always smiles at me, but I feel as if some other feeling sits behind her eyes. It is almost like she wears a mask. I just want to be real. I want people to be real with me.

I really do not want to go out with those people. I always feel so superficial with them. On one hand I want real friendship, but I am unable to be that friend to those people.

Can I sidestep society's reaction or does the world's response matter? Can I/we move away from what other people think, say, and do? Or, is this an attempt to fit in? I knew I/we cannot be concerned with other's thoughts, judgments, or reactions. What if I volunteered my shame? What if the secrets I kept, especially those kept to myself, were spoken? Might people see how very much the same we all are?

Continue this dialogue, using your feelings and words. Journal your thoughts before moving to Mind Fullness. If words do not come, draw. If you cannot draw, doodle. Breathe. Feel. Allow. Receive.

Mind Fullness

There is nothing wrong with self-improvement. Outer changes have their rightful place. However, when it is done to fit in or gain Love and acceptance, it stems from feelings of being inadequate. This clearly depicts a lack of self-Love. Physical accoutrements are merely Band-Aids for wounds that exist internally. Inner work is required, not outer work. Making changes for the sake of others and their happiness sets a precedence for bartering and manipulation to continue within the relationship.

By indulging in codependent activities, we create energetic cords linking us to the person we feel indebted to. An energy transference pipeline funnels energy in the direction of the other, leaving individuals energetically depleted. These cords are wrapped with like-energy dynamics matching past generations, increasing the intensity of situations to be met. Each experience provides the opportunity to either follow numbly, get triggered, or perceive what is really going on. It can result as an emotional, mental, or physical energy drain, as we take turns becoming psychic vampires.

Consciously witnessing the self, and acknowledging what dysfunctional behavior is really asking for, will support a person in getting clearer about personal and relationship boundaries. All cords have two sides. In codependent unhealthy relations, misperception keeps a cord in place. One person may create release through shifts in perception, but the other individual will still have a cord dangling in the wind, if she has not tilled her own mind. The one who consciously moves forward is protected. The one who does not consciously take action to heal is opening him- or herself to being a communal energy bank for discordant misaligned like-souls seeking to feed on energy as well.

Bringing a relationship or circumstance to completion does not mean that the individual can no longer be in your life; it means their misaligned behavior can no longer be in your life.

Cords are created, by holding guilt, shame, blame, projection—or the need to save another. The more individuals clear their own blocks to Love, the less susceptible they are to psychic and spiritual dis-ease. Should means "I really do not want to, but I tell myself it is what is expected of me." The result becomes a cycle of depletion and exhaustion instead of creativity and energy. Get rid of the "shoulds" in your life.

Charity begins at home. This is true as much for an individual as it is for families, communities, and nations. In order to give the family, community, and nation, *you* must first and foremost give to *you*. It is imperative that receiving and giving to the self be top priority. Selfish action—listening to the needs of the inner self—is necessary to enjoy a full range of emotions, thus ensuring a full and filling life.

What happens when one dies to his or her old self? He find resurrection and rebirth. This is what Christ and many other Masters were trying to show us. It is what nature illustrates, year after year, and what many sacred philosophies also speak of. Ongoing cycles of birth and death are the beauty of human incarnation. We get an infinite number of "do-overs." In each moment, there is no end to our beginning. Step by step, we all learn to turn back toward ourselves, initiating deeper desires to discover what lay within.

The willingness to be vulnerable leads to authenticity and boldness. These behaviors pave the way for a life to go into hyper-speed. In a beautiful manner, everything happens in right time with universal flow and guidance, all the while being the training for every upcoming adventure.

People physically endure self-imposed torture, brainwashing, slavery, and forced silence. We torture ourselves with judging thoughts, becoming shackled to a lineage of victimhood. Worst of all, we silence our own voices from fully crying out because our forbearers did not. This would be true for all cultures and societies. Every race has experienced the roles of victim and abuser at some point in time. It keeps appearing to show all peoples of the world that there is much inner work and healing to be done.

Terror happens in the mind. Torture occurs through our thoughts. Fear occurs when we believe in harm, giving it the energy to be created in our lives. What if you lived knowing there is only go(o)d—living with such presence that there is no story, only the moment? Might the world change? Yes, your world will change because you have been the change. If you want to see a different world, then learn how to see it differently.

We obviously still carry a deeply negative and discordant consciousness in our world based on the level of violence, terrorism, and misuse of power. Our need to fix and control gets the better of us, showing itself in the world around us. The only one we each have liberty to fix is the self. Veneering the outside, whether a body or a building, is not change. That's cosmetic. Underneath remains the same. A human being must focus on the small self to shift and heal, traveling its own landscape to truly change.

Any two at odds, are more alike than not. Their egos, fears, anger, and lack of forgiveness would have them view the other as opposite or the enemy. What they do not realize is the enemy is "in-a-me." Those who they judge, they in fact are. "In-a-me" also references that our own worst enemy is unknowingly the misdirected, wounded self. For those unable to achieve peace in the human form, the miracle would be death so that the belief in suffering could also die.

Life is a journey of opposites. Every soul need only look in the personal mirror and collective mirror to discover the contract engaged in and the healing being called for. The "other" is here to show you a part of your self. The awareness that surfaces is the ultimate miracle, as was the one who chose to be the example of that.

We have all been programmed, but what is actually running is a virus of the mind. When we erase the programs and get rid of the viruses, we endeavor on a whole new operating system. You are neutralizing distorted coding that have you experiencing a virtual reality based on your perceptions. Healing is created through awareness and remembrance of truth. You are already whole.

Truth Fullness

>> Why do things need to change?

>> Where do things need to change?

>> What needs to change?

>> How does it need to change?

>> How will you remain accountable in making these changes?

Will Fullness

Write out what is working in your life. What is not working in your life? Inquire about significant relationships, finances, career, spiritual practice, and friendships. Are you isolating or out in the community? Are you utilizing creative capacity positively or negatively? Are you focused on the interior or exterior as you move through life?

As you contemplate these, notice if any patterns are running through every area of life. How you operate in one is how you will operate in all areas of your life. What needs to happen to clean up dysfunctional aspects of your life? What are those places of chaos showing you, about you? Look back over your life and tune into the patterns that keep repeating. Journal.

21

Rest Room

Heart Fullness

How could this have happened? I cannot believe I did this. Another deadline—in a stack of deadlines. My body keeps trying to get me to slow down but I do not have time for that. I will try to make time over the next month if nothing else comes up. If I just work a little harder this month, things might get easier and then I can take a break. I wish the world would stop for a week just so I could sleep.

I am so tired. I hear the thoughts in my head constantly: "I really need to rest. I need to get some sleep. I wish I could take a break." My body is screaming for some time off. I don't listen. I just keep pushing. I keep giving. I keep placing everything else in front of myself. I can take a break next week. I just need to get past this. When I have time, I will take care of myself. One day, my time will come.

My life has become a rat race. I try so hard. I give so much. I made choices to please others to make them happy. I have to hold back the tears. I can't let others see the pain I have inside. I wear this mask to fit in. I just want to feel loved. If I don't keep doing these things, I may lose everything. What if I end up without any friends? What if my family turns away from me? What will I do? What if I discover I am not worthy of love, without doing all of these things?

Take away this pain. Please, fix what is broken in my thoughts and my body. I do not know what to do, what to ask for, how to heal. I speak to you from my heart. Help me. Please help me. Now I ask in prayer for…

Continue this dialogue, using your feelings and words. Journal your thoughts before moving to Mind Fullness. If words do not come, draw. If you cannot draw, doodle. Breathe. Feel. Allow. Receive.

Mind Fullness

A seed of understanding rests at the depths of our soul. Beyond all appearances, there is Go(o)d. It is representative of ancient knowledge, compassion, and truth. This seed does not flower or germinate; it remains whole and encased, solid in form. It does not dry out and wither. It resides as everlasting endless possibility. Marinating within the heart, the seed remains alive and supple, healthy and whole. Regardless of how the heart dries up or becomes broken, it is always safe and protected. It is the Divine spark of infinite potential and endless possibility.

When coming from hopeless, hope is the soil that allows growth. Attention and believing are the fertilizing agents. Action and Love are fluids that unfurl the encasement from which it may flower. Hope rallies people to continue moving, persevering, and aspiring. As part of our DNA, it is the essence of something beyond comprehension—a Divine innate power to co-create, dream, and manifest. Hope becomes the soil for the heart and mind to build, grow, and prosper—to flourish, overcome, and succeed. Hope speaks as a soft, almost-silent prayer—the simplest, most powerful as "Help me, God."

Spiritual journeys unfold, twist, turn, and are seldom smooth. The soul journey is a path filled with rocks. Attempts to discover and rediscover ourselves become the mission. And the purpose? We come in knowing only to forget, learning something new to release it, in order to find truth. We come in feeling, become numb, and stop feeling, so that we can learn to feel fully.

Your greatest stretch of road lay in creating freedom. That means cleaning up codependency. There is an opportunity to discover your greatest and subtlest degrees of addiction. All things pushing you to the wall are still Love. This is the form of Love that helps you rise up and out in a greater way.

When others need you, they are using you to fill emptiness, to remain in their place of disempowerment or in the throes of codependency. They are asking you to play into their self-perception of smallness. The same is true when you need someone or something. True detachment means your

Love and presence remain with them, regardless of your physicality or necessary conscious actions for higher good. Honor where they are, seeing the Divine in and as them. There is no thing and no one to save, fix, heal, or help. You need do nothing; your presence, as sacred witness, is enough. The purest Love is being able to see people in their power, peace, health, prosperity, presence—even if they cannot.

The greatest form of codependency occurs when these other two types merge: the need to feel needed. This is just a seesaw of abuse back and forth, keeping you both locked in misaligned paradigms of pain and struggle. Get off the seesaw! It may leave the other on the ground for a bit, but you will have given them the place to now rise. In doing so, you actually set them free because they learn how to get off the seesaw. They will stand and move on to something else.

Love discerns the highest good. It is flowing in the direction that feels Light—and feels right. It is living in alignment of the gentlest thoughts, feelings, and actions that serve all, but also understands when discipline, action, and strength are required. This stance, of and in Love, may not always look the way others desire. Trust yourself to know what to do, how to act, why to move, when to stay, and when to go.

Love is truth. It is pure, whole, and ever present. The distortions that make Love appear distant, painful, or manipulative are human filters of misaligned fantasy and projectionist expectation. When you become conscious about what you place on Love—as shackles, chains, limitations, and control—a new experience of Love and Loving unfolds. When Love does not look and feel Loving, it is because you are caught up in examples of Love from your past, instead of being in the Love that is ever present.

Call forward all aspects, highest to lowest, youngest to eldest, unconscious to super-conscious—all dimensions, spaces, times, and fragments to be present to moving into a unified experience of Light. Ask the mind to believe in Love and support. Ask the heart to be open to compassion and sovereignty. Ask the body to be strong and vital. Ask the spirit to be boundless and laser-focused on the experience and expression of truth. You must ask for it.

Life is not here to live; it is the container for the experience of aliveness. Experience is not for you to get through; every experience appears so that you discover and dive more deeply into you. Every event in life is meant to "herd" us—because the Universe has "heard" the deepest most soulful part of us—to unfold our greatest dream of freedom and creative expression. Rather than discount your stories, stay immersed in their richness, while you move into the one that has yet to be told. All prior stories are gifts of grace toward a higher understanding and more beautiful human/humane experience. Drop into them. Now rise.

Only one thing exists—the essence of all that is. It weaves through all pieces of creation with a single intent to know itself and its complete connectivity. We are the pieces of a grand puzzle interlocking to form the most magnificent image ever known.

May your heart be continually opened. May your mind find stillness. May your body heal every discomfort. May your soul be fulfilled of every longing. May your path be clear. Release. Release. Release. What is this word really saying? Experience "real ease." That is what happens when you let go. To let go of something, you must first fully have hold of it. Own it. Clutch it to your bosom, like a long-lost Love.

Truth Fullness

» Who is riding the seesaw with you?

» Where in life have you created struggle because you "needed to feel needed"?

» What and who needs to be released right now?

» How can you remember to breathe while releasing?

» How can you turn release into "real ease"?

Will Fullness

Today is an opportunity to push the "reset" button. Instead of checking out, check in! As life rises, turns, and twists in front of you—as you experience feelings of heartbreak, loneliness, or separation—feel the pounding heart. Notice the pull of your gut, as a sign to stay focused within. That is where the truth of I AM resides. In knowing your inside world is real, and your outside world is the illusion, live from your center. Create the connection, wholeness, Love, and completion that you want on the inside, and watch it flower on the outside. You have created life challenges to stay focused, disciplined, and aligned. You need not create these issues if you remain in your heart at all times, in your core, always at one with your Source.

Breathe in and breathe out. Breathe deep and extended, rhythmic, and flowing. Are you breathing air or is it breathing you? You are constantly on life support, so why do you tell yourself you are not supported? Why do you play this game of being less than you are when the entire Universe conspires to breathe you into life? Do your part; all you really have to do is allow it.

❧{ 22 }❧

Letting Go

Heart Fullness

Please don't leave me. All I need is you. I do not know who to be without you. I do not know who I am without the life I have created. No, don't go. Oh my God, you are gone! What now? How could I have not known? Was this happening all along and no one told me? I feel so betrayed.

I am afraid to love again. I don't want to be hurt. I don't trust my judgment. How was I so blind? I feel so stupid. What if I am used again? How do I trust after being betrayed? What if I attract the very same thing in again? I might die. My heart feels frozen. I don't even think it's open.

God, melt this heart. I deserve love, don't I? Am I so bad? So unworthy? So undeserving? I had so many dreams. I wanted the fairy tale. I wanted love to be forever. I just wanted to be cherished and cared for. Why so much pain? I am battered and bruised. My heart has been beaten to a pulp, my innocence is lost, my hopes trampled. I have been beaten down. Who would want me now? I am not sure I even want myself. I do not know how to love me. Is there anything left to love? Is there anything worth salvaging? When I look in the mirror, I do not see it. I feel old and tired. I do not want to live the lie anymore.

God, bring me back to myself. Help me see myself as you created me. Help me know what love is. Help me find the truth. I know. I know I need to learn to love myself. Do I even know what that means? If I know what it is, why am I not giving to myself? I knew self-care had to do with proper exercise, healthy eating, appropriate rest, right livelihood, and nurturing experiences.

Mind Fullness

Whether or not we face wounds as children or adults, those foundations support new manifestations of cause and effect in being initiated. We place ripples of intent in every moment. You will see, with unfolding proof, what you are asking for consciously and subconsciously. In setting the stage for new life to appear, living rightly through aligning all of your faculties remains your highest option. All dysfunction arises out of suppression. You will get to know it, one way or another.

When what you do not want appears, it is an opportunity to reevaluate what you are doing, what you are thinking, and where else in consciousness requires healing. As you clear wounds, you clear the path for expansion toward your highest expression. You become the god of your own understanding, birthing a realization that, to discover oneself as an angel, one would first experience a beast.

When do we give the devil his due? That devil in your life got you to this point of introspection—and for your own g(o)od! This one is mirroring something you must see. To discover the experience of a god, go with open arms and sit with the devil inside. You are always one with your Divine creation. Will you lock arms with the divine devilish one who also plays within your shadows?

Facing the deepest shame rests in two places we dare not go. The great gargoyle-like guardians of the soul stand atop pillars of deep-held beliefs in woundedness. One is the devil inside, that which is worse than any newscast or reality television show—more vile than a fiery novel, soap opera or nightmare revealed. The other is the deep knowing we are God in form, fully fathering and mothering this reality in its horror and its heroism.

The final place of shame lay in the fact that we created the whole painful reality—or illusion, depending on what you want to call it. Realize it all: the pain and hurt, the ones cast and all shattered pieces that lay in the aftermath. Meet the one who imprisoned all others within distortion and perceptions, most of all yourself. Behold the Master Teacher who would create a world that isn't, into a world that is.

Freedom rests in your shame. Take responsibility for every lie, manipulation, belief, word of gossip, and ill of fate. It rests in the willingness to hear every thought against the self or another. Grace is given to the self, in acknowledging the one who hates, and the one who is hated. Atonement comes when we Love and believe in the one who has been denied, repressed, branded, and banished.

Releasing the shame and the secrets is about being seen, heard, acknowledged, and honored despite who we were, what we have done, or how we have behaved—longing to fully stand with all that we are, faces raised to the sun. How noble a cause that would be? How immensely healing, especially humanitarian, and world-changing to allow that degree of compassion, honesty, and vulnerability? How does anyone expect to change anything if unable to repair the separation inside? How do any of us authentically Love any other, when we have yet to discover how to Love the parts of ourselves still residing in the shadows, hidden, buried, and imprisoned. These are the ones we disdainfully look back at and name bad, ugly, stupid, useless, crazy, wrong, guilty, and dirty.

I not only see the secrets that I carried but also the pain that I hid from everyone in the name of "Love." I never considered the most important one who quietly held the shame of living through so much. She was the true essence of unconditional Love, in the space she held for so many years; She is sacred and holy.

I had been betrayed repeatedly, only to discover those around me knew it was happening and never told me. These people were family, friends, and colleagues. They spoke to me, their eyes silently revealing shame, but their lips never saying a word. Never looking at me when speaking, they held secrets as weapons. Perhaps speaking among one another, stealing from each other, sister women are the demise of the very feminine we seek to empower. How can we condemn the masculine energy when we actively and aggressively participate in the very same way?

I carry a compounded shame for being witness to the same and in remaining silent. Now, I address that shame: the places where I knew of women close to me that were being betrayed. Why did I not say anything? By not speaking the truth, I was branding myself with shame that was not even mine—that of the other, the adulterers in relationship, and the recipients of adultery. By carrying their secrets, I might as well have been in bed with them. By speaking the truth, would I free myself of the noose that would otherwise be my own hanging?

Secrets, lies, deception, and withholding are the disease we keep spreading, teaching, and becoming. It takes a village to raise a child. Aren't we all children? It takes a village. Where have the villagers run off to? We are children raising children—orphans. Could it be that we are all in the same boats—all castaways, lost at seeing?

All people are good. There are no "bad" people. They are following footsteps. They are doing their "job": contracts, assignments, roles, and so forth. We needed them to play their game to straighten what has gotten so out of line, for generations upon generations. This is not about those people over there. This has everything to do with you. We are all one family—a world family. My shame is in your history and vice versa.

Our parents had no idea how dysfunctional they were. They had no idea what wounds, patterns, and imprints they were passing on any more than they had control of DNA, eye color, or skin tone. We are them—until we choose to be ourselves. They unknowingly hurt us, abandoned or betrayed in many ways, but they had no idea how to handle shame, much less that they held such. One by one, we can heal lineages of the past, freeing generations of the future. But it requires authenticity and radical honesty bathed in the discipline of Unconditional Love.

Why let emotional attachment to past hurts be the threads that keep you tied to control? You can end the walk of shame, so that the prisoner of war who deeply honored the orders of the past, may receive the honor of a soldier who has come home.

Wholeness is the inclusion of all parts. Those that speak against you could be right about you. They might be seeing you exactly as you are. Be open to that. We are each the Allness that exists. We have to be willing to embrace the darkness to the same degree that we desire to be the Light. You may, in fact, possess the qualities you have been condemned with. More than likely, those traits have shown up in some experience or within certain relationships. If they do exist within you, you also have the complete opposite. The error is not in having these traits but in the desire to avoid, dispense, or banish them. Light has to cast a shadow, so we all have one. Shadows do not need to command our experience. However, unacknowledged ones will do just that. Think about how you clamor to be seen and heard when you are ignored and disrespected.

We are here to be the villain and the hero, the devil and the saint, the victim and the victimizer, the mother and the child, fallen angel and god walking. The human experience allows us to feel and experience everything. The Divine experience includes knowing and understanding all perspectives. Various polarities of personality and related actions are aspects of Divinity. Relationships assist in discovering hidden pieces and parts. They bring to light who we are being, by bringing up our shadows.

This is the only plane of existence that supports multidimensional, experiential learning. It is why souls choose incarnation. This earthly trip is a privileged one. People mistakenly view the world as "what" happens to them instead of understanding "they are happening upon the world" to have a textural, visceral knowing of "how" they respond to the very experience they are in charge of creating. It is the ultimate science fiction!

The lens, through which you view yourself, has been darkened, by taking on the thoughts and beliefs of others as your truth. Your distorted vision is a rejection of your wholeness. Because you cannot see the wholeness/holiness of yourself, you are unable to see it in any other. The distortions you place on other people are what you subconsciously believe about yourself. This outward projection supports chaos and confusion, embedding fragmentation within the spirit before it has an opportunity to see itself for what it truly is. This is the obstacle course we chose to maneuver. Where are you getting tripped up?

We are all begotten sons and daughters, made in the image and likeness, brothers and sisters of Masters before us—Ones of the ONE. Wholeness and holiness are inherent blueprints of every man, woman, creature, and object, seen and unseen. Wholeness *is*. Holiness *is*.

Not all souls are granted this experience. It is one that has to be earned. Only on this plane, do we experience duality, the ability to have a body and the expansive ability to feel extreme polarities. Again, people mistakenly view the world as what happens to them instead of understanding they are happening upon the world to have a textural, visceral knowing of how they respond to the world.

Wholeness is knowing completeness. We are born complete and move to the next experience complete. Human life is a path of incompletion—in completion—in order to remember the knowing of being complete. The recognition of wholeness is what needs adjusting. We come from that which is whole, holy and complete. In fact, *you* are that which is whole, holy, and complete.

Wholeness, or Holiness, is not only our birthright but also embedded deeply within the soul grid. It is programmed into the human body circuitry, expressing in, as, and through us when we maintain open channels of this highly sophisticated "softwear." Rather than judging ourselves or others, we merely need to witness how people express and receive feedback from the internal guidance system and observation deck.

There is an opportunity to break this pattern of generational distortion by clearing the lens of projection. Anchoring into wholeness, and releasing any past residue placed on and within you by other people will untie future generations from the S-I-N (self-inflicted nonsense) given by the father and the mother. In doing so, you become the teacher and way-shower for others to follow suit, creating a clear path of freedom. Wholeness and Holy-ness are not dependent upon any other; they are inherent blueprints of every man, woman, creature, and object, seen and unseen.

There is a matrix that exists. It is the program that you are choosing to follow. In becoming part of the program, in getting with the program, in following along with the program, you abandon the very uniqueness you came in to experience. Divinity did not express to create an army of drones. Divinity desired to be the grand designer of dreams upon dreams personified.

Truth Fullness

- » Where in your life is magic appearing?

- » What would freedom look like for you?

- » What signs in your life have been urging you in that direction?

- » What part of you needs to die?

- » What part of your life needs to die?

- » What is ready to be born?

Will Fullness

In the moments you cannot find your breath—in the moments you cannot stand—in the moments you cannot scream, or cry, take it to the tub. The water does wonders. Sit and do nothing, but feel. Do not rise until you can rise. Let the water hold you, comfort you and keep you. Pain only exists because something in your life is ready to die. Put it to rest.

Move back into the truth of your Oneness. Focus on the following sacred sharing, and let it awaken what is pre-encoded within you of the truth: your Oneness. You are the One.

1

11

111

1111

11:11

111:111

1111:1111

We are One.

We are the Ones.

We are the Gateway.

We are the Key.

We are in time.

We are out of time

We are timeless.

We are The One.

1111:1111

111:111

11:11

111

11

1

Facing Reality

Heart Fullness

I hate what I have become. I can't believe how my life has turned out. How did I end up here? I have made so many wrong choices. I should have known better.

Why do crazy things happen in my life? When will this ever end? Dear God, I surrender I surrender. I lay myself down before you. My body is to the ground, my feet to the fire. I lay prostrate before you. My ego is cast aside. Take me from my life and make things new. I want to start over. I need to do life over again. I made mistakes, wrong turns, mis-steps. I have hurt and been hurt. In the moment I did not know better. I am better than I was but still not good enough. Help me. Please help me.

I could see myself but I did not know what I was doing. I became blanketed by my own insanity, sadness, depression—delusion. I was caught up in my own mind. I followed misleading thoughts. I created a committee of runaway thoughts and let them rule me from the head. I saw with clouded vision. I hold regret and remorse. I am so sorry. I wish I could start again, take it all back, have a new beginning. Can I have another chance, God? Can you erase my life and let me begin again? Can I really see my true face?

Continue this dialogue, using your feelings and words. Journal your thoughts before moving to Mind Fullness. If words do not come, draw. If you cannot draw, doodle. Breathe. Feel. Allow. Receive.

Mind Fullness

Deep dives bring treasures revealing hidden parts of the soul. If you ask, "Who am I?" you might discover a different answer than yesterday, or even tomorrow. You may also find it leads to another question: "Who do I want to become?" Beneath that lay the fear and excitement of another question: "Am I ready to shed all that I have been?"

Being "authentic" means you are ready to place aside all masks. These slowly build from childhood. In allowing others to place expectations, projections, personal views, and rules over who we know ourselves to be, we lay a framework of replication. We make a choice to either live in the illusion of others, or go against the grain and be considered different, unique, odd, or special.

Masks are worn in order to survive. Often, that survival is about holding on to the Love and acceptance of others. However, the Love gained from wearing a mask is never real Love. As the Love wears thin, the mask grows thicker. This results in extreme numbness. Only when an individual becomes strong enough to do the inner work required can the mask be lifted to reveal a more authentic person.

The mask is the covering that you show the world out of fear. It is the persona you hold and keep trying to prove to yourself. Masks keep the "shoulds," the "have tos," and the "musts" in place.

In hiding your vulnerable, true face, you deny acceptance of your greatness. You forget and lose touch with who you really are, what your dreams were, and the tingly vibration that connects you to feeling your heart and core. How often do you allow yourself to feel? Really feel? If numbness rests anywhere, there is a mask in place.

We grow up believing that our roots consist of the families we birth from or are reared in. The stories of grandparents and ancestors, heritage and lineage, that are handed down are the setting of a play. The people and props of life create one of many stories that exist. You are one of many stories. You are the story-teller.

Although an experience may be happening, and feel quite palpable to the touch, it does not mean that it is real or true. It is a version of you. Various bubbles of experience are happening simultaneously. You have tapped into a particular one. There are many other versions and outcomes to this story of you.

There are also many other stories occurring where you are a different role. However, whether or not you believe in alternate realities and parallel lives, there is only one true essence of you. What is real and true is something that does not change. Roots that are real and true have been in place and will always be, despite birth family, adoption, displacement, or lineage. This Essence is the sacred root that can never be severed. It is buried and awaiting your discovery.

Regardless of your story or circumstance, the sacred anchors you, runs through you, and has you at both ends. Finding the roots of your sacredness will keep you grounded and clear. These roots stabilize you, regardless of the landscape or weather. These roots link all the trees in the forest. Move beyond the roots you were born with into something greater and more expansive. The roots of your family, culture, religion, heritage, and society were a place for you to grow from, not be bound by.

If you find yourself restricted, bound, suffocated, tied, or held hostage by any root systems, it is time to find new ground, awaken new seeds, and anchor new roots. At both ends of your energetic trunk, the one constant is the essential root—the essence root of your nothingness and your allness. This is your safety. This is the column of unending connection, continuous energy boosts, and the monumental flow of Divine intelligence.

Healing requires focus on each of the energy bodies a human being possesses. Third-dimensional reality is the realm of veils, duality, and chaos. We are outer-focused and connecting to primitive basic senses. Fourth-, fifth-, sixth-dimensional living and beyond involves the care, integration, and conscious use of our many energetic systems.

Third-dimensional living is physical body–focused. Energy and emotion must be embodied, by breathing all experiences through the various bodies. This will provide lasting healing integration and power. In strengthening the physical body, the mental body is cleared, the emotional body is relieved, the energetic body is opened up, and the spiritual body becomes aligned and illuminated for a true multidimensional experience.

We chose a body for a reason, but we need not keep it in the density of the third dimension. That is what is meant by "heaven on earth." We have the ability to rise into a higher state of consciousness, bringing the fourth- and fifth-dimensional energies down into the body. Our feet cannot be in two worlds but our energy can. Keep the heart and mind in the higher kind, and the lower world will change. What you cannot fix here in the physical, you can work with in the ethers. In that realm, we speak to the higher self of each individual. "As above, so below."

It is imperative to keep the flow of energy moving and shifting. Breath and exercise not only release stress from the body, but also shift blocked energy. You came into a physical body to experience physicality and emotion. Feel...breathe...move...ground...breathe...feel. Be still in the emotion and heart. Rise into the truth of who you are by living in the higher mind and high heart. That is the true meaning of who you really are.

Truth Fullness

» If you chose a challenge you were experiencing and spoke to the person on the higher planes, how might the situation change?

» How might you change?

» How you creating heaven on earth—"As above, so below"?

» How are you supporting the physical vessel in lightening up?

Will Fullness

On a regular basis, go outside. Stand in the sun. Place your bare feet in the ground. Close your eyes. Wiggle your toes. Raise your hands to the sky. Invite the sun to send a cord to your gut, the solar plexus. This is the power cell of the human body, the sun center. This is the place of will and attention.

Imagine sunlight being pumped into your core, energizing and filling you completely. Let the sun continue to pump in sunlight, until each limb has been filled. You are a human—"hue man." You are a light man. Let the sun recharge your trunk.

When you feel filled, imagine your feet growing roots and connecting to the earth. Let those roots extend down from the soles of the feet. Continue extending them until they meet the molten lava center of the earth, the place of sacred birthing—the sacred mother root of all things.

Once you have connected to the Holy Mother root, extend the trunk's core of light up through your body and out of your head. Send this column as high into the Universe as you can imagine until it connects with the Holy Father root. Let your entire body and extended root system flood with energy and light. You are but one root system in a mass of many. Imagine roots extending from you, both high above you and down below you. As you do so, notice they are connected to other root systems, creating one giant energetic tree, filling the entire Universe, ethers, surrounding the earth plane, and grounding within the core of the planet. You are and have always been connected to All That Is—and for all time. You have access to all that you need, desire and are. Open to it. Anchor into it. Breathe it in.

Inhale IV: Attention to Love

Love is the essence that exists within and without me, in and around me. The remembrance of birthing through Love, returning to Love, and the constant supply of Love is reengagement with Love as the energy expressing in, as, and through me. I open myself to being Love, and unconditional in my loving.

On this day, I set heart-full attention to:

1. Experience stillness of mind by dropping down and within.
2. Recognize my body's wholeness, even when it feels otherwise.
3. Receive the abundance within each experience, regardless of appearances.
4. Discover balance by moving, adjusting, and changing.
5. Respect my need to exercise and need for rest.
6. Allow bold beginnings at the onset of each ending.
7. Listen attentively.
8. Have compassionate forgiveness, especially with what does not make sense.
9. Become aware that the only unhealthy emotions are ones I do not express.
10. Engage fully in life, Love, and joy by staying present with their opposites.
11. Openly embrace each step as organic goodness conspiring to reveal truth.

Exhale IV: Communion of Heart Opening

Dearest Ultimate Soul Mate,

I lovingly commit to US. I desire to know US. I am willing to see and feel US completely. I willingly allow all emotion to rise so that I discover US. I call forward my personality self, lower self, pain body self, hopeless romantic self, wounded parts and needy self to be present and available for wholeness in the highest interest of US. I know there is no end to the Love of Self. Show me Love. Show me how to Love and BeLoved. Show me how to Love my most feared and fearful self. I humbly submit my mind, ego, and heart to the union of US. Help me remember what I have lost. I open my mind to move beyond all limits and limitations.

I ask for the assistance of my angels, guardians, guides, body devas, nature spirits, cellular structure, dimensional selves, parallel selves, Highest Self, Holy Self, Ascended Masters, and Light Beings, in all places and at all times, to fully support this journey of Love, Loving and being Loved by attuning my frequencies to the highest available now.

I ask for healing holograms and sacred geometric forms to be placed around me that support the highest recognition and recalibration in remembrance of the Love that I Am.

As these heartfelt words are spoken, I know them to be activated and charged with the energy of fulfillment and completion in the most profound and nurturing way. I find union with the greatest, most expansive expression I AM. I decree and declare this, from the sacred center of my Divine soul being, for US. So be it...And so it is!

Forever Yours In Love, Of Love, With Love, As Love,

The Lover's BeLoved

Say Preparation

Heart Fullness

I'll be okay. I never expected it to work out, anyway. Luck is meant for other people. I don't know why I even try. It never works out for me. I'll give up trying. I can't do it on my own. I keep believing in people—in myself—but it never works out.

There are so many life issues to deal with. It seems I only have a brief amount of time before the next thing on the list needs to be attended to. I am so tired—so tired. I just feel so trapped. There are so many responsibilities and so many people to please. Everywhere I turn I feel judged, pulled on, ripped apart.

My perceptions block me from seeing my wholeness. I am caught up in seeing through other people's eyes; I cannot see clearly. My unworthiness, not-good-enoughness, ambition, and co-dependence are not me, but things I bought into. These are the things I believe about me. Why do I give constantly to others without regard for myself? How did I let myself get into this destructive pattern? I have made so many mistakes. I have missed so many chances to get it right. I have let many others control me. I have given myself away so many times, there is nothing left to give.

Who am I? Why can't others accept me as I am? I cannot let my life be run by other people and their thoughts about me any longer. I have to find out who I am. I want to remove these masks, these coverings. I cannot bear to fail again—in my life, in love, in my relationships, in my career. Can I stand tall, bare-naked, and just be me? What if I find nothing? Worse, what if they were right all along?

Continue this dialogue, using your feelings and words. Journal your thoughts before moving to Mind Fullness. If words do not come, draw. If you cannot draw, doodle. Breathe. Feel. Allow. Receive.

Mind Fullness

Separation can only happen in illusion. What are you believing that is not true? What story have you bought into that causes a divide? There are four parts to every story:

1. Your side.
2. Their side.
3. The neutral perspective.
4. The Divine Truth.

Ego is in play during reaction, isolation, triggers, and in all dense emotion. Pour Love on by communicating, staying present, and engaging. Respond within instead of reacting outside. Otherwise you will find yourself once again in blame, shame, isolation, and "why me?" You always have the choice of fear/running/isolation or Love/communing/communication. Which have you always chosen? Which will you now choose?

When there is conflict, when there is question, when there is concern—do you check in with yourself? When there is conflict, when there is question, when there is concern—do you check in with yourself? Do you turn and walk away without inquiry? Do you go into a story? Do you stay, ask questions, and feel into the truth? It's not what happens to you; it's how you handle what happens to you.

Relationships are created for the purpose of seeing more about ourselves. Communion is the ability to honor the Self, and the other, from a place of authenticity and voice. The problems of today, whether personally or globally, exist simply due to an inability to commune and communicate.

True healing, growth, and expansion occur when we take relationships to the next level by staying long enough to let the chaos settle. Only your experience exists to you. How is the other supposed to know anything about it or you, if you don't tell them? Conscious living is about open conscious communication. That relationship begins within.

Appreciate what you read or what others say, but close your eyes and feel. Your body cannot lie. Your greatest teacher and resource is yourself. Your feelings tell the truth. But only you can really determine if it feels good and right, or feels bad and out of alignment.

We have been mindless creatures, trying to become mindful, when we need only be mined. What we seek rests deeply within us. When the mind falls in Love, it is not something that can be controlled. Be aware that a connection, a calling, a longing has come from deep within. What's on your mind today is really of no consequence. What's in your heart is all that matters and which is real.

You are in, with, and of Love always. When the heart rises from Love, truth is remembered. There are many versions of what is called truth, but there is only one Truth. Tell the same truth all the time, to all people. And this, too, is a journey of revealing because your greatest deception is your own denial. There are no real crossroads in life because all paths lead back home. However, you mistakenly believe you have crosses to bear. Lay them down and choose the less bumpy road.

Too many are trying to escape into the ethers, have supernatural experiences, and disappear into any place but here. Why do you think you have come? The illusion is that you have to ascend and reach somewhere. There is nowhere but here, right now. Through the body and through humanity, you rise.

We believe that it all has to connect—that it all has to have meaning. The only things required are presence to ourselves and the willingness to be seen as meaningful—and each and every moment as meaningful to the presence of the moment. Then, all else rises into place. We are too attached to a lifelong version of meaning. Rising into the purity of this moment, completely present is ascension.

It is in the night that we dream, when we are asleep. Life now may feel like sleepwalking through a dark night each day while you sleep at night as the night sky looms dark overhead. You are either asleep, sleepwalking, or sleeping through life until you wake up and realize the dream is yours to make real. You cannot be in a process of awakening; you are either asleep or awake. The night and the Dark Night are for your dreams, and for you to awaken. Time to get up!

The only difference among dreaming, having a dream, and living the dream is the degree of allowing in your experience. If the moment asks you to smile, then do so. And, if it asks for a cry, a scream, or a tantrum, do not deny it. If it asks you to fall or stop, then okay. If it wants you in despair, then sink there, too. And if it asks you to laugh, never stop. The most honoring thing you can do is say *yes* to the moment, because in doing so, you honor yourself.

I will discover my personal magic when I am willing to recognize and celebrate yours. Whether or not you celebrate, approve, or recognize mine does not matter because the Love surrounding that magic is enough to keep me whole and complete. You are the Divine walking, fully capable of the highest expression because that is what you are, what I am, what we be. When we give and receive Love, there is no mind, a full heart, and a sense of oneness that is unexplainable and often illogical. You need only "have it."

Truth Fullness

- » Do you check in with yourself?
- » Do you turn and walk away without inquiry?
- » Do you go into a story?
- » Do you stay, ask questions, and feel into the truth?
- » Do you look for the magic in others?
- » Do you introspect so that your personal magic is revealed to you?

Will Fullness

Choose a new life vision. Paint pictures in your imagination, feeling the experience within the heart. See yourself living that life completely—in body, mind, and spirit. As you let this new manifestation in, follow conscious action steps to let the past find completion.

Hold the space for your truth to unfold. Allow an open field of possibility to be created. And use simple tools and rituals while you are waiting:

» Discover alone time.

» Find your rhythm (your time of day, climate, sounds, and tastes).

» Laugh a lot!

» Establish a nightly wind-down ritual.

» Have an Attention Stretch and Gratitude Workout.

» Dream, dream, dream.

» Write, write, write. Walk, walk, walk. Play, play, play.

This Connection

Heart Fullness

The quiet is too quiet. My mind keeps talking and I can't get away from it. The experience of stillness evades me. I find quiet places, take nature walks, and go into meditation spaces, but I never reach anywhere. I want so deeply to connect with my Source. There is always a distraction. The mental chatter is constant.

Moments of silence are challenging because I am left with my thoughts. They race through my mind: what needs to be done, where I need to go, and what has happened that I do not want to face. It seems as if the land of stillness will never come. My life is not cooperating, the people in my life are not helping me, and what I really want remains so distant.

If I take this step, people will think I have lost my mind! Why do I feel so undeserving? Can I take a chance on a new dream now? I have held back for so long, wasted so much time, spent so many years investing in what I have always done. How can I leave that career now and leap into nothingness?

Who am I to stretch beyond those around me? Who am I to live big and express full out? Can I let myself be more successful than those in my family? What about family loyalty? I do not want to make others feel less than. Maybe it is better to just play small like I always have. I could learn to be content.

What if I fail? Do I really want to take that risk right now? I need to use my head. I have responsibilities. I missed my opportunity. What would I do if I lost everything? I can't live with myself if I don't try. There are no guarantees if I do.

There is something out there calling me and I have no idea what it is, much less where it is. Can I trust that? Am I crazy? The unknown is such a big nebulous place. It feels scary—and yet something inside me feels excited. What do I trust?

Continue this dialogue, using your feelings and words. Journal your thoughts before moving to Mind Fullness. If words do not come, draw. If you cannot draw, doodle. Breathe. Feel. Allow. Receive.

Mind Fullness

Although experiences may be different, at the core, people are the same. We desire to be Loved and accepted. None of us wants to be hurt. We seek community and inclusion, but often exclude ourselves, and others. The things that we seek are only for us to take away or be granted. For some reason, we want them from other people. Oftentimes, the very thing desired is right within arm's reach. However, the arms that need to be reaching sit crossed and waiting, due to the ego's false expectation of another. What is being sought out is what the individual must give to the Self. The outer representation is merely illustrating what is lacking in self-attentiveness.

Disconnection is a state of mind. In creating stories about what we think is happening, we make illusion real. It becomes magnified to the one holding it in mind. In doing so, the body hears the command and responds. In allowing the ego to run amok, the personality and energy change in a person. Closed stances, short conversations, little eye contact, weakened hearing, and disconnection result from misinterpretation and misinformation.

Expectation is premeditated disappointment. Some part of you knows what the other is capable of. If they are not the type to deliver, some part of you realizes this already. It is a way to stay condemned within your story. You unconsciously test the other so you can prove to yourself that they are bad or wrong, and can feel righteous in your isolation. This way you lay claim to how "special" you are, in that you are not Loved or accepted like everyone else.

Expectation is a way to check out of life, saying, "I have the right to avoid responsibility, because I make you in charge of my life, emotions, reactions, and choices." It is a manipulative way to enmesh others into personal dysfunction. It is also how we get to hold a grudge.

Expectation stems from two things. First, there is a need to do things for other people with a conscious or unconscious belief they are required to behave a particular way or do certain things back for you. It is how we raise ourselves above others, achieve the right to stay angry, and prove to ourselves that the world is not supporting us.

Secondly, expectation holds a degree of narcissism. There is a belief that other people's worlds are all about you. The only world they are required to pay attention to is their own. You only have control of what you are able to do. The response from the other person is their right of response. It is what they are capable of in that moment or where they choose to be in their life. To believe they need to live their life according to your whims, needs, rants, raves, desires, actions, or feelings is arrogance and narcissism.

The same holds true for you. You are not to live your life based on the reactions, words, or behaviors of other people. You are to make choices based on what is most loving and kind to your own experience. If you are acting from authenticity and deep Love, only good can arise. With authenticity, your truth is your truth, but it does not mean others will like or embrace it. Their upset is a gift to them, an opportunity to uncover their own wounds, beliefs, and desires. Remain in a place of self-Love and authentic living, and do not be swayed by the reactions of others.

Having expectations allows you to isolate and cut off the world, resulting in a deeper state of anger and loneliness. Disappointment stems from not receiving the Love, acceptance, or Loving response wanted. You really are in the same place either way. Both positions point to the fact that the only one you can control is you. The only one who can fully give what is desired is you. To receive a complete understanding of what you desire, give it to both—you and the other person. In doing so, your relationship to self, the other, and life shifts.

What has actually presented itself is an opportunity for you to know yourself in a more attentive way. Make choices and actions with full responsibility to the Self. By engaging fully with everything you hold at a distance, more meaning can be brought into life through experience instead of expectation.

Read my first book, *Conversations With the Universe*. Watch the signs appearing to you. Begin to understand your language with the Universe. Notice what you are thinking of when your signs come. Notice all the ways the Universe is giving you the same messages. Begin keeping a journal of how things appear so you create your own specific dialect.

The Universe has your back and is always leading you to your greatest expression; only you hold it back. Take leaps of faith and fall into the void. You will be caught by the invisible.

Truth Fullness

How do you do or not do the following?

» In the face of storms—stand tall.

» When feeling isolated—reach out.

» When feeling overwhelmed—release your attachments.

» When there is drought—go back to refill and refuel your core.

» When blown in many directions—become grounded.

» When it starts to pour—drink it in and be drowned by it.

» When becoming something else serves a greater purpose— adapt and change.

Will Fullness

› Make healthy choices.

» Spend time outside.

» Breathe deeply.

» Drink more water.

» Engage in sun salutations.

› Open yourself up.

  » Find friendship.

  » Smile more.

  » Give compliments.

  » Focus on the energy lines.

› Express creatively.

  » Journal your thoughts.

  » Sing a song.

  » Use color.

  » Use imaginal cells to grow energetic roots.

› Create balance.

  » Practice yoga or walk.

  » Sit quietly.

  » Let others assist.

  » Exercise.

Dying to Live

Heart Fullness

I feel so trapped but I do not know how to go. At least I know what this is. Anything else is unknown. If I go, everything will change. I won't have what I now have. What if it is a mistake? But I am unhappy. My life feels empty. I know it is not loving to stay here. I am just so afraid of what's next.

I think I am actually afraid of being free. Can I be happy? Do I deserve that? I would have to make decisions. I would have to make choices. I guess my failures would be my failures. Right now I can blame it on someone else or the situation I am in. I have a reason to hold back. If I leave, I have no reason to hold back. And then, if I don't go for it, I will have myself to blame.

What if I am good enough? Can I handle it? Can I handle what that asks of me? I think I have stage fright. I am afraid of being alive. It is so easy to hide from life—and complain about it. Do I have the courage to live my life?

Continue this dialogue, using your feelings and words. Journal your thoughts before moving to Mind Fullness. If words do not come, draw. If you cannot draw, doodle. Breathe. Feel. Allow. Receive.

Mind Fullness

Intimate experiences are the vignette of what is created in the world on a greater scale. It is the responsibility of each one of us to value the experiences of turmoil, fear, and pain as gateways for personal growth, empowerment, and creativity. These things appear for the purposes of healing. When we are ready to let them go, they will let us go. Everything that exists prior to that surrender is a prison or a barricade—an excuse to deny one's power, and a poor payoff to a false "god." This dysfunctional way of living continually beckons for the answers, resolutions, and lessons outside, leaving a person feeling shaky, off balance, and continuously on edge.

Although we are living in a world of duality, we are not required to be a roller coaster, bumper car, or even slow-moving vehicle on a bumpy road; our essence is the answer to every question, the compassion in the chaos, the willingness to live out the script that may have no meaning.

It is one's personal responsibility to be guardian and guide of the inner and outer worlds. Consciously commit to the 13-inch highway between the head and the heart. In engaging with the rainbow path that guides from root to crown, many areas that are blocked or in need will be discovered. In clearing and reenergizing these chakra centers, along with caring for the amazing body-vehicle, we become charged up and ready to go. Being on solid ground means keeping one's systems centered despite the chaos, so that nothing outside shifts you from the ultimate experience of who you are.

The greatest fear we have is that of our own mortality—not getting it right and in enough time. However, we experience death multiple times throughout our lives. It is imperative to allow the death of words, patterns, beliefs, behaviors, habits, old wounds, unhealthy relationships, and addictions. When we let things die, something more beautiful can birth and grow. In becoming comfortable with the waning of what exists, we begin to see that the death we ultimately fear is not dying. It is releasing limiting constructs and stepping into the unknown to live fully. There is no death, only life, in its many forms and reflections.

We are told death means things have ended, decayed, and been lost—gone forever. Death is identified with grief, tears, and sadness. This fear of the unknown relates not only to physical death, but also the multitude of life experiences that court change. Denial of death keeps individuals stuck in circumstances that are disempowering, painful, victimizing, and uncomfortable. We get comfortable being uncomfortable where embarking on the unknown appears as a risk. The true risk lay in staying who and where you are.

Death is not really the end, but the beginning. We are meant to experience dying on a continual basis. What is falling away is not real. It is the illusion blocking the ultimate creation of and connection to who we really are. Dying and birthing are one in the same: implosion and explosion expressing "the void" and "big bang." It is the ever-expanding experience of nothingness and all-ness. Death sheds unnecessary layers so we continue experiencing the immortality of the spirit—dispensing of thoughts, beliefs, habits, patterns, dis-eases, discomfort, relationships, environments, and energy that no longer serves. Even physical death is a rebirthing to Divine essence, and the opportunity to birth into another experience of the Self.

Many walking are already "dead," living unconscious lives without feeling, disconnected from themselves and others, and void of passion. They cannot see. They move day-to-day, by habit rather than choice—settling for what their circumstance is instead of seeing it as the platform from which to create. For so many, the "end" is already here. But this death hangs onto being dead. It never moves into a state of new birth. Instead it marinates in its own decay.

Denial, anger, bargaining, depression, and acceptance are the steps necessary for creation to change. When each person steps more fully into the dying process, our world will become more alive, allowing new ideas to rise up out of the ashes. The one constant is change. The choice to venture into it is our gift, the golden key opening heavenly gates. Old constructs, past restraints, and outdated paradigms must fall away for new growth to occur.

It is what happens in life and what is occurring in our world's systems, from banking to healthcare to government. The government as we know it must die for a new paradigm in conscious nationalism to be born. The codependency of money must end for materialism to find a new definition. It is imperative that we continue to redefine, fine-tune, and clarify who we each are, what we are about, and how we relate. Acknowledging these choices affects the rest of the planet. It is paramount that we change— thought to thought, step by step, layer within layer—continually becoming the example of courage, voice, vision, mission, and passion that others need to see—and more importantly, that we need to witness.

To remain fully alive, we need only remember we are soft clay to be molded and sculpted into many beautiful forms. We must wake up to the possibility that all we have believed may not be true. We are so much more than we allow ourselves to be. We are the clay and the hands that mold the clay. We are the sculpture, in process and already complete. We are the master sculptor and the clay pot. Be willing to die in order to live. Be willing to Love into every stage of the process. Love into dying, Love into birthing, and Love into life.

It is not about remembering who you are. The remembrance rests in who you were. We were created as art by the Divine. Our lives, and each step taken, are the casting of the artist's hand. Just as we create art as monuments to others, our very lives are monuments to the soul—in fact, "masterpieces."

Truth Fullness

» What did your mother or father have to grieve about?

» Did they properly grieve?

» What in your life needs to be grieved?

» Will you let your heart break open at the tragedy and the sadness your body holds?

» What was not fair and needs to be felt that sits in the stages of grief, loss, and mourning:

  · What is in denial and isolation?

  · Where is the anger?

  · How have you been bargaining?

  · Have you experienced or allowed depression?

  · Have you pushed into acceptance before you were ready?

Will Fullness

Go through your things. Find some items that are symbolic of what needs to die for your life to change. This may include pictures, a gift that reminds you of a promise that has been broken, or an item that brings a painful memory of hopes dashed. Bless these things and let them go.

Identify the part or parts of you that need to die to transform you and your life into something new. Write a eulogy that offers your sentiments and honor these pieces of you that have tried, persevered, toiled, or pushed for so long. If you have been angry with God, and had made a silent pact, write your "angry letter" to God or go into meditation and rant. This is also about allowing the God of your understanding to die, so that you may be born to a more loving God of creation.

Say goodbye to the people and/or places that keep you locked in unhealthy patterns or in a state of abuse. It does not mean they are out of your life forever, just until you are strong enough to return with a sense of self. Remember: You are creating your life anew.

❧ 27 ❧

Save Yourself

Heart Fullness

I cannot believe I am sick. I need to do something. Oh God, what if—I cannot even say it. What if I don't heal? What if the diagnosis is negative? I can feel this life inside of me. I have not done what I came here to do yet! I need strength, God. I'll do anything. I'll promise anything. Just save me.

My mind won't stop! I keep thinking the worst-case scenarios. Get it out of me! The doctors keep giving me options that don't sound like options. These are my choices? I have to make a decision and can't. Who am I living for? I might be at the end. The adrenaline is pumping through me. How do I not be afraid? What if I die? It is not my time. I have not done anything with my life yet. Have I wasted my life?

Mind Fullness

Healing, in the human sense, is different than healing in the soul sense. In human terms, desires are usually for a specific issue, the problem causing angst in the moment. Human healing asks for the miracle, to be rid of something or to return to a "normal"—a perspective of the world created to feel safe. However, "normal" is the very thing that must release. The change happening is actually breaking barriers to their wholeness and freedom, set in place through the wounded child's creation.

Healing is begged of, prayed for, and paid homage to as if the solution. But the solution is in the inquiry of what created the need to heal in the first place. When healing appears, it may not look the way the human mind or personality wants it.

The soul understands healing in a broader spectrum seeking greater good for all. That often appears as opposite to what the human mind is asking for. For example, someone seeking healing from an illness may mean coming back to health in the current body. However, the soul may view healing as the release of the body from pain, by passing on to the next level of existence. Divine healing relates to an outcome for the greater group within the experience. In soul healing, the dis-ease or challenge is the miracle. In Divine healing, it becomes the gift that creates the atmosphere for all involved to heal, allowing an opportunity to go inside for contemplation, reflection, and awareness.

The Divine perspective has no good or bad, no ill or health, but a journey of experiences within the realm of wholeness existing at all times. Divine healing creates a web of change for a larger group. It is not preoccupied with the details of one person or situation. Divine healing knows that creation is the miracle.

When seeking healing, discern what part of you is asking and what it is asking for. Is this the ego self, soul self, Divine self, human self, or pain body self? The part of you asking for healing has an agenda, but the soul is seeking experience and growth for itself. In true healing, the appropriate people, circumstances, and energy will elicit massive transformation, unconcerned with time, space, or appearance. The broadest spectrum of healing is beyond all of that.

In the soul sense, people are fulfilling contracts necessary to their growth and self-realization. Miracles would vary within life lessons of personal power, Love, forgiveness, and surrender. Perspectives on life warrant situations to either prove internal belief systems as truth or birth new paradigms of realization. If they do not, it becomes the task of future generations. All lives have a global purpose beyond the name or role they play.

Through death, consciousness becomes illumined with all parts of the story we cannot see while living. In the next realm, peace will be received. Although the human body lives in a state of oppression, the Spirit is always free.

Oftentimes, individuals only feel a portion of an experience. It is natural to place aside feelings, instead acting out what we think needs to be done or how we believe we should behave. It is the way we protect ourselves. Sitting with each experience gives the body an opportunity to release on every level. Many people carry wounds and uncomfortable situations with them from year to year. We all have pain, trauma, and a sense of deficiency. We all deaden while living. It is likened to baggage that just keeps getting heavier and heavier. At some point, collapse happens. It is so heavy that the burdens of carrying it take a toll on all facets of life. Life does not beat us up. The longer one holds onto identities and masks, they create lives that are not aligned to the highest vibration of Love. Course corrections will take place in the form of the pebbles, rocks, and boulders that life presents.

These things are not easy to admit to oneself. However, the alternative of wearing many masks while trying to maneuver all the baggage collected over the years always ends in a more torturous experience. Either choose to see yourself as you are, or be forced to see the distorted face of tragedy you now embody.

The energetic and emotional body can be viewed as a large glass container. We are the clear and pristine liquid energy of joy, bliss, happiness, and Love. Experiencing harsh circumstances, or the energy of others, can create residue that begins to cloud the container. In an effort to understand this residue, stronger experiences that allow us to feel the dense emotions of the residue in a deeper way are created. When the emotions of sadness, anger, jealousy, fear, and the like are experienced and suppressed, they layer on top of the initial light emotions within the container. As more experiences occur, heavy emotions continue to pile on, clouding the container and the darkening the liquid within.

Forgiveness, Love, compassion, and the ability to express emotion are likened to clear water. As these forms of Love are poured in, the contents will initially swirl and cloud, making an individual feel as if the world is in chaos. As more Love is brought in, the container will overflow and the denseness will begin moving out. In continuously pouring liquid Love into the container, heavy emotions weighing down the vessel will filter out. Anger, sadness, shame, and guilt start to flow out of the vessel as experienced emotion. The container becomes clearer and clearer. Eventually, the only things that remain are peace, Love, joy, bliss, and true compassion. The container will return to its pristine clear state. Pouring Love on the self will bring up everything unlike itself first. However, the truth will come through after washing the Self clean of energetic and emotional residue.

Compassion is the awareness of the deep suffering of another, while holding the space of Love. This awareness cannot fully exist within unless we first acknowledge our own angst and pain. This can be a challenge because no one wants to acknowledge inner darkness. This part of man is hidden and buried within the subconscious, but seeds manipulation and codependence to attain its ultimate desire of acceptance and Love.

There is a part of us naturally willing to be in service toward others. Unless there is deep immersion into the processes and experiences of self-realization, the majority of actions performed are for the wounded self, subtly serving addictive needs and reasons. These actions are based upon a core feeling of not being good enough and being broken. When another individual is helped in some way, the one "in service" can tell herself she is a good person. That is the payoff—the manipulation. Receiving the gratitude and praise of others becomes a gluttonous way to feel better about the self. It is a source of manipulative self-affirmation, which would not be necessary if the belief of "good enough" existed.

The greater the "need" to save, help, heal, or give to others, the more intense the lack of self-value or the ability to see the Divine quality of the other. In this case, all actions to save, help, heal, or give are not selfless but, in fact, for the self. The individual is using the experience for the gain of external and internal approval.

We save others because the brokenness we see matches the part of us we do not want to recognize. Instead of working on the self, many individuals choose a cause on the outside. It is much easier to project that darkness onto someone or something else.

This is a harsh perspective for many to receive. Please know it is expressed with full and complete Love, so that you may move to a place of true service, after attaining a knowing of your true worth. At the very least, acknowledge the *why* of your passion and creative force.

True service occurs when the other is viewed as the self, not someone outside needing assistance. The necessary work is within. The actions we take on the outside are purely to remain the experience and expression of self from a detached perspective of the outcome, still fully engaged, Loving, and compassionate. This just means the situation need not change, regardless of the outcome. This appears to sound selfish, but the difference is there is no personal need or gain involved. It is selfless service, meaning the needs of the self—either self—have been placed out of the way purely for the communion of experience in relationship with itself. This is Divine union as well.

Compassion can be viewed as "come-passion." "Come-passion"—exude from within me. The source of compassion is personal passion. Passion fills us up and exudes forth effortlessly, providing energy so one does not feel depleted. Passion creates self-worth and self-value, where nothing is required from the outside. It allows for more intuitive inspiration to arise. In this way, we can truly birth solutions for the experiences at hand. Compassion arises from "being."

The being place of compassion is much more powerful, present, and expansive. It also brings to awareness the wholeness, divinity, and ability that we each possess as spiritual beings having a creative human story. In that consciousness, an individual can support others selflessly, recognizing the needs and circumstances required, as the healing of passion and compassion for the individual is blocked.

Truth Fullness

- » How do you feel about death and dying, being sick and sickness?

- » How many times in your life have you already experienced death?

- » Did you survive; now can you thrive regardless of what you face?

- » Do you believe—*know*—you are energy, and eternal?

- » Can you sit with that concept and see the bigness of you in this small experience?

Will Fullness

Find a collection of stones, sticks, or large rocks. If you do not have any, have some delivered for the purposes of building a small labyrinth. This will be your sacred circle of attention and prayer. It will be the place that you walk out the words that sit low and deep in your groin, begging to be spoken, aching to be heard—by you.

If you do not have yard space that allows this, you can create a labyrinth in your apartment or home with tea lights, crystals, or small rocks. Allow the walk around your space to begin at your front door. Place stones or candles at each window as you move through the space in a meditative way. This may be done in silence, prayer, song, or breath techniques. As you return, light each candle or collect the pieces that have been placed, completing your path. Let the candles burn down.

This daily walk is your opportunity to embed your ground with new roots. As you move through the labyrinth, hold your "palms" before you as if engaged in a soul "psalm." Let the soles (souls" of your feet take the necessary steps. Notice how language reveals the hidden sacred. In addition, the soles represent the higher soul and lower soul walking together, creating footprints on the bosom of the Great Mother. Pour your hopes and dreams inward and outward through your hands and feet as you speak them out of your mouth and breathe them out of your nose (knows). The breath knows all things, which is why it is important.

Visualize a column of Light from overhead washing through your spinal ("spin all") column. Cleanse your fears, worries, and problems. Lift them up and lay them down in reverence for the gift they bring.

Begin each walk with attention in the heart, at the entrance to the labyrinth. End each walk with a gratitude prayer. Let your roots grow strong, thick, and deep. What goes up must come down. What grows down must grow up. You are the central point of infinity, but you must fertilize the field with thought, feeling, and action. You are the center of your Universe. Now, let your garden grow.

Inhale V: Attention for Understanding

Knowing is truth that exists within. The human experience is the remembrance of knowing which comes from its allies of Living and Being.

Today I stand, fully extending my arms wide open, my mind filled with expectancy, and my heart believing:

1. I am the co-creation of my life, as shadow and Light.

2. Unlimited possibilities lay within me ready to express my creative capacity.

3. Life is an opportunity to know myself in a deeper way.

4. I am worthy of Love and connection.

5. Change is a loving way to renew my mind, body, and spirit.

6. My thoughts, words, and actions are the bridge.

7. Inquiry and contemplation deepen my truth.

8. *Yes* opens the gates to all that I AM.

9. I bring meaning fullness to the world.

10. I have power to open portals for boundless experience and self-realization.

11. I AM deserving.

Exhale V: Communion With Loving Reflection

Dearest Ultimate Soul Mate,

I lovingly commit to full reflection of innate Divinity through US. I welcome the ability to create and become aware of mirrors within my life for US. I am willing to witness the great unfolding of cause and effect that surrounds US with joyful ease. I am open to allowing the deepest degree of intimacy with my world, engaging compassionate correction and passionate creation between US. I now ask that we discover one another as the full spectrum of Light, revealing the brilliance and radiance of US in the highest possible expression of mystical marriage. I bridge—I build the bridge—I AM the bridge.

I ask for the assistance of my angels, guardians, guides, body devas, nature spirits, cellular structure, dimensional selves, parallel selves, Highest Self, Holy Self, Ascended Masters, and Light Beings, in all places and at all times, to fully support this journey of loving reflection, placing US firmly within the Divine footprint of sacred loving, living, being, and knowing, supporting the truth that I AM.

As these heartfelt words are spoken, I know them to be activated and charged with the energy of fulfillment and completion, in all times, spaces, and places, in the highest state of unconditional Love and the most profound nurturing way. So be it...And so it is!

Forever Yours,
The Lover of the BeLoved

28

Sound of Silence

Heart Fullness

In the silence, my thoughts scream loudly. In the silence, the images boom in my mind. In the silence rests all I do not want to see and hear about myself. This silence speaks volumes. When does the silence become quiet? When will I hear you? Where is that still, small voice? Or has the voice not been listened to so that it screams at me from everywhere and everything?

I know this world cannot be random. There is meaning, and yet it has no meaning. Speak to me in the silence. Let me hear you. Come to me. Let me hear your words that I many learn. Let me know your sound that I might reach you.

I feel all alone in this giant auditorium. Whisper to me in the night, where eyes can't see. Speak softly to me behind the closed doors of my mind. Breathe your harmony into the chaos of my life. I beckon your melody. I seek my own song. Hear ye. Hear ye. Please. I'm listening.

Continue this dialogue, using your feelings and words. Journal your thoughts before moving to Mind Fullness. If words do not come, draw. If you cannot draw, doodle. Breathe. Feel. Allow. Receive.

Mind Fullness

Silence is the place where messages come. It is the extended period of time where the rest of the world is left behind. An attentional holy meeting takes place in earnest and reverence. Be clear in the asking and even clearer in listening. When ready and present, the message always comes.

Things may not always appear as we want, but definitely as we need. The human mind has its own expectations as to the end result. When things do not arise in a way an individual desires, grievances block the connective flow. In the grievances we hold, the doubts, weaknesses, and insecurities we invest in, we keep ourselves from opening to Source and supply. We think God sits high on a mountaintop and creates our pain and our miracles. It is God whom we believe is there to be prayed to when in need, sitting so powerfully away from us. The Divine is not on the mountaintop; S/He sits deep in the valley of your own Being.

Let go of grievances, remove the clouds of doubt and insecurity, and take down the walls of judgment, anger, and resentment. Let go of being "fine" or "okay." We disrespect life as Our Creative Source when we settle for less than we intend to be. We curse ourselves with limiting beliefs held, often berating ourselves with the stories of our lives. There are no mistakes. There are no wrong turns. The fact is, you cannot make a mistake. Lift the veils that exist within the mind to clearly see how Divinely beautiful it has all been.

As the image and likeness of creation, you are to become, or "come to be." What holds you back from being in community with all things and in communion with the BeLoved? The mind, stories of fear, grievances, and control. You placed veils there. Return to the blessing that waits you. A blessing is present in this moment, in this very moment; it is *you*. You are blessed, and you are the blessing. Furthermore, you are the blesser.

Move from expectation into expectancy. Expectations stem from two things: a conscious or unconscious belief people are required to behave a particular way. Second, there is a belief that the world is all about you. The only thing you have control of is what you are able to do. The response from the other side is their response. It is what they are capable of in the moment or where they choose to be in the moment.

Ask yourself: "What was I seeking from them? What did I do for them, thinking I would receive what I wanted? Did I really want to do what I did?" In isolating, you block yourself from the world, not receiving what you want. The disappointment from expectation also stems from not receiving the Love, acceptance, or loving response desired. You are in the same place either way—both pointing to the fact that the only one you can control is you. The only one who can provide what desire is you. The only way to fully receive a complete understanding of your desire is to give it to *you*. Love and accept people for who they are and what they are capable of. Love and accept yourself.

We are the ones who placed the veils there. Return to the blessing that waits. Become the blessing you seek. When you live in expectation of others, you are to be disappointed because your expectation is seen through your filters of wounded ness, so it can only create that reflection. Live in expectancy of your greater Self instead, and you will create an entirely different and empowering experience. Move from expectation into expectancy.

Expectancy is being pregnant with possibility. It is the triune of mind, heart, and being that births something out of Love. It is not demanding or controlling. We are engaged in the God process because it is birth and creation of something from nothing. It is bringing forth creation from creation itself. Expectancy allows us to experience being God to something of our own creation, learning to Love it unconditionally—hold it, cherish it, and discipline it from the perspective of Divine Mother and Divine Father. When in expectancy, we come into union with the BeLoved and are bringing forth a child to be birthed, reared, nurtured, and cared for.

Manifestation is not just to have, but to experience. The children, businesses, or ideas that we are inspired with are the seed of the Father (Divine Law) implanted within the Divine Mother (Tree of Knowledge). This Divine Child (the seed of fruit) is ready to be impregnated with desire, vision, and belief. Then, and only then, does it have a fighting chance to survive.

The ideas, children, and births will be another mirror, in how they grow, how they fall, and how they rise. They will trigger us, show us every weakness we hold, and challenge us with the energy required to look after them. They will make us proud, show every strength, and live out our own unfulfilled dreams. They will also experience our foibles and shadows. Expectancy and creation are natural to us. We need only follow our bliss and continue to look expansively, clearing the inner landscape of any blocks to Love's connective creative presence.

You can either "be longing" for the BeLoved, or you can belong to the BeLoved.

Do not keep yourself from your Divine right. Take the time to be still. Find the essence of your true self. Allow the gifts that are being brought into your life. Remain available to accept the unconditional Love sitting and waiting at your feet. Even the rock is a diamond in the rough. Know the truth of who you are; know the truth of who walks, talks, moves, and creates through *you*. Be still and know I AM that I AM.

Truth Fullness

» Imagine the seed of a new birth within you?

» Does it move and kick?

» Is it speaking to you?

» Do you feel it low in your gut, within the womb of creation?

» Can you be with it for a while, all to yourself, so you both are bonded and nurtured?

» Are you preparing the space in your life?

» Are you getting ready to nest?

Will Fullness

Place your hand just below your belly button. New life awaits you. A seed rests in the sacral chakra, the energy center of creation and relationship, the well of abundance, and the pelvic bowl of expectancy.

In this place you can birth something new. This birth holds the key to experiencing relationship in a deep, new way. This is the container that will hold all the abundance you deserve: wealth, prosperity, connection, and Love. It is the sacred space of new life.

As it grows within you, it is fed by every thought and feeling you have. You imprint this child with the emotional character, strength of will, and clarity of mind you use. It understands itself based on what you stand on. You are imprinting this new life with your DNA.

Beyond Illusion

Heart Fullness

I want to have more out of life. I want to be more. I know I am capable of more. If only I could believe in myself enough. I know I have gifts to share. I just want to do what I love to do and know why I am here. I want to know my life has meaning and purpose—that I matter.

I don't want to waste this life. The worst thing would be to reach the end of my life and feel if I have just wasted time, or never even gave a chance to my dreams. I can do this. I know I can. I have to do this. I am willing to do whatever it takes, and I know I will make it.

Can I really do this? Can I? Am I fooling myself? Can I really take a chance on me? Everything I have gone through must have been preparing me for something. Maybe that moment is now. Maybe that moment is me. Maybe all of the past was for the present. Can I wish upon a star? Can that star be me glowing brightly in my own life?

Continue this dialogue, using your feelings and words. Journal your thoughts before moving to Mind Fullness. If words do not come, draw. If you cannot draw, doodle. Breathe. Feel. Allow. Receive.

Mind Fullness

This is the moment that mindfulness moves out of the intellectual mind into the heart mind, where a deeper knowing and understanding occur. It is the place that exists beyond science or spirituality. It is the wisdom of experience. It happens when we look forward to looking back, knowing it was all for the "present," the gift of this moment.

Life is not about living in your pain, becoming a victim to it, or even becoming it. Life is about witnessing the experiences as they move through, regardless of what the human self and personality self judge them as. Being authentic is acknowledgment, acceptance, and celebrated expression.

I am not my experiences. I am a product of my life experiences. I embrace them as a part of me because they lead me to discovering my expansiveness. I choose whether or not to live beyond them. I choose to either respond or react. In responding I create healing. In reacting, I create additional opportunities for healing.

Those who find life challenging have a perspective that they are their experiences. All individuals experience pain and loss. It is part of the human condition. Some people are addicted to pain. They live their pain long after it has gone because it is their high. It is their only way to feel, so they think. Others live partially, keeping one foot cemented in the bucket of past pain while placing the other in the future, running to escape their pain.

Finally, there are those who understand their power rests within their pain, able to be transformed into the fuel that heals, motivates, and inspires. Rather than remaining focused on life circumstances, many individuals are inspired to create from painful experiences, as a way to serve others.

Every individual is here as a teacher, as a minister, as a guide. In the course of life, we cross many who have lived similar circumstances. These opportunities allow us to step out of our story and use it to support others in their personal journey. In the process, our own wounds heal.

As we each take responsibility, we bring the world more toward oneness. As we each choose to be more authentic in right word, right thought, and right action, we move into right living. Individual integrity brings the world into greater integrity. As we each take the time to heal and reintegrate wholeness into personal experience, we heal *our world* of all of its ills. In doing so, we support *the world* in healing as well.

We all need darkness to germinate, water and food to nourish, and Light to lift us up and out. In leaning toward the Light, we see what is warm and true. Its awareness comes from having a reference point of what was cold and isolating.

Just as the lotus springs from the murky waters, the muck is part of the necessary fertilization process for us, as humans. This is a good time to acknowledge mess-ups, inconsistencies, reactions, and invisibility within your experience—and be okay with all of it. Mess-ups lead to cleanliness. Cleanliness is Godliness. Inconsistency leads to consistency and reaction to new actions. Most importantly, invisibility allows for visibility and vision.

Too much time is spent in regret. There are no mistakes—only "mis takes." We are on the movie screen of life. If actors are allowed to do several scene takes to get the movie they are looking for, are we not afforded the same as stars of our own movie?

Every moment is part of your great story. Every good movie holds themes of sadness, failure, despair, tragedy, determination, dreams, Love, and triumph. Every great book has a villain and a hero. Don't put your book down before creating an "authentic happiness" ending.

Being compassionate to oneself, regarding everything that has occurred, is imperative to shift into a new experience. Holding thoughts of shame, guilt, or anger will only create more of the same. Forgive yourself and others. Be released from your own judgments. Refrain from gossip. We each have the right to be human. Being perfect is overrated. Embrace your imperfections, but live consciously. We have the Divine right to experience the present moment. We have the spiritual right to discover our greatest self and the intimate connection to what is so much greater. Most importantly, we have been given humanity to witness the ecstasy every step. This cannot be done if we're still caught up in the "dynamics" that occurred eight chapters ago. Think rightly, speak rightly, and act rightly, to shine brightly.

In consciously seeing ourselves as we truly are, "steady wisdom" develops. Steady wisdom provides the perspective and awareness to allow experiences to move through us without attachment. It is the opportunity to just observe the classroom setting we are engaged in. Regardless of whether life brings something horribly tragic or something blissfully exciting, we take in the situation as another subject in the school of life. We are books to be read and entertained by—"subject" to ourselves.

Why is it people Love the movies or watch television? These are ways to escape into another story, become another character, and live a different experience. They are mini illusions, within the illusion. We choose in every moment to be entertained by a script of your own making, or a random script that has allowed a commercial break from life. The real Self is in a state of stillness, very aware. It is watching a story unfold, incredibly amused by the whole thing. Life is soul Disneyland: filled with roller coasters, fast rides, haunted houses, and beautiful gardens. Your soul came on an adventure. Can you approach each experience from the same mind-set and heart-set as when on vacation? Relax into your life. Relax into your body. Relax into Love.

We are the sky. The emotions, experiences, and circumstances are the clouds that move through. The challenge comes when we forget. The error is in believing we are the passing cloud. We must continually remember we are the entire sky. Most people get caught up, battered by, and washed away with the storms. At other times, we do not even acknowledge the beauty of the fluffy cloud shapes against the blue horizon. So *who, what,* and *why* are you? For what purpose? You are here to discover yourself, your creativity, your voice, and your expansiveness. *You* are the purpose of your life. Your Loving Essence is your purpose.

"Loving Essence" exists within every single human being. The one and only perspective of truth rests in seeing that Loving Essence in the person, deed, or situation at hand. Loving Essence responds instead of reacts. Witness from a place of Love, compassion, and fullness, instead of judgment, control, or gossip. There is no room for judgment, harshness, or limitation when you are the living expression of the "God-self." Instead of being held back by the viewpoints of the human condition, you are able to hold consciousness of the "Divinity" of other people and situations. How does one reach this stage of being God in human form?

You begin with you. Can you see yourself from the Loving Essence? Are you able to recognize you as the Loving Essence? Can you release judgment for any and all past actions, regarding yourself and others? Can you express gentleness, Love, and compassion to the Self unconditionally?

Can you open yourself to receiving a life of fullness and flavor instead of remaining stuck in lack, limitation, regret, and victimhood? Are you willing to turn every seemingly bad or hurtful event in your life into a place of empowerment, by extracting from them all of the lessons, abilities, and strengths you gained? Can you embrace and celebrate all of who you are, who you have been, and who are becoming?

Anger is as much a gem as gentleness. Sadness is as beautiful as joy. Fear creates as much inspiration and ingenuity as Love. In many ways, it actually has driven us into our greatest creations. This is the full spectrum, without which we would not have experience. This is the all-inclusive rainbow. Our complete awareness of the beauty of all things is the pot of gold we have been searching for. In seeking the illusion of what is obviously beautiful, we have missed a hidden beauty—a hidden treasure, embracing the inner rainbow of emotions, bridging the gaps within the diversity of experience and expression in life.

We can spring forth from the intellectual understanding of spiritual beings having a human experience to the experiential understanding of the human "being" spirit. We can no longer create separation of being human or being spirit. The integration of both is required to qualify for the next level of integration.

Truth Fullness

> » Have you taken a moment to welcome something new (creation or birth) into being?

> » What do you know about yourself that you want this child (creation) to have?

> » What do you not want this child (creation) to take from you?

> » What do you desire to learn from this child (creation)?

> » What do you want to teach this child (creation)?

> » What will you name this child (creation) (a name you know it by, not necessarily what it later becomes called)?

Will Fullness

The first individual you must hold the space for is yourself. Honor the sacred essence that you are by creating a sacred altar. This is the place where you come to have intimate connection with you as creator, as the prayer, and the pray-er. Write your own prayer. Create your own mantra. The sacred space you create is for you to step into your Higher Self energy, knowing you are a being beyond space and time, mind and physicality.

In this space, take time in reflection. Think of someone who really makes you angry or sad. Focus upon what you believe he or she has done to you. As you do so, notice how your body changes. Does it tense up? Do you feel anything in particular? Does a certain place in your body feel noticeable, all of a sudden? Breathe into that part of the body. Breathe Love and light into your body. As you do so, imagine that everything you do or give to yourself, you are giving in triplicate to this individual. Will this impact how much you give? What you give? Will you forsake yourself or bless yourself? Notice how you use your power, for or against yourself.

On a sheet of paper, write out all the words you would use to describe this person or that body feeling. How do you judge them? How do you perceive them? What do you feel toward them? Where are those qualities in you? Check in with your body again. Do you feel discomfort in the same place or has it moved?

Close your eyes and imagine you have walked down a long hallway known as the corridor of truth. The sacred room at the end of this hallway is the room of Loving Essence. Enter the room. You will see two chairs sitting opposite one another. Breathe deeply and invite the Loving Essence into the space with you. Open your heart, asking it to reveal the highest degree of Loving Essence that can sit and be Loved.

As you anchor this in your heart, the door to the Loving Essence room opens. The individual who has hurt or harmed you most deeply, whom you have judged or held at a distance to the greatest degree, enters the room. This person takes the seat across from you. Breathe in the Loving Essence.

See the Loving Essence as God coming through the actions and behavior of this person. No matter what he or she has done or said, imagine it was for the sake of Love. Consider this was a contract of tough Love. What do you have to say? What do you feel? What do you want to ask? Ask any questions you have. Listen for the answers.

Be willing to embrace the Loving Essence. Understand it. Imagine that the person in front of you changes like a chameleon, revealing the faces of all those in your life who you perceive as hurtful, angry, harmful, jealous, spiteful, deceitful, and betraying. See the Loving Essence in each one until the face shifts into another. As each face shifts, know you have released them from the experiences you have tied them to. As you reach the final face of Loving Essence and it clears, see your own face in the body opposite you.

Can you see the Loving Essence? Can you recognize how loving and supportive this being has been, despite you? Are you aware of all the times your soul was present, as your backup and support, in every situation? Will you recognize how the perceived wounded and shadow side tried to protect, honor, and save you from each experience, in the best way it could? Do you understand they have taken all of your abuse, self-battery, and harsh self-talk, and still remained loyal, present, and available to you when you call?

The Loving Essence never leaves. It holds the space. It uses tough Love and tender Love. Seeing the Loving Essence is how you "return into Love" what it has given you.

See yourself as the Loving Essence that you are, have always been, and will continue to walk forward as.

30

Balance Beamer

Heart Fullness

I feel shaky about these new steps. I can't quite get my footing. Whoa! I almost slipped. I am not sure what I am fighting for. The ground moves beneath me and I find myself on the floor. I need to find balance in my life. I need to say goodbye to certain things—certain people. I need to do more for myself. I must bring everything into balance.

And I don't "need" to do anything. I should want to do these things. But there should be no "shoulds." What do I do? How do I do it? What do I want? What do I really, really want? Why do I want that? Then I will know what to do. Then I will figure out how to do it. But this time, I balance my life.

Continue this dialogue, using your feelings and words. Journal your thoughts before moving to Mind Fullness. If words do not come, draw. If you cannot draw, doodle. Breathe. Feel. Allow. Receive.

Mind Fullness

Balance is the middle point between action and being. It is the ebb and flow of life in its natural state, when we do not manipulate, control, compartmentalize, or create codependent relationships. Balance is communicating and listening to the softer inner voice, as opposed to the outer loud ones. Soft whispers come from the heart, the body, inner spirit, and life.

Too many people try to "do" balance, create it, or master it. But, balance already exists. You cannot "do" balance any more than you can "do" Love. People are unable to access it because they are caught up in the to-do lists, future attainments, and results they are seeking. When we are preoccupied, we are not attentive to the only thing that actually exists: the present moment. Two things happen in the now: Balance naturally arises, and we move back into the body.

The beauty of now is that there are no to-do lists, anxieties, or obligations. Those are end results that exist in the future or pieces of the past where you created an assumption. In this moment, you can only be where you are.

When you lean outside, all other voices are louder than the voice of the self. Their ranting appears more important. Their needs seem justifiable. Personal importance diminishes, if there is not a strong sense of self. Hurried, anxious responses to requests result from not centering and not listening. You might as well have a sign above your head saying, "Take everything I have from me until I am bled dry. In exchange, will you Love me, cherish me, and take care of me in whatever way you choose—if there is anything left of me."

Although it looks like service and Love, it is actually a manipulative form of codependency. You are doing something to get something, rather than from pure desire to do it. Even worse, what is truly being sought is never verbalized, thus never received. This is done in families, relationship, jobs, and business.

Manipulation and unspoken contracts create a depletion of personal power, resulting in an imbalance of energy. In attempting to achieve a specific outcome, the individual sets a trap where he imprisons himself. He barters himself into unnecessary busyness and business, in order to continue receiving the perceived benefit the outside offers. All the while the benefit is also a distorted, watered-down version of what is really desired. Real Love never costs, asks of, or barters.

Unbeknown to the one(s) outside, they consented to this bartering, manipulative relationship, receiving a washed-down version of what they seek. In the end, neither is happy. Both individuals feel unfulfilled, resentful, and disillusioned about Love, life, and the relationship. They will either continue to wear the masks or a rub in the relationship will begin to form beautiful cracks and separation.

The body will never let a misalignment go unknown. This human spacesuit is a high-tech instrument with monitoring systems, communication devices, and subtle vibration sensors. The body has an intelligence that goes beyond the brain. It is intuitive and guides in very specific terms. Sensations, feelings, and health issues can easily assist one in determining what needs resolution or reconciliation. In the long run, if you are not listening, the body will let you know. The body Loves you enough to stop you, especially when you won't stop yourself. This appears as illness, disease, accidents, and pain.

Most people have lost touch with the body. They use it—even abuse it—but do not fully understand its abilities. The body will assist in establishing natural balance if you are present to what it is asking. Sensations and intuition will guide you to understand the rhythms and cycles of your nature. In following this subtle language of life, all interactions become easier.

Balance is achieved when one pays attention to the self. Knowing and following rhythms of the body will create periods of activity and rest aligned with the Universal plan. It maintains a flow in which you attain synchronous support from the Universe.

What *have* you got to lose?

What have you *got* to lose?

Those two questions have two entirely different inferences. One asks, "What is at risk in your life?" That question comes from the head. It is the place of fear. It is what stops you from being open, vulnerable, and authentic. Our belief in the false reality we live, the surface connections, and the facades we have built are what we are so afraid of losing, without any concern that we have already become lost due to those very things. This perspective asks that you turn your back upon the spark of Light that rests within you, turning your back on the remaining part that would make you whole. This is conformity.

The other question comes from the heart. It is in a compassionate and soft tone. Whispering gently, it urges you into the Light, by way of the ember glowing within the dark. It is beckoning, "What you are willing to let go of? Will you let loose? What is surface, shallow, false and of the masquerade? What have you 'got' to lose in order to touch what is real?" This is the place of courage.

The truth is there is everything to lose and nothing to lose. In order to truly know our full expansiveness and the entirety of loving essence that we are, we have to drop all containers and parameters that have given shape to something meant only to be fluid and free. The expansiveness of you can never be contained. Love is not to be held or encased. Love is not to have boundaries that limit it or walls that confine it. We must lose, or let loose, everything that keeps us from seeing and honoring all of who we are. And on the flip side, we have nothing to lose because that which is real can never die, never change, and never be lost. Truth unites.

Maybe that is why I feel so free. Regardless of what is shared or experienced, it really will be okay. Why? Because I am doing it for me. I am freeing myself from the very pieces in my history that taunt and tease. It is those pieces that keep creating any remaining chaos. No matter how much inner work has been done, it is the hidden parts of ourselves that are attempting to get our attention. Without these parts, I would not have become who I am, nor would I have walked in the direction of my highest Light. Light is not evident in Light but it can be seen if there is darkness. Without your hidden pieces and parts, your shadows and your shame, you would not "becoming." Don't just think outside the box; think outside and beyond all reality and illusion. Your life requires your death. You cannot keep spirit in a bottle, cage, personality, ego, career, lifestyle, structure, routine, rut.

Truth Fullness

>> When have you controlled or held captive your heart or another's heart, or left someone behind?

>> Let your heart reveal what it believes to be your deficiency and defense.

>> What have you traded off in the name of Love?

>> Listen to the body. What parts ache, hurt, or have not been Loved?

>> What has it been asking of you, repeatedly, that you have not done? Now, do that.

Will Fullness

Ask your wounded heart to ponder your life fairy tale, the villains, and the happy ending you desire.

It is time to learn to move your body. Increase your movement practice beyond what you have. If you still have none, begin one. If nothing else, walk 20 minutes a day with no distractions of music or talking. Give this time to your Self.

When you complete any activity, spend a few minutes in the silence. Deepen your stillness practice beyond what you have. If you still have none, begin one.

The voice is still, and small. Hear it—and listen.

❧ 31 ❧

Me and My Self

Heart Fullness

I tithe. I feed the homeless. I smile. I'm polite. I even say, "Bless their heart" instead of what I really think. I go to work. I come home. I do my best to be kind and pay my debts. I forgive constantly. I have cleared, cleansed, and prayed. I have been down on my knees, hugging trees, wading through waters and up on mountains. I have sweated through lodges, walked on hot coals, and sat naked in a forest for three days. What else does it take to create life the way I want it? What's the deal, already?

I've been baptized, shakti'd, initiated, and moved through rites of passage. I have had Reiki sessions, done breathwork, and sat under pyramids. I tap myself, twist like a pretzel, and lie in hyperbaric chambers. I sage my house, incense my car, and put salt in the corners of windows. The white candles are lit, the water is on the sills, the black clothing has been discarded. I've Om ed and Amen-ed, meditated and mediated. All the while, moving through my stuff. I have even looked inside to myself to clear their stuff. Hell, I give up! Forget the world! I need to save myself! Drop the oxygen mask already! I surrender. Do you hear me? I SURRENDER! I SURRENDER!

Continue this dialogue, using your feelings and words. Journal your thoughts before moving to Mind Fullness. If words do not come, draw. If you cannot draw, doodle. Breathe. Feel. Allow. Receive.

Mind Fullness

Self-care raises the flag against all injustices from anyone or anything that goes against the needs of the sacred body temple, anointed heart, elevated mind, or spiritual being. This is probably the greatest lesson we all must learn. It is also the true gift to another, in the example that is set. In addition, an individual is unable to have real empathy or support another in Love, without codependent motives, unless having released one's own manipulation of self.

This is your lot—and your lottery? What will you do with it? How will you use it? Who will you share it with? Will everything remain the same, or is it time to change? What do you consider most important in this life experience?

The wounds that were inflicted by others, knowingly or unknowingly, stemmed from the wounds inflicted upon the Self. The abused became the abuser, becoming the abused once again. What better way to believe one is unworthy, un-Lovable, or not good enough than to deny oneself their own time, attention, Love, and compassion. We thought what we were receiving from the outside world was hurting us. However, what are we doing to hurt ourselves? What about the negative self-talk, negative emotions, self-neglect, and self-abandonment? We use these as building blocks to create the people and life circumstances that project back onto us from the outside world. We then batter ourselves through guilt, shame, and apathy. We are consciously unconscious of the abuse.

In doing so, harmful, unsupportive relationships are allowed in. Overwork, addictive behaviors, and negative environments become our manner of leisure. All the while, we know what we need to do, but do not believe ourselves worthy enough to do it. Yet, a deep core part, the initial spark of Divinity that birthed us, is seeking to recall that knowing through experience and integration.

What would need to happen to make you stop and take notice? Why wouldn't you finally give yourself all the things you continually say you will get around to? What will allow the growth experiences and interactions you fight so hard to avoid? Maybe the most loving thing you can do in this moment is let something or someone go. What if you released the attachment to a particular outcome?

Consider getting to the heart of what you want from others, your life, and yourself. Unfortunately, for many people, self-care does not begin until illness, tragedy, or heartache occurs. It is not important enough until we create a time and space where there is nothing else to do but receive care. Is that really what you want to create? Or, would you like to consciously choose to make experiential growth changes?

Self-care consists of two layers. The first layer is the most challenging because it means taking time for oneself. We have to recognize what we have invested in. Look at where you spend your time, your energy, and your focus. If it is outside of you, it cannot possibly be on you, much less inside of you. The integral point of change comes in conversations the human being has with its spiritual being-ness. In giving up time to jobs, experiences, and people that really do not feel good, we are exacting a cost to ourselves and investing in someone else's life rather than our own. In giving up energy, we do not allow our full life force to surround the true Divine plan in store. By giving up your focus, the vision blurs.

These are parts of it, but a very small part. They are the initial hurdles we move through to approach a greater awareness of what true self-care and self-Love encompass. There are aspects involved that we may not even be aware of—or perhaps have fought our entire lives, because they are foreign to the personal experience. Unfortunately, the Self is the first attention and intention thrown out when other people, responsibilities, or life circumstances appear.

Why do we so easily abandon ourselves? What is the sense of urgency for everyone and everything outside of us that pushes personal needs into the recesses of the mind? In creating endless distractions, we remain ignorant to answering the call the Self keeps sending out. Those initial calls began at the very first wounding ever experienced. That was the moment of lost Love, the moment of forgetfulness, and the beginning of fragmentation.

Our riches and our richness correlate to the degree of self-care we have in our experience. Self-care is concerned with self-value, worth, and the depth of Love with which we view ourselves. How is it possible to be abundant and wealthy if deep down there is a feeling of unworthiness? How are you to be cherished and deeply Loved if beneath the surface is a raging ocean of self-doubt and self-criticism? How can you expect others to serve you, comfort you, or be compassionate when you do not give yourself the time of day? A new saying is in order: "Do unto the self as you do unto others." Although we may not always treat others as well as we could, we certainly treat them better than we do ourselves.

You give your attention away unknowingly. You allow others to affect you. Do not take anything personally. They do not know your triggers. *Forgive them; they know not what they do.* Those people that have hurt you, triggered you, and seemingly caused pain in your life do not have any idea of your wounds. They do not know what is going to ding you. They have no knowledge of your beliefs or history. You are not fully aware of yourself; how is it possible for them to be? They truly know not what they do.

They cannot know how you perceive or what you feel. They have not lived your life or seen through your filters. The only one who can set things straight is *you*. Release all people from making your life easier. Furthermore, forgive yourself, because you know not what you do. You cannot possibly know how you are triggering another. Their reaction is only your responsibility in how you handle it. After all, you will not know your own cause for triggers unless constantly inquiring and contemplating.

Instead, find the centering point with the breath. Take in the environment with your inhale. Express your roundedness with your exhale. In this way, you will be more solid and in the flow.

How are you exhaling? The extent of your exhale reveals the depth of your inhale. The exhale makes the space for the inhale. The exhale is letting life go; the inhale is breathing life in. The space in between is the point of magical choice as to whether or not we anchor into deserving or unworthiness. Do you deserve and are you worth the next breath? How deep? How much? How far? What are you willing to inhale? What are you waiting to exhale? It is a moment-by-moment choice. Healing and manifestation are only an instant away. They are hidden within the next breath.

Truth Fullness

» What do I want?

» What do I really, really want?

» Why do I want that?

Will Fullness

Court yourself. Date yourself. Romance yourself. Treat yourself the way you would treat a new Love. Move toward the day that you want to exchange sacred vows—vows that will never be broken because you have not only fallen in Love, but also become friends.

Use the following verses as an engagement vow. When you are ready to marry the self, fully and completely, write your own vows of commitment, spiritual friendship, and Divine union with the soul.

> *I, [your name], take you, [your name], to be a faithful partner in sickness and in health, in good times and bad, and in joy as well as sorrow.*

> *I will help you when you need help and I will turn to you when I need help.*

> *I choose you as the one with whom I will spend my life. I promise to Love you unconditionally, to take all your faults and your strengths, and to support your goals. I promise to honor and to respect you, to laugh with you and to cry with you, and to cherish you from this day forward.*

> *I commit to you in mind, body, heart, and soul—until death do us part. By the power vested in me by the Holy Spirit, my Holy Creator, and in the presence and blessing of His/Her will and all Light Beings. So be it...And so it is! Om Hu Amen... and Ashé!*

Inhale VI: Attention to Self

As the Sacred Self, I midwife all others through my presence. I become the space of purification and power by standing witness to the beauty present, allowing compassion for all involved to experience and express. I AM detached from the outcome but am fully engaged in experience, expression, emotional presence, and union to facilitate the oncoming birth. I see all that is occurring as a miraculous unfolding for one and all.

It is my compassionate selfless intention to:

1. Be present to the space between the breath.

2. Remain in truth.

3. Potentiate the space of Unconditional Love.

4. Immerse in moment-by-moment reflection of my container.

5. Allow others their experience.

6. Clear the way for understanding.

7. Ground.

8. Engage union.

9. Review my Law.

10. Radiate tenderness and vulnerability.

11. Stand as an example.

Exhale VI: Communion Through Self-Love

Dearest Ultimate Soul Mate,

I AM present to US. I support myself in a structure of caring for US. I am ready to lead and to be led down the path of physical well-being, emotional wealth, mental health, energetic alignments, and spiritual atonement, so that I am the giver and receiver of pure Love in the field that surrounds US. I am willing to give myself what I never received, engaging a meaningful communion between US. I forgive my transgressions, self-inflicted abuse, ignorance, waywardness, bystander-ness, and unconsciousness so that I remove the shackles that have bound me, tear down the walls that surround me, lift the coverings that shroud me, clear the denseness that weighs upon me, and unplug the passion dwelling within me. I open my body, mind, heart, and spirit to US.

I ask for the assistance of my angels, guardians, guides, body devas, nature spirits, cellular structure, dimensional selves, parallel selves, Highest Self, Holy Self, Ascended Masters, and Light Beings, in all places and at all times, to fully support this Self-Love journey that has been placed directly in front of US. I stand firmly upon the Divine path of sacred living, Holy being, and intimate knowing of the truth that I AM.

As these heartfelt words are spoken, I know them to be activated and charged with the energy of fulfillment and completion in the highest state of unconditional Love in the most profound and nurturing way. So be it...And so it is!

Forever Yours,

The Lover of the BeLoved

Journey of Essence

Idol Eyes

Heart Fullness

I wait for the day that I can really be in gratitude. I keep taking steps to love myself bigger. Until then, I will just keep saying thank you. Right now it comes from my mind—and out of my mouth. There will come a time that it truly comes from my heart and every cell of my being. Until then, I know this is enough. I will be compassionate and kind to me from now on.

I see you in everything. I feel happy when I allow myself to connect with you. Your beautiful gifts do not go unnoticed by me any longer. I relish in seeing the magic and mystery you gift to me each and every day.

Continue this dialogue, using your feelings and words. Journal your thoughts before moving to Mind Fullness. If words do not come, draw. If you cannot draw, doodle. Breathe. Feel. Allow. Receive.

Mind Fullness

Various sacred texts speak against the worship of false idols. However, few realize that idols are not only in the form of people or "Gods," but can be the things that individual attention becomes focused on—our pain, victimhood, beliefs, and stories. False idols are also those very things we cannot live without: money, certain people, a particular job, projects, a home, a pair of sneakers, a particular food, glass of wine, time—even the investment in someone else being sick, in poverty, or pain, or obsession with a world that needs saving, fixing, or correcting.

Anything used in excess that beckons continual focus or that creates stress and anxiety has become a false idol. We can become our own false idols within the addiction to certain personality traits, habits, patterns, and identities. Let go and let God...Be.

This does not mean you would not care for those people or things if you walked away. It means you know you are stronger than the association with those people or things. Nor does it mean you have to abstain from everything in life; it is releasing attachment to its need. This also reflects a healthy relationship, instead of codependence.

When individuals allow something on the outside to rule their life, or at least control a major part of it, that item has become their "God," a false idol. If any one thing is withholding quality experiences for an individual in other life arenas, then that experience is depleting the essence of the individual. If some "one" or some "thing" holds greater importance than the care, Love, and presence within oneself, false idols are being worshipped.

Prayer is not for God; it is for you. God does not need your prayers. S/He does not need you to bring anything to attention. Nor do you need to ask for anything to be done. In Divine mind, everything is whole, complete, and already done. There is no ill, lack, or limitation. Prayer is not necessary for God; it exists to bring you to that communion with the God of your understanding.

Prayer is required for the human mind. Prayer is a tool for you to lift yourself up and out of vibrations that do not serve you. Prayer is to help you take yourself to the Divinely Right Mind and see clearly. Prayer would enable you to see things as the truth that they are, instead of the illusion you allow yourself to get trapped by.

The only real reason to pray is to connect. Pray yourself up. God, at all times, is connected to and within you. It is you who would stray away. You are the one who leaves or forgets. Prayer is your self-made lifeline back to the Divine. It gives you the conscious method of phoning, or honing, in to that which is the I AM presence.

It is not your job to save your family, friends, or other people—not even the world. The only one you have the ability to save is yourself. You are here to save *your* world—your inner world. The higher your mind, the better you are to your family, friends, and this planet. Make a pact to be more conscious of your prayer-ful connection. Raise your vibe.

Each one of us is a prayer walking. Prayer holds the space for energy to heighten. Every word spoken, thought, and action taken is a prayer. We are the "pray-er" in that we use abilities to raise our vibration to connect to Creation, and in creation.

This requires bringing the mind and heart to a high-frequency state. In anchoring into who we really are, the mind of who we are, and feeling all of the abundance, health, wealth, prosperity, Love, and knowingness we each are, space is present for another to vibe up, tapping into this frequency as the "pray-er" lifts us into alignment with like power. In that sphere of existence, we catch the wave that has the ability to dramatically alter physical reality. Focus and frequency can shift reality if we are able to hold it.

We are also the "prayer." In being named and having our name spoken, each one of us is an activated walking prayer. Every word we speak is creation. *In the beginning was the word.* This is our first gift as Creation creating sound. The words we say are sending out focused frequency into the world. However, we hold the power of those frequencies being low vibrating or high.

My feet are killing me. My bad. I am so awesome. No more war! These are prayers. We implement manifestation in every moment. Initially, words and thoughts are placed into energetic form. They hang in the ethers, waiting to get energized again and again. Repetitive words, thoughts, and actions support them in moving toward physical manifestation. A giant storehouse of implemented prayer hangs energetically around us, waiting for further implementation so creations may drop into reality. They remain anchored in the ethers because we are not living fully within our bodies. In order to ascend, we must descend.

The senses have one unified mission. These are gadgets of the spacesuit we wear. They assist and guide the journey as we man the controls. They are the stepping-stones back to energetic form and expansion. If we stay attentive as captains, they become powerful supportive instruments.

If we step away from the command center, these controls go underutilized and unconscious. The senses are our compass. When this happens, a person travels in a completely different direction. Engaging the senses brings people back to present time, the "now" moment, the path of true knowledge—in other words, the self.

Move your focus from what is above and outside of you to what is inside of you. Reconnect to something absolutely "sensation"-al: *you*! You are endowed with the most sacred of gifts through your body: your seven senses.

The senses provide the experience of awareness:

Sense of Sight	Clarity	The Nature (of) Self-Perception
Sense of Smell	Discernment	The Polarity (of) Self-Love
Sense of Taste	Truth	The Perfection (of) Self-Acceptance
Sense of Hearing	Omniscience	The Silence (of) Self-Awareness
Sense of Touch	Devotion	The Physicality (of) Self-Realization
Sense of Intuition	Presence	The Freedom (of) Self-Expression
Sense of Humor	Lightness	The Darkness (of) Self-Reliance

The outer world has become the master to which we have become enslaved. Chained to all that we perceive externally as freedom, we dismiss the one we keep imprisoned within our own "land." The only means of escape is the underground railroad we each possess. This rainbow coalition of energy centers, known as chakras, is illuminated by the righteous—the "right-use-ness" of the senses. It is time to be freed from self-imposed slavery and bondage, to discard the armor used to fight the world. In doing so we return to the innocence of the Divine child, with all the gifts that endows, as written about in my second book, *Your Journey to Enlightenment*. Your enlightenment is not going to be handed down from something outside. It is going to be given by the grace of your own being, through bridging the Light with the very shadow it has cast.

Truth Fullness

- » What have you placed as false idols in your life?

- » How do you use language to disempower you?

- » How can your listening to self-speak alter your experience?

- » Do you really listen to others from all of your senses?

- » In connecting to the senses, how can you embrace them fully to see yourself?

Will Fullness

Close your eyes and invite your senses. Connect to everything as if it were a missing part of you that has returned. Savor and enjoy each moment by engaging "sense-ability."

Plan a date for yourself. Set a day, time, and location for the date to take place. This is a date just for you and your senses. Make a dinner reservation for one. For the evening, you are to dress and engage a full sensory experience. Plan to go dancing or to hear music afterward.

On the day of your date, go to the store, and buy flowers and a box of chocolate. If you like wine, select a bottle of wine. Choose things that engage the senses. Allow the colors to inspire you. Close your eyes and breathe in the scents. Feel the petals as if you are selecting the perfect gift for a Lover. When you arrive home, place the flowers in a vase and arrange them in an aesthetic way. Keep them around you all day.

Giving yourself plenty of time to get dressed. Select something that makes you feel sexy or sensuous. Choose a fabric that feels good, has texture or shine, and flatters you. Play some music. When showering, use a soap that is scented; breathe in the aroma. Lather the body, engaging touch; feel the water against the skin. (As an alternative, have a bubble bath and make it a leisurely afternoon.) Don't forget the chocolate.

Notice how the air feels when you leave your home. Be aware of every nuance of the evening. At the restaurant, choose something you would not normally order. Savor each bite. Notice how you feel being with yourself. Are you fidgety, nervous, looking down, or looking around? Are you self-conscious or comfortable? Are people glancing over? What are you telling yourself about this? How often do you leave your senses? Can you take yourself back?

Take in every sound, smell, taste, and experience. When walking out of the restaurant, notice the pressure of each foot as it steps along the pavement. Are you moving slowly or quickly? Let nothing go unnoticed. Be completely present to yourself. When listening to music, let your body move in the manner it chooses to. Dance if you feel like dancing. Continue the evening, fully engaging with your senses. Upon returning home, thank yourself for a beautiful evening and the ability to spend time completely present to you.

Mad Scientists

Heart Fullness

Thank you for the synchronicity. Thank you for my life. Thank you for every wound, challenge, obstacle, and block that I have experienced. These are the very things that helped me get closer to you. Thank you for opening my eyes to something I did not see before.

I am so grateful that you held me close. I was never in danger, nor in harm's way. I never was lost or dead. Your hands always held me. Your heart always loved and cherished me. Your mind always inspired me.

Thank you, God, for the journey. I am grateful for each and every step, and look forward to each and every moment, whatever that may be. What an honor I have been given; what a gift I am able to give; what a blessing I AM.

Continue this dialogue, using your feelings and words. Journal your thoughts before moving to Mind Fullness. If words do not come, draw. If you cannot draw, doodle. Breathe. Feel. Allow. Receive.

Mind Fullness

We as parents—all of us—create our own versions of Frankenstein. Each a mad scientist, we create a fallen angel from an angelic being. Children are the "Adam of our labors," eating from the tree of knowledge. As parents, we are that tree. Society, culture, and ongoing influence have become the fruit of these labors as generation upon generation increase the harvest of patterns, beliefs, and wounds. We were birthed in paradise as the sons and daughters of Divine creation. However, we fell from this grace by descending from those who came before us.

The mother and father are to steward creation. We came to help them remember, as guides and teachers of innocence, wonder, and playfulness. Instead, because most parents mistakenly believe they are the teachers, we get branded with their amnesia through the example and control placed upon our lives. We make them our gods; their perspectives our law. This is the sacred trinity each holy text is written from, one filled with wisdom, story, and a whole lot of made up stuff—father, mother, and child.

Each one of us stems from a vast and rich lineage that is no less than any holy book that has been scribed. The teachings are the same. We are each ladders leading to the same place. Our lives, the stories we create, the fantasies made up, and the legacies left are but parables, verses, and chapters in the book of Tom, Dick, Harry, Susan, Mary, Simran, and more. Revere your life as beautifully sacred and holy as that of Jesus, Buddha, Shiva, Mohammad, Krishna. Theirs are no greater, yours no less. We all come from God stuff. We are all the same. Don't take my word; it is what they have said.

Parents represent the "tree of knowledge" from which we are the fruit. As fruit, we come bearing the seeds of salvation. Instead of knowing we are nurtured by the Light, we eat of the very tree that births us. As we fall from the tree, we become lost in its shadows. Parents may or may not realize we are the sweetness to be partaken in order to see where seeds of truth have been planted. Instead, their wounding eats away at the child.

Trees always hold a shadow underneath. These branches are the paths we extend out as experience in the world. Although it appears dark beneath branches, brilliance and flowering stem from extending oneself. Trees continually reach high. Shadows provide shelter and shade during storms. However, the tree is far bigger than its shadows. You are greater than the shadow you cast, bearing the fruit of royal ancestry—a holy lineage whose crown touches the sky.

We are one in the same, each holographic representations of the sacred story: Adams and Eves of different faces and time. The old story is representative of the Old Testament—"test I meant." These are the challenges and obstacles we placed before ourselves to be worthy of God's

Love. However we did not realize, in falling into their conditions, we made parents our god in form. The error of understanding came in forgetting we are worthy of that Love regardless. We never lost it and cannot lose it because Divinity is Love without conditions.

The new story is represented as our New Testament—"test I me not"—when we are willing to recognize the Self always in Unity with the Divine Mother and Divine Father, knowing you are/I Am that Divine child with whom God is well pleased. And who is God but you, all of you represented in every piece and part of the world, animate and inanimate expressions and individuations of the "Oneness, blessing" at all times?

Whether parent or child, sister or brother, you have done nothing wrong. There is no blame. You are not responsible for others or their behaviors. You are to be responsible for your choices. To yourself, and all those who came before you, say: Thank you for being. Thank you for seeing, for holding, for loving, for living. Thank you for standing. Thank you for creating. Thank you for working. Thank you for playing. Thank you for serving. Thank you for knowing. Thank you for remembering. Thank you for choosing. Thank you for....

Who you have been had nothing to do with me. Not your actions, thoughts, and behaviors. Who I have been really has nothing to do with you. Not my dysfunction, chaos, or projection. That truly was all about me. Who I am willing to be and truly am—now that has everything to do with you, and the rest of the world. I am an example who is the journey to Love—my journey to Love and part of your journey to Love.

Stand in the Love that you are. There is no other truth. If you are in struggle, doubt, or pain, you have bought into a lie and there is an old tape playing in your head. Time to erase the tapes; listen to the truth instead. Come, little one, come out of the shadows. You are Loved. You have always been.

Be embraced in the fullness of your pure, unconditional Love. It has always been here. Now turn and face it. It will appear downtrodden, weary, and burdened. It may feel dense, laden with heavy emotion; it is standing in the shadows of a broken heart but strong spirit. This is the part of you that has been the spiritual warrior and fought the good fight. This One has stayed in the background, quietly moving, scurrying, running, and toiling. This One has done, been, and had every experience specifically for your "becoming."

If the shadows are behind you, then in front of you is the brilliance of Light, the all-pervading brightness being emitted through you. There can be no shadow without Light. There can be no Light without shadow; and neither can exist without witnesses. Bridge the parts of *you*, by embracing what lay behind you and opening to what has always shined before you. And say unto the ears of the Divine.

"Merge with me great OverSoul.... Your higher guidance has always led me when I most needed it. I no longer wish to lead. I no longer desire to be guided. I am ready to know myself as Leader, Guide and Steward of my own sacred path through the Divinely faceted path/past to my Soul's true mate. I am the prism that casts light in all directions, the full spectrum of the rainbow color extending across the heavens. As a precious jewel, my radiance shines with the heart fullness of a Grand One Design...GOD."

Truth Fullness

» Can you see the spiral patterns of your life repeating?

» Do you recognize how your life as a most sacred and perfect story?

» Do you recognize what you as a being brought into the world for your caregivers to see?

» Is your life following your "Old Testament" ("Test-I Meant") or your "New Testament" ("Test-I-Me-Not")?

» Can you truly embrace the gratitude for all that has been, all that those around you were, and everything you have been, are becoming, and have always been?

Will Fullness

Create a New Life Dream Map. Take time to look through magazines and clip any images, words, or statements that excite or inspire you. Choose only things you Love. You will have seven sections for the New Life Dream Map: physical, financial, relationship, self-care, social, service, and career.

Create this album or scrapbook as your new sacred story. Have fun with it. Make it decorative and beautiful. This is a gift for yourself, your soul, your BeLoved. Create the highest possibility of yourself. Take time with it and enjoy it. Make it colorful. Go all out and place within it what you really want. If you want to write a letter or list any details for a certain area of life, be specific. Always ask for that or something greater.

Close your eyes, taking yourself to the experience that you want. This experience does already exist. You need only lift your frequency so you can align with that bubble of existence. You exist in many times, at many places, living many scenarios. You have brought your consciousness to one of them. If it is not what you want, you are the creator force and need only lift your vibration into alignment with another sphere. If you have integrated this completely on all levels, including the body, it will manifest and hold.

When the opposite seems as if it is showing up, the Universe is testing and confirming that you really want and deserve what you recently called for. The opposite appears to see if you revert to old beliefs or truly anchor in the new desire. It is the checks and balances of monitoring whether you can maintain the frequency. The Universe wants to make certain you are completely aligned with your request: thought—feeling—action.

The Trinity

Heart Fullness

Who I was yesterday is not who I am tomorrow. Who I am today is not who I was on the day of my birth. Upon each death within my life, I am never the same in any day of aliveness, so why do I drag these identities along? They are simply excess baggage. From now on, I shall travel Light!

What they say is only true about me if I choose to believe it. If I choose not to, then it is theirs to own. I am willing to climb every mountain and each hill. I am ready to find heaven on earth. It is here all the time. I need only choose to see it. I can do this step-by-step, moment-by-moment, always with love. I will see the world with new eyes. I will hear everything with new ears. There is only Love or cries for Love. I will be a Love catalyst in the world. It needs me. They need me.

I shall look at them with Love, hold them with Love, hear them with Love, see any and all actions from them with Love. Love stills. Love heals. Love loves. I am and have always been only Love.

Through my giggles, infinite possibility bubbles out as pathways of Peace. And from my tears, rivers of Light form to heal the world. Deep in the heart of Source, I rest, I sit, I wait. Deep in the heart of Source, I dream, I imagine, I play. Deep in the heart of Source, I create, I see, I Know. And Truth reveals in the Light of Grace, in Perfect ways, in Divine Time.

Continue this dialogue, using your feelings and words. Journal your thoughts before moving to Mind Fullness. If words do not come, draw. If you cannot draw, doodle. Breathe. Feel. Allow. Receive.

Mind Fullness

The trinity is a multi-layered experience of convolution, involution, and evolution. We are each a "merkaba," a chariot of ascension. *Mer* means "Light." *Ka* means "Spirit." *Ba* means "body." We are a spirit body that is surrounded and infused with Light. We are wheels within wheels, spirals of energy existing in and as DNA; having locked within, the ability to move us from one dimension of being to another.

This structure, both simple and complex, allows the experience of vast portals in expanded awareness, a range of potentials within conscious-ness, and memory into infinite possibility. Two perfect tetrahedrons, one inverted and one upright, are the meeting of the heavenly body and the earthly realm. These two four-faceted pyramids bring together 12 unique trinities within us, as portals of longing and belonging. These 12 create 12 outward reflections. Within these wheels of life are many beginnings and endings, cycles of birth and death, each leading to a greater experience of reality and illusion. This is our sacred geometry.

It would begin with the truth: his truth, her truth and the whole truth. This trinity is reality. It is the expression of the Divine Masculine, Divine Feminine, and Divine Child—except most do not experience this first trinity, because people are not living from their truth; they "lie" in their illusion. Instead, the second trinity is experienced: the dance among fear, distorted Love, and the experience of these as You.

The third trinity is the ancestral lineage: his story, her story, and the (w)holy story, that becomes holographically replicated through you. This is the central meeting point of the merkaba, where the gate between worlds is available to all those who wish to cross into the upper realms of expe-rience. The Divine Father and Divine Mother are replaced by physical incarnates sent to steward us. We begin to make those parents who birth and rear us our gods; false idols that have also fallen victim to the gods of their own understanding. Their stories become our stories; layers of time wrapped intricately upon one another until a soul decides to cut through the cloth, creating a new fabric of reality.

We are spirals, both inward and outward. The interior is reflected in the outer; the outer is reflected on the inner. This is "experience" experiencing itself in the (w)holiest of ways. We judge certain emotions or situations as wrong, bad, or less than Divine when they are what make up the fullness of Divine experience. This spiraling energy-in-motion (emotion) can be illustrated through 12 levels of trinity, wheels within wheels of evolution and involution.

Evolution consists of "experience" experiencing itself as masculine energy, feminine energy, and formless-into-form-into-formless energy. We have interpreted the Father, the Son, and the Holy Ghost in biblical terms, but what if it describes the different aspects of the spiral? What if all of reality is purely perception, even how we view the most sacred things, such as sacred texts or prayers—even the Trinity?

What if "the Father" is simply "the Law"? We interpret laws as commandments or Universal Laws. Open to the perspective that "the Law" is whatever you believe to be true. The beliefs one lives by become his or her point of creation, the law of attraction, his or her government. These beliefs, which inspire actions and stem from feeling, activate the Universal Laws. "Who art in heaven" is the reference you hold as consciousness. What you believe in your mind, you become. Law is creation—static and changeable. Thus the container is established.

From this perspective, Holy Spirit is the Higher Self, the invisible guide that knows your truth and worth. Each One is a spark of the Divine. The Holy Spirit is the Essence that is all-knowing, timeless, and formless, playing out in your life all of the time. This part of the trinity is you, as grace, blessing, miracles, signs, symbols, and synchronicity that appear. This would be above the Law.

The "Son" is the human form within the container, the conditions of self in expressions of dark and Light. This is the part under effects of the Law, the lower self. Yet we are interconnected—never separate. The desire to change beliefs (the laws) allows changes brought forth by the Holy Spirit, as well as changes actualized in body by the Son. Through this cycle of change, evolution takes place and the spiral continues. We live via the sacred chariot of ascension, encountering each expanding trinity. Each step is a process of involution and evolution—a dance of opposites.

The 12 Trinities

Trinity	Evolution Involution	Experience Living	Experiencing Being	ITSELF Formless Form Knowing
1st Trinity	Reality The Truth	Masculine Feminine	Action Stillness	Whole Divine
2nd Trinity	S-I-N* The Lie	Fear Love	Constriction Expansion	Experience
3rd Trinity	Illusion The Dream	His Story Her Story	Perception Clarity	Holy Story
4th Trinity	Worth Relativity	Unworthiness	Worthiness	Mastery
5th Trinity	Dark Night Shadows	Reaction	Response	Death
6th Trinity	Hero Journey Light	Unconscious	Conscious	Aliveness
7th Trinity	Chaos Synchronicity	Challenge/ Bondage	Gift/Bond	Grace
8th Trinity	Busy-ness Stillness	Servitude	Service	Peace
9th Trinity	Breakdown Breakthrough	Armor	Amour	Unity
10th Trinity	Surrender Embrace	Replication	Creative Rebel	Freedom
11th Trinity	Creation Imagination	Conformity Timeless	Courage Boundless	Majesty Space
12th Trinity	Universal Law Presence	Religion Law	Spirituality Allowing	Mortality Immortality
Whole Fullness	Creativity Creation	Connection Self-Value	Union Self-Worth	Communion Self-Love

*Self-inflicted nonsense layered beneath pathologies of perception, after being parented and people-pleasing. We falsely believe we are here to keep ourselves from dying, while too busy making a living.

Ascension will be the same for all of us, as is the path to our soul's true mate, because they are one in the same. However, the difference is in the details. Uniqueness and individual genius lay within the ability to create the saga of life into aliveness. We become the walking dead.

Actually, we are here to get busy dying: to stories, identities, and beliefs. Then, we have a real chance for aliveness "being." In learning this dance, dipping down, and being lifted up, the opportunity for knowing wholeness unfolds the Divinely inspired Master Creator. In the final steps, "Law" disappears. All that remains are two, united as one, in the dance: Lover and BeLoved, Soul and Soul Mate.

Involution and evolution occur simultaneously. Presence determines the speed and depth of growth. Each stage of "experience experiencing itself" has a masculine and feminine side. The polarity of one or the other exists until it is brought into balance. Balance arises as we allow the full spectrum into awareness, leading to greater knowing.

Truth Fullness

- » What beliefs have become "the Law" in your life?
- » What do you focus on when looking at the 12 Trinities chart?
- » Are you taking as much time to be present to your involution as you are to your evolution?

Will Fullness

- › Create a *vision* for the experience of yourself:
- › Create a sacred space and an altar for yourself.
- › Place things that lift the spirit, heighten your vibrations, and inspire you.
- › Write daily gratitude prayers in a Sacred Prayer Journal.
- › Create a God-box. Place inside issues you want God to take care of.
- › Create a special place within your altar in honor of your Shadow side.
- › Pick five people you admire. Be one persona per week for five weeks.

Change "Age-nts"

Heart Fullness

There has been no wrong. Every step and choice has had a purpose. Let there be no guilt, no shame. I am special. I am unique and individual, in a world of sameness. I will let it shine!

I shall always see in myself what others may be too blind to behold: the brightness of my Light. My mind and life will not conform to the small ways in which others think. I am bigger than life!

I am precious beyond thought, magnificent beyond words, and Loved beyond any action. I ask myself to Love me to the same degree I am Love's Essence. When I have reached the depth of the earth and the farthest galaxy, I will know a thimble full of the Love my shadows have held for me to experience my divine greatness.

Whatever comes, I will live my dreams. Whatever comes, I will receive my worth. Whatever comes, I know I am Loved. My Love, I hold you close and that truth is eternal because I am you.

Continue this dialogue, using your feelings and words. Journal your thoughts before moving to Mind Fullness. If words do not come, draw. If you cannot draw, doodle. Breathe. Feel. Allow. Receive.

Mind Fullness

It is believed that people do change for better or for worse. However, it is not that they change; their perspective does—the approach to life and the attitude with which one lives. It would be easy to want to blame or shame another in regard to the experiences of my life, but there really is nothing else here. I know it all looks and feels very real, but even scientists know we live in a holographic universe. The truth is, I created my reality by what I believed, allowed, and chose.

Age	Experience
0–11	Forgetting who we are.
11–22	Beginning to feel into who we think we are.
22–33	Not caring who we are.
33–44	Searching for who we are.
44–55	Finding comfort for who we have been. Reflection.
55–66	Connecting to more of the Truth Self. Letting go.
66–77	Contemplating who we were with who we are now. Acceptance
77 onward	Guiding, directing, witnessing, reliving, and reconciling the Peace/pieces.

We believe we are here to be somebody, hoping to be anybody, and oftentimes feeling like nobody. In actuality, we are some "body," but mostly an expression of our perceptions, experiences, and the result of environments. Now it's time to be "all in body."

We have the ability to be anybody if willing to live beyond perceptions, projections, and beliefs. Ultimately, we discover we are actually no body—not form—but Light, sound, and color, ever changing, ever evolving, ever expanding. We are no body, a pure expression of the infinite potential that is beyond form. We are to be nobody by not identifying with any identity, role, persona, or expression, because in the identification is the limitation. We are the unknown, in its full expanse and broad spectrum of lifelessness to aliveness. The bridging of these two end points results in the true experience of humanity and oneness.

All of life is holographic. Each representation is simply an expanded or minimized version of the same hologram. If you look to art, song, writing, sacred text, and life, they all hold the same elements and themes. You will discover the same story among diverse peoples, but the details, approach, and expression bring the difference. This is what has been categorized as our uniqueness and truly only encompasses 1 percent of your entire being. One percent of you is the manner in which you experience and express your life; that is your genius within the collective. The rest is sameness. Ninety-nine percent of each person is the Essence of Divine knowledge, Divine expression, Divine curiosity—Divinity, in its all-ness and nothing-ness. This means we all have the same chance to be, do, and have whatever we desire. Ninety-nine percent of you is dynamic, mutable, creative capacity made manifest.

The other 1 percent is the what, how, who, when, where, and why— the significant elements to plot any storyline. And the whole point of this divergence is our convergence. From the void, that which is the black hole, to matter expressed, leaping back into the void from whence it came as Light—a white hole. It is all black and white, and it isn't. We are on the stage. One side is black. One side is white. And, in the middle is the spectrum of color that unites the two—a rainbow coalition.

It is time to celebrate life. This is your time to live fully, authentically, completely in new discovery. You are on the cusp of your spiritual union. Once we have come this far, we cannot fall back. It is simply not possible. The only step to take is the one in front of you—the empowered step, the powerful choice, the actions engaged in responsible Love.

Begin by taking responsibility in your own life. Look at yourself and acknowledge all that you have been. Forgive your experiences, yourself, and others. Choose healthier steps. Pray. Meditate. Breathe. Play. Broaden the mind and open the heart. Come together in unity, community, and collaboration. Choose to no longer participate in gossip, judgment, blame, or shame. Stay focused only on what good can come forth in, as, and through you. Participate in the things you require to be joyful and empowered.

Your experience is not supposed to look like anybody else's life. It will not be the same. Dare to be bold. Dare to use your voice and express your gifts. Be the unique spirit that you are. Allow others to be who they are. "The God within me honors, Loves, cherishes, recognizes and is ONE with the God within you" is the mantra to repeat in your mind. Create your heaven on earth.

Truth Fullness

- » What are you waiting for?

- » What is there left to say?

- » Will you be defined by your past or allow your past to bring definition to your future steps?

Will Fullness

I Channel. I Move. I Embrace. In the days following, take 15 or 20 minutes for yourself. Put some music on that you Love. Close your eyes and let your body move how it wants. Imagine when you move your body that you are moving your life. Pull toward you what you want. Love into what no longer serves you, blessing its future. Invite into your heart the new dream. Dance your dance. Sing your song. Your soul is dancing and life is the party it has gone to.

Inhale VII: Attention for Receiving

As the Sacred Self, I recognize my actions, my mistakes, my wins, my losses, my failures, and my celebrations. The sacred is the complete embrace and integration of my opposites for my soul's expansion. I ally with wholeness and all-ness so that I may give and receive the many blessings that I AM.

I embrace my sacred holy birthright and human-born right. I openly accept and receive:

1. All I give out.
2. Abundance and prosperity.
3. Loving and being Loved.
4. Voice and expression.
5. Forgiveness of others and myself.
6. Gifts and talents.
7. The responsibility of being a teacher and way-shower.
8. The right use of my thoughts, words, and actions.
9. Expansiveness and being-ness.
10. Transformation and healing.
11. Open doors of opportunity, God ordained encounters, Divine appointments, synchronicity, and messages.

So be it...And so it is!

Exhale II: Communion in Loving Consistently

Dearest Ultimate Soul Mate,

I lovingly commit to being present to US. I welcome the ability to create consistent Love for US. I am willing to witness the waters that surround US completely. I am willing to allow all experiences that engage a loving communion between US. I ask now that we engage in re-aligning and recalibrating US to the highest possible state of balance and respect.

I ask for the assistance of my angels, guardians, guides, body devas, nature spirits, cellular structure, dimensional selves, Highest Self, Holy Self, Ascended Masters, and Light Beings, in all places and at all times, to fully support this journey of loving consistently, placing US firmly upon the Divine scale of balanced living, being, and knowing the truth that I AM. I ask that my life and being be attuned and calibrated to the highest essence available at this time.

As these heartfelt words are spoken, I know them to be activated and charged with the energy of fulfillment and completion in the highest state of unconditional Love in the most profound and nurturing way. So be it...And so it is!

Forever Yours,

The Lover's BeLoved

36

The Divine Mother

Heart Fullness

I Love you, Mom. I have always Loved you and always wanted your Love. I wanted to be just like you—and nothing like you. I cherish every moment we have had together, and I would do it all over again, in exactly the same way. Thank you. Thank you for being in my life experience. Thank you for loving me the way you did. Thank you for being everything I needed you to be—everything I asked you to be before we came here. Thank you for engaging in such a sacred soul contract.

I know you had to be strong. I know you felt you had to take care of us. You were forced to step into a more masculine role. You felt like you had to give up on your dreams and desires for so many others. I see you. I know you. I acknowledge your pain and loss.

Forgive me for willing to be happier than you. Forgive me for letting myself be free. Forgive me for taking care of myself in ways you did not. Forgive me for following my dreams and never giving up on them. Forgive me for loving myself in ways you did not know how. Forgive me for living beyond what our legacy of womanhood has looked like, until now.

Let me show you unconditional Love—that it places a salve on every wound, caresses you gently, and holds sacredly every tear, dream, desire, and wish you ever had. Relax with me now. Play with me. Let us laugh. Open to me. Let us be friends. Let us be sisters. Let us be soul mates on the grand journey called life. May you be blessed, always. I Love you.

Continue this dialogue, using your feelings and words. Journal your thoughts before moving to Mind Fullness. If words do not come, draw. If you cannot draw, doodle. Breathe. Feel. Allow. Receive.

Mind Fullness

Your mother may not have given you Love the way you wanted or needed it. She may not have been able to see you, because she could not see herself. She may have been too young, single, divorced, sick, absent, or wrapped up in herself. Some mothers abandon, some neglect, some devote themselves to their children, but all give themselves up in some way. Some are too protective, too perfect, too overbearing, or really messed up. They all just do the best they can with what they have.

They all came with their own baggage, consisting of fears, beliefs, insecurities, wounds, and generational imprints. They agreed to be that so you could have the exact experience you wanted, and needed, to fulfill your soul contract.

Soul contracts create the space for remembering the divine experience. We are each given one or many mothers to guide us along the journey. They are surrogate representations of the Divine Mother, but in her fallen human form. They engage in contract to rediscover themselves and to steward other souls. They collaborate to create the storyline needed. In addition, they seek to rediscover the Divine Mother essence. In order to do so, they will first have to be everything the Divine Mother is not.

Regardless of your mother or mothering experience, the Divine Mother is always with you, watching and holding you. The Divine Mother is the essence that we call to in the midst of our brokenness. She guides and carries us through the dark night. She is ever present, holding the space. The Divine Mother Loves unconditionally. In doing so, she knows our strength will overcome. She wants to touch us, and does so in our deepest spaces of vulnerability, emotion, and humility. Her heart is so deep that it journeys to the center of the earth, hot and bubbling over with Love for her children. We are ever connected by the divine energetic umbilical cord; it has never been severed, and only needs to be remembered.

The Divine Mother's arms are widely extended. Her eyes are open and filled with unconditional Love. Her heart beats for you. She lives within you, moving as you in the moments you are inspired, Love deeply, intuitively connect, or are able to comfort and hold the space for another. It is she who engages synchronicity, calling forth your angels and guardians. It is her essence that supports, every step of the way.

You can see her in the green landscape of the forest, the droplets of water resting on the earth after a rain, the mist that hovers over the water early in the morning, and the dawning of the sun when light peeks over the edge of the earth. She is the soft cry of a newborn, a pair of eyes that smile, and the gentle hand that holds. The Divine Mother is the moment of feeling full, juicy, overwhelming emotion.

You need look no further than your own heart. The Divine Mother desires to be one with you in loving, expressing, and moving in the world. She asks that you let her in, by loving yourself the way she Loves you. She asks that you take long walks together and intimately speak.

Truth Fullness

The Divine Mother says:

I hold your precious heart, Dear One. I have known every place of pain you have experienced. My Love for you is all-encompassing. You have been asleep for so very long, caught in your dreams and nightmares. I have been nudging you awake, but you have not been ready for me until now. You have always Loved to play dress-up. You leap so passionately into your play. But you did not realize you were playing.

Awaken to me, my child. Let me be with you, so that you do not hurt yourself any longer. Let me Love you, nurture you, and cherish you, as you have always deserved. When you do anything that fills your heart, warms your spirit, and feeds your soul, I AM Love expressing through you, wanting to give more of that to you.

Will Fullness

What words do you need to say to your human mother?

Hello, Mom. I have something to say to you.

Continue this dialogue and journal your thoughts to and about your mom before moving on.

Become the Divine Mother to yourself. Create life, being fully connected to the loving presence of the feminine essence. The feminine is receiving energy. It is the unconditional Love space. Deep compassion, forgiveness, and "care-frontation" are how the Divine Mother speaks to and through you.

Invite it. Embrace it. Live it. Be it. Know it.

The Divine Father

Heart Fullness

Dad, I Love you so very much. Thank you for being such a strong guiding force in my life. Thank you for always encouraging me. Thank you for taking my side. I want you to know that I am grateful for the walk you have taken. I know your heart has a sense of loneliness and separation. I wish I could ease that. I cannot know what it is like to have lived the life you lived. I do know you did the best you could with what you had.

You have traversed life with grace, through tough times and easy ones. It is what always gave me strength to walk mine. You have been an amazing teacher. In watching you, I discerned what I must do and what I must not allow. I want you to know I am here—open-hearted, expecting nothing, placing no conditions. I long for deep conversations, long walks, and time in each other's presence. I want to know you and know your life. I desire to hear what your heart hides and holds back. Trust me, Dad. Let me Love you. Open to all that is here for you.

It must have been scary with all the responsibility of a family, and not knowing what to do or how. I know you had to be strong. I know you felt you had to take care of us. You were forced to give up on your dreams and desires for so many others. I see you. I know you. I acknowledge your pain and loss.

Forgive me for willing to be happier than you. Forgive me for letting myself be free. Forgive me for taking care of myself in ways you did not. Forgive me for following my dreams and never giving up on them. Forgive me for loving myself in ways you did not know how. Forgive me for living beyond what our legacy of fatherhood has looked like.

Let me show you unconditional Love—that it places a salve on every wound, holds you gently, and holds sacredly every tear, dream, desire, and wish you hold. Relax with me now. Play with me and let us laugh. Open to me. May you be blessed, always. I Love you.

Continue this dialogue, using your feelings and words. Journal your thoughts before moving to Mind Fullness. If words do not come, draw. If you cannot draw, doodle. Breathe. Feel. Allow. Receive.

Mind Fullness

Your father may have been present, or absent, deceased, or missing. Your father may have abused you, spoke harshly, been neglectful and uncaring. He may have worked too hard, worked to little, or been jobless. He may not have been able to communicate, let his feelings show, or play with you. He may never have shown up for ball games, cheerleading practice, or piano recitals. But, he did do the best he could with what he had.

Our fathers are born with the imprint of war, oppression, responsibility and struggle on their backs. They have had to witness pain, inflict harm, and carry guilt of their father's pasts. Many fathers never had fathers and their mothers were wounded as well. But they all fulfilled soul contracts so that you could have the perfect configuration necessary to create the life and learn the lessons chosen for your soul contract.

The Divine Father has been watching all along, holding the space for your truth. The Divine Father Loves without conditions and grants every child's deepest desires. The Divine Father energizes us, gives strength, and helps us be courageous. The Divine Father is the underlying support structure that constantly supports.

The Divine Father is the source of energy holding us high in the ethers, and is also that which surrounds us as space. The Divine Father is action, creation, and motion. The Divine Father constantly builds through us.

The Divine Father is the whitecaps of the mountains, the rustling of leaves, the rushing of white water in rivers. The Divine Father is the plant that pushes through the earth, the multicolored sunset on the horizon, and the waves on the shore. The Divine Father's energy is immense and powerful but vast and loving.

Truth Fullness

The Divine Father says:

My child, you have had me all wrong. I am not wrathful or vengeful. I do not judge or punish you. I wish to create with you. I Love you and know your infinite possibility. I am here to be present to you, in every moment. I listen to your requests. I take action upon your feelings. I gift you all that you desire in heart and mind. I give it generously and lovingly, never judging what you ask for. I do not question it. You asked me for the experience of anything, and I give you that experience. It is not real; you are real. You are really me—all of you are really all of me. I shower you with the gift of free will.

Will Fullness

What words do you need to say to your human Father?

Hello, Dad. I have some things I need to say.

Continue this dialogue and journal your thoughts regarding your father and the relationship you have had before moving on.

Become the Divine Father to yourself. Create life being fully connected to the loving presence of the masculine essence. The masculine is the action and doing energy. It is the solution and resolution space. Deep contemplation, authenticity, and conscious living are how the Divine Father speaks to and through you.

Invite it. Embrace it. Live it. Be it. Know it.

38

The Divine Child

Heart Fullness

To my BeLoved children,

Forgive me for my own amnesia. I Loved you enough to live out experiences that support you in ways neither of us know yet. I give you permission to be happier than I. I give you freedom to live your life boundlessly an timelessly. I bless your experiences with the all-ness of Love, laughter, connection, community, happiness, health, wealth, and success far beyond whatever has been experienced in the "his-story" or "her story" of your ancestry. I decree and declare you are free and Divine, complete and innocent, whole and Holy. So be it... And it is so. I Love you deeply.

Continue this dialogue, using your feelings and words. Journal your thoughts before moving to Mind Fullness. If words do not come, draw. If you cannot draw, doodle. Breathe. Feel. Allow. Receive.

Mind Fullness

I look back on my life in awe at times. It may seem hard to believe, but I would live every minute over again, exactly as it was. I would not change anything. I have no regrets. I would make all of the same choices, because those experiences led me to exactly this place of reverence and gratitude. I have been able to experience a grand expanse of myself, achieving a level of peace that is instilled so deeply that I am able to witness creation from a unique vantage point. Most importantly, I accept me fully.

I had been waiting for so long to be in Love. I had been waiting for it to show up on the outside. What I learned is that "in Love" is a field of energy—a frequency. I had mistaken it for a feeling, when it is actually a be-ing. It is something that anyone can embody. We are in it all of the time, but may not always rise into the presence of it.

I can be in Love while dealing with every experience. I can ask myself, "What would Love do?" When I respond, "In Love," as Love and with Love, I transform everything around me into a place of Love. I have been reaching for the BeLoved when all I had to do was "be Loved" by me.

This is the moment to do what you have not done, be who you have not been, speak what you have not spoken, and allow the change that has been waiting to create something new for you. This is your moment. This is my moment. This is "moment-us"! It took 14 billion years of Universal time to get to this moment. That is a very long labor for the Universe to experience me. My fingers are here to write. My legs are here to dance. I have eyes to see great beauty. I hear the laughter of my boys. My very large heart desires to feel every nuance of life.

I have lived the dream and created my reality. I have experienced illusion and known insanity. The topography of my landscape has been rolling hills, peaks, valleys, mountains, and cliffs. I have sunk and swam, died and lived, leapt and fallen, crashed and been caught. I have had it all. Grace met me at every turn. It is the same for you!

I see how it could appear as chaos, if from the outside looking in. But, when looking from the inside out, it is a magnificent Love story of creation, romanced by Lover and the BeLoved. How could I have known life would be so immense and beautiful? Who could have known Love could be so sweet? Why did I not realize before now what was there for me all long? Dearest BeLoved, you have finally come....

I AM Truth Fullness

From the Divine Child:

You believe you are on a journey. My BeLoved One, you use this word as a consolation for where you are in life and what you have been through, thinking there is somewhere to go. It is no consolation. You are always where you need to be. It is a celebration. You are not on a journey. You ARE the journey.

You are MY journey through time, space, emotion, experience, and evolution. You are the manner in which I journey. You are MY creation and I journey through you. Your choices either limit my journey or allow me to experience myself again and again and again, as new.

When you get caught up in the seriousness of "your" journey, you send yourself in an endless loop. The journey you believe yourself to be on is only a speck of time you have wrapped yourself around. It is not you. It is not all of me. My dear, free yourself to experience. Become the journey so that I may "be-coming" through you.

You feel you have been through the fire. You fear it, but do not realize that your limitation is frightened of being released. The limits you believe in are your investments in your human-ness. I am asking you to release your hold on being human and become god-man, so you reclaim your humanity. You do not see me because I AM you, all of you.

In the past, your walk into the fire has been forced. Change was thrust upon you, but it is the fire of transformation that burns both ends, duality and nothingness, so that you melt into completeness. I AM complete; I AM completion.

You have the opportunity to take hold of the journey that you are, with consciousness. Step boldly, leap passionately, and dive completely into the flames that will release you. Willingly decree and declare your truth by burning through everything you have ever held. Be open to the unknown expanse you are—that I AM. Find your true Light in the flames you fan. When need arises again, step with Love into the fire and burn through all your limits, lacks, addictions, doubts, weakness, insecurities, and judgments. From the ashes of your longing shall you emerge strong and free.

All the past will fully release into the nothingness from which it came. What remains is possibility. The place of new life lays waiting, fertile and ready. Are you ready? Don't you understand that your journey never revealed you to be broken? This was the prism of perception that cast many facets of experience, one of which you focused upon. Be broken open, bringing forth the gift and blessing that you are.

Light dwells inside of you, bubbling with brilliance to be expressed, coursing with courage, calling you to be committed to yourself, and in service to all awaiting you. It does not require your doing because it IS your being. Open your eyes! Open your ears! Open your hands! Open your body, mind, spirit, life, and ability to be Loved! Set LOOSE your SOUND. SHINE your LIGHT! COLOR your WORLD! RELEASE your SPIRIT!

You never truly believed that you deserved ALL that acknowledging the Divinity within you bequeaths. Now is the time. This second— THIS MOMENT—this OPENING GATEWAY OF TIME, YOU ARE THE HOLY EXPRESSION DIVINE ONE. You are deserving of what Love unfolds in, as, and through you!

The world is awaiting your Mastery! Raise ALL of your voices— that they express their frequencies to the fullest, completely integrating the fragmented pieces and parts that you are holding. "Re-cognize" the powerful blessings and sentiments those parts present. Forgive yourself for what you did not know. This is the moment "for-giving" back unto you the peace of your being. Let those voices return to become the chorus that celebrates YOUR BECOMING. Your soul song is to be sung, your dreams are to be more than dreamed, your blessings are to bless the world. You are too Be-Loved.

Let the world know the true expanse and fullness that you are! Bring forth your desire to experience yourself to the fullest, allowing talents to shimmer forth, fully manifest, in all the ways and means that are your Divine possibility. Open yourself to the greatness desiring to unfold from within to without. Let your beautifulness shine. "Be-YOU-to-Fullness"!

Dearest Divine Child Within me,

I have finally found you. I crossed deep valleys, great gorges, and scaled high mountains. But, sweet Love, I am here. I long to spend all of my days deeply in your heart's embrace. I want to know the softness of your soul, the depth of your emotion, the expanse of your mind, and the sensuality of your essence. I am here to discover you in all of your glory.

I hold your every dream and desire as a sacred prayer. I see your beauty and I bow down in gratitude. Your great wisdom and power are my treasure of time and space—an eternity spent searching for what holds meaning and truth. Let my Love be like a soft blanket you wrap yourself in. Be always protected and cared for here and into the Beyond.

Remain with me always, nestled in my tenderness. I shall cherish every moment and kiss each memory. Let us dance among the stars and swim in the ethers. Laugh and play with me. Let us create and dream together. May I inspire you and breathe deeply with you. I am here for you, to discover all of you, to be with you. I want to experience ALL of you. Have my Love. Have it. Feel this Great Love. Be "In Love" with me now, forever more united as One. In Love, Of Love, With Love. Yours Truly in complete devotion.

Will Fullness

Write a Love letter to any and all age stages in your own words. There are little orphaned parts of you that desire to have attention and hear certain words. They want to create with you and asset you in stepping into your dreams. Spend time getting to know them, their desires, and what they love to do.

Inhale VIII: Attention to Unity

My Oneness accepts "all that exists" as extensions of my one Self. The world and experiences are representative of the collective consciousness that I AM in its current state of my Oneness, the illusion of which is division and separation. My collective Oneness is dependent upon my singular Oneness; I AM that whole, Holy, and complete Oneness! Sacred, unified Oneness is the manifestation of my unconditional Love. I AM unconditional Love manifested!

As a commitment to my Oneness:

1. I open my heart and my mind to celebrate all emotions and experience.

2. I embrace Self-Love, self-acceptance, and self-forgiveness.

3. I seek experiences that expand joy, passion, and purpose.

4. I engage authentically celebrating my similarities and differences.

5. I embrace engaging with all things in order to know *all* of me.

6. I spend time with my Self and Holy Self and my Whole Self walking the essence of my Divine Self.

7. I question everything, in order to create new reservoirs of empowering beliefs.

8. I enact ways of conserving and caring for my energy, my body, my mind, my heart, my spirit, my Self, my home, and my planet.

9. I listen to my heart by allowing time for silence and feeling.

10. I close my eyes, ears, and mouth when seeking my own answers.

11. I pray for peace: inner peace, outer peace, "Master-peace."

Exhale VIII: Communion as Unconditional Love

Dearest Ultimate Soul Mate,

I lovingly commit to being the unconditionally loving masculine and feminine completion of US. I welcome the ability to be mother and father of the beautiful Divine child that I AM and create that Divine trinity of consistent unconditional Love for US. I am willing to witness a world that feels safe, secure, peaceful, and generous, despite the chaos others need to experience. I understand that I am in the world, but not of the world. I anoint myself in the sacred and holy waters that surround US. I am willing to allow all experiences, knowing that all things reinforce and continually engage a loving communion of Oneness between US. I ask now that we marry, fully and completely bringing together, all of my orphaned children, disenchanted beliefs, discarded suppressed emotions, unfulfilled dreams, misaligned perceptions, and misdirected expectations with their Divine mates of the Divinely blessed child, creative mind of infinite possibility, sacred energy in motion, manifested dreams, clear sight, and personal responsibility. I AM the child with whom God, Source, Universe, Sacred Mother, Divine Father, and Holy Spirit are so well pleased. I can do no thing wrong.

In claiming my rightful place as a Divine Being walking, I decree and declare the release of all present life karma, past life debt, and generational curses. I live out my pure purpose of life in each moment experiencing, engaging, and discovering the expansiveness and creative ability that flow in, as, and through US. There is no end to what I conceive, achieve, and receive. There is no end to that which I AM. I seek myself lovingly to no end.

In gratitude, I stand with my angels, guardians, guides, body devas, nature spirits, cellular structure, dimensional selves, parallel selves, Highest Self, Holy Self, Ascended Masters, and Light Beings, in all places and at all times, fully supporting this journey of learning how to unconditionally Love US as my one true life purpose. It is my prayerful Attention to experience myself loving, living, being, and knowing the truth that I AM.

As these heartfelt words of my Divine soul contract are spoken, I know them to be activated and charged with the energy of fulfillment and completion in the highest state of unconditional Love in the most profound and Divine mana. So be it...And so it is!

Forever Yours,

The Lover and the BeLoved

Mystical Divorce

There come many moments in life where the intense sheer pain of suffering creeps in and tears away the very foundation of life. In that moment, everything is upside down. The world goes topsy-turvy, as a chaotic whirlwind continuously keeps the mind in a spin. This natural disaster is meant to place us on the ground where we cannot move, where we must sit, feel, and allow something to die away—something that was never meant to be held in the first place. As what was once known fades into ashes, something new rises, and its brilliance is far greater than anything we could have ever imagined.

There is a place for divorce in the journey of the soul; it is that of mystical divorce. This place is the only place where separation and Oneness meet. Everything requires merging, bridging the space between all meaning, definition, and that which is odd, and at odds, with any another. Mystical divorce is different from traditional divorce.

Traditional divorce is the separation of two halves that tried to make whole. However, these two halves brought with them their sameness. What happens when you place two batteries of the same charge together? They repel each other. This is why there is conflict in relationship. It is not that the two are so different; it is because they are so very much the same. It begins as power surges. Unless grounded, these surges will continue until a fire ensues within the relationship. It is this same fire that attracted you in the first place—the right chemistry. The fission and fusion of your chemical makeup brought you together as the two prongs of a three-pronged cording.

When one of the individuals begins to change positively or negatively, there will be a charge. It becomes an active charge, so powerful that it requires balancing. If the power is too strong to come into balance, it must blow up, resulting in what we see as divorce. I am not just talking about traditional marriage here. It could be a workplace or an organization. Typically this will be any situation that is reactive and friction-oriented. Neither good or bad, it is what it is. It is an opportunity for those like charges to attract and repel until each meets and calibrates to another of equal power. Then, they relate in a balanced way, where a pure flow of energy keeps all operations running smoothly.

Mystical divorce is different because it takes divorce and works on the inside rather than reacting on the outside. Mystical divorce absorbs the responsibility for core wounds and codependencies that engage outer dysfunction. Grounded in a place of unconditional Love, all perceptions, projections, responsibility, and reaction are taken off of the other and placed back upon the Divine line of the self. This individual releases all need to save, fix, or heal anything externally. The individual focuses his or her attention on what he or she received. Deep, soulful gratitude is held for what has been gained, learned, and grown through the outer relationship. This stance allows the other to continue, holding deep awareness of his or her Divinity in all choices, knowing there are no wrong turns and no mistakes.

Through mystical divorce, you are able to finally marry yourself. There is detachment to all that is outside of you from the stance of codependence to one of interdependence, knowing that that there is only One Love to focus on. Place all of your attention and Love back into your body and heart. Focus dreams, desires, wishes, talents, gifts, and creations inside the Hara line (the line of Light on the front of your spine that extends to the far reaches of space and time).

A bridge forms between separation and individuality to connection and reunion. This is Oneness: that of Self and other, Light and dark, wounded and wholeness, heart and mind. As you marry the shadow self with the more evolved self, a heightened being is born. In coming back into connection with the two sides of the self, we are able to view all others as connected, despite their behaviors, reactions, stories, or experiences. It is imperative at this time that we each reach the place we can see all others in their Christed Light.

We also see that the Light and dark reside within and nowhere else. In "reflecting" on the inside, we see clearly what has been reflecting on the outside what was held in the consciousness of mind and heart. Everything that has been experienced was created in the mind to then be brought into the heart. And in doing so, we are able to move down into the gut to find the essence of power. The more we are in our power, it becomes rooted, grounding us in full connection with Mother earth. That is the eternal gift. In this way we claim our Divine inheritance, the kingdom of heaven, reigning as the great Lords of understanding. In this way, "as above so below."

We have all been busy trying to ascend. But where exactly does Spirit have to go? It is already ascended. We are here to descend—into form, into the body, into earth, back into our true nature. Through that we loop back up in infinity.

A perpetual intercourse opens between heaven and earth, a Jacob's Ladder upon which angels ascend and descend. The kingdom of heaven is simply where we are right now in form; it is you. You are the kingdom of heaven. The "ladder" is the 13-inch highway between the head and heart that we, as angels, travel back and forth. Our willingness to continually ascend and descend between the mind and heart within our own being is the journey to the promised land. It is the bridge—the space between the breaths of the walk where reflection can take place.

We journey to the mind to think and perceive. When the reflection of the world shows us what we believe, we begin descending into the heart to feel. Feeling gives time to be in the reflection from the senses. Our sight now looks within. Ears listen to the quiet. The depths of being are touched. What we truly long for is tasted. We smell with discernment how we are being. Our sixth sense of intuition rises to guide us back up Jacob's Ladder, where we place in heaven that which we will have on earth. Heaven, the mind, is where we plant the seeds that are to appear on earth, the heartland. You see, there is nothing "out there"—no thing. As the seeds are placed within the heart and begin to grow, feelings grow. In this place of reflection is the power of creation on the outside. Here is where we create what we see "out there," that illusion that feels so real. We Love ourselves enough to create outside of us what we are feeling in our bodies and our hearts. You create in reflection "in and on earth as it is in heaven."

The prayer reads "hallowed be thy name," but most walk as if "hollow be thy name." *Hallowed* is sacred, venerated, and holy; the latter is empty and void, nullifying your Divine sacredness in its totality.

Thy will be done speaks of the power of your will as God walking. You have a choice between free will and Divine will. Free will is control and controlled. Divine Will is "free" and freedom. You are that Divine spark, the God of your own understanding.

Don't you know that you speak out loud your ills, your wants, your pains and complaints? As God walking, you are stating these prayers. From the "lips of the Divine" that you are to the "ears of the Divine that you are," you speak prophecy in the word you say. You create your reality with the power of prayer amplified when you speak it. And because there really is no one here but you, who do you think you anoint those prayers upon?

Judgments, gossip, blame, harm, and violence spoken are powerful prayers you bring into creation upon yourself. As you give, so you receive; it all eventually has to come back to you because there is no other. "Thy will be done." Your will is always being done. If your will is Divine will, then life shall flow. However, that really means giving up control and letting go. Love thy brother as you would Love yourself, because your brother is you. I am not my brother's or sister's keeper; I am my brother and sister. Are you ready to fly by the seat of your spiritual pants?

Sacred Marriage

A moment arises where awareness bridges what was to what *is*. Through connecting the dots along the way, the beautiful path of devotion reveals a Divine courtship that has taken place from the moment of your birth. It has been the journey of the soul. You separated as a Divine act of Love in order to experience the greatest romance of all time. This walk has been a courtship toward union and communion, giving you the gifts of the greatest Trinity of all: Love, Loving, and Being Loved. In unification, through the vessels of energy, growth, truth, and wisdom, holy matrimony is the reunion of the many reflected facets of a prism of Light. This Divine marriage brings together Shadow and Light, Divine Masculine and Divine Feminine, mind and heart, body and soul.

When individuals "heart-fully" embrace themselves in Love, they energetically extend the invitation. They are inviting the world to bring like kind individuals who understand the consciousness of heart-full embrace. In that moment, God meets God, Lover unites with Lover, and the BeLoved becomes One.

Marriage in the metaphorical sense is the uniting of two beings into Oneness. In the soul sense, marriage would unite various aspects of the Self into Oneness: the Divine Self with the human self, the masculine and the feminine natures, the Lover and the BeLoved, the Light and the Shadow. Heart-full embracing integrates the completion of what is already whole, so that further expansion occurs. True sacred marriage is the uniting of all that is and has been whole.

We have misconstrued it all: believing things as good or bad when it was all Divine, especially all that stood backstage in the shadows, living behind the scenes/seen. The blame has been place on ego, another outcast villain that we desired to separate from. EGO does not mean "edging God out," as it has been written many times. Instead, it signifies the preoccupation of "experiencing God outside" ourselves. There is not a false self; it is a very true part of us. Even these parts in reality are the courtship of the shadow.

This fully devoted part of us was the "Fallen Self." It is only fallen because we cast it down. That is the reason that we have the hero's journey at all. The Fallen Self is to be revered as sacred. Lift it back up into the Light and see it for its radiance. In the shadows, all of the "smaller" parts "cast" bring your STORY to life.

The story represents many things throughout our lives. It, too, will constantly change in its meaning. The spiral is ever spinning up and down. When you see its movement, you shall see that it does not matter whether you focus on the downward spiral or the upward one. Its sheer movement is what has you mesmerized. The illusion is that, based on your perception, it can be spinning in a downward spiral or an upward one.

> **(Old) STORY—Spinning Tales Outwardly Reclaiming Yourself**
>
> **(New) STORY—Sacred Truth Organically Recalibrating You**
>
> **(Divine) STORY—Superabundant Totality Omnisciently Reuniting Youthfulness**
>
> **(No) STORY—Soul Truth Openly Recognizing YHVH (sacred name of God)**

Where on the spiral are you? There is no wrong choice. However, there is a particular experience attached to each one. Which experience do you desire to have? Which story will you live out? What experience will you, as experience, have now?

I and Thee Wed

I call forward my angels, guardians, and guides; my light body, higher self, body deva, and team; and their higher selves. I call forward the archangels, Ascended Masters, and all beings of Love and Light that hold the highest state of unconditional Love. I ask for all of my selves, in every space and time, throughout all stories, states, thoughts, beliefs, and perspectives to come. I invite my children, their higher selves, and all beings that are in support of their highest good. I ask that this celebration ceremony of Divine matrimony be the bridge and the blazing flame of Light for all lineages past and future for me, my children, and all those that are the oneness that I Am, for the awakening of Love united in, as, and of all separate parts. May this space be held in the highest sacred order, surrounded by sacred geometric forms of energy, growth, wisdom, truth, and unification, and energized by all symbols, words, and intentions of this sacred space.

I decree and declare my Love throughout all time, in all lives and experiences for all of me. I, Simmi, take thee, Simran, to be my BeLoved, to have and to hold, to celebrate, honor, and cherish, to rise into and with, in all experiences. Into our ever-expanding experience of Oneness, I Am in Love, Of Love, With Love, As Love united with you.

I decree and declare the union that I AM of shadow and Light, Heaven and earth, mind and heart, body and soul, Divine Masculine and Divine Feminine, birthing many Divine children that bring forth ever-increasing capacities higher and higher in vibrations and frequency of Light, sound, color, and Love.

In being a beacon of Light and Love for myself, I hold all of my thoughts, desires, wishes, and divinity within and on my own Hara line, backward and forward, above and below, in all saves and times, throughout all experiences thought of as past present or future. I open, allow, and receive the full expanse of Love that I AM. With this I step into full union and communion with my own Divine beingness. With this I am wed. So be it…And so it is.

41

The BeLoved's Letter

Dear BeLoved,

BeLoved, I see you in everything. I feel happy connecting with you. Your beautiful gifts do not go unnoticed by me any longer. I relish in seeing the magic and mystery you lovingly provide each and every day. We have been intertwined from the beginning of time, rising and falling into each other's arms. We share in the Love through Shadow and Light. You have been there through the Darkest of Night. I see you in the Holiest of Light. May we unite for ever more in full recognition of the beauty and purity of this unconditional Love. I am the Lover and you my BeLoved.

Thank you for the synchronicity. Thank you for my life. Thank you for every wound, challenge, obstacle, and block that I have experienced. These are the very things that allowed me to move, stand, and awaken to our reunion.

I was never in danger, nor in harm's way. I never was lost or dead. Your hands always held me. Your heart always Loved and cherished me. Your mind always inspired me. Your choices and silly antics provided opportunities every step of the way. Your vigil kept me supported. I am grateful for each and every step, and look forward to each and every moment, whatever that may be.

I Love YOU. I am not afraid to say it. I am not afraid to feel it. I am not afraid to give it. I am not afraid to be it. I am not afraid to let you know it. I am not afraid for the world to discover it. You do not need to do anything about it. You do not even need to respond to it. Can you just have it? You need do nothing in return. Your presence is enough. That is why I Love YOU.

I dream of you when I am awake. I see you in my sleep. I feel you in my presence. I hold you in my being. I have been waiting for you all of my life. You have been with me throughout eternity. You are my opposite. We are the same. I love you. Will you receive it? Will you let it in? Will you embrace it?

We walked with grace. I know the pain that you held and the courage it took to go deeper than I ever imagined we could. I am deeply honored to have this experience of experiences. Your arms were around me every step of the way and your back against mine in support. We will always be united in this manner, although now not in "need" of it, but in a place to be receiving wholeness.

It is within the deep pools of your gaze that I see my own reflection, a knowing of all that has been from my shame to my glory. And within that gaze I see the depths of real Love, One that no other could ever give me— that sight of a true BeLoved who is here only to see me, hold me, cherish me, and celebrate the all-ness of who I am. I fall into you, my BeLoved, as you drink me in with the passion of a Lover.

Great spirit of mine, knowing no end, realizing new beginnings that embrace the emptiness and allow fullness, I contemplate your vastness and ponder the smallness. I shall always breathe you, inspire you, sing within, and through you as you dance boundlessly throughout my experience. May the Most High of the ethers, moment by moment, become manifest in physicality for the greatest joy and bliss, deepest connection and Love, highest truth and expression.

May nights be filled with sweetness. Dreams dance in joy and our body held deeply in Love's arms. May our mind be cradled in truth, our heart marinate in Essence, and our Spirit fly wild and free, and then may we awaken in that reality—moment by moment, day by day, for all eternity.

There are moments when I know, yet it has always been. There are experiences where I feel, but you are both in the feeling and non-feeling. There are lives being lived, but you are all of life. I have been seeking arms to hold and a heart to dive into, and all the while I have been carried by your timelessness and into your heart of boundlessness. I am the Lover and you, My BeLoved, are the Divine Union of all time.

If you are open to seeing, it is emblazoned across the heavens as a sea of stars. If you could hear me, you would know my whisper as the wind and heartbeat as forthright as thunder. If you could feel it, you would receive my kiss, placed in every raindrop and embrace through every ray of sun shining down. Have no doubt that you are in my arms. Lean on me. Be with me. Rest in me. You are my BeLoved.

I AM your Lover. I Love you.

❦{ 42 }❦

Why?

"Why?" is the greatest answer of all time. It sounds like a question. We think it's a question, but it is actually the answer and the reason for everyone and everything. "Why?" is the question children constantly ask as they discover their new world, repeating it ad nauseam. It's likely to be the question that is first asked in regard to this book. And, it is what we say in every step of our lives, at every turn, in the face of each challenge, and when we don't know what else to say. We ask it, not realizing its answer are the steps we take. Every great leap in my life has begun with "why?"

If I look back at every step that appeared as dysfunction—work-a-holism, three miscarriages, *11:11 Magazine,* 11:11 Talk Radio, writing books, The Rebel Road, divorce, losing my children, this book—they all had a "why?"

One came before each moment, silently from within. Hidden away was a part of me that knew and forged forward because I was not done; I was being done. The other came loudly from the outside. Outside is the chatter, providing a choice point to stay committed to self, or again be sucked under by the tide of those already lost at seeing.

Why did I become a work-a-holic? Because that is what I needed to do to survive. That was all I knew modeled in front of me. That was my fight-or-flight response.

Why did I have three miscarriages? Because I needed to see how I could not receive Love from myself or anyone else.

Why a threesome? It involved Me, Myself, and I at different times in my life. It is such a holy number, isn't it? The Trinity. Because Love brings up everything unlike itself.

Why have a Love affair? I wanted to feel. Because I wanted to Love and be Loved. Because, even in the most unloving situations, Love is still present.

Why *11:11 Magazine?* Because I wanted to heal; I wanted to do better and be better. I wanted to create something bigger than myself.

Why 11:11 Talk Radio? Because I wanted to feel in community with others, and in that moment as far removed as it really was from people, it was connecting in ways I could not have imagined.

Why write books? Because I wanted to witness what I had learned and share with/of myself in an honorable way.

Why the Rebel Road? Because I wanted to develop the courage to write this book. I had to create the conditions and conditioning to truly help me understand the real meaning of unconditional Love. And, I desired to truly trust, not only writing about spiritual law and principle, but also having undeniable proof of the things I wrote and spoke about.

Why write *Conversations With the Universe?* Life is magical and I saw it. Miracles abound, and my life was living proof.

Why write *Your Journey to Enlightenment?* I never had a childhood, but some part of me knew of its importance. That book is my experience of childhood and the awakening of that in my life now.

Why did I write this book, *Your Journey to Love?* Because I knew I was ready to finally receive my soul's true mate. I knew the only way was in. I knew I was that One—and the block to that one. I am worthy of my own time. I am giving to me in generous and loving ways that no other ever could. I am to be cherished for exactly who I am. I Love myself enough to be true to myself. *To thine own self be true.*

The super "why?": I see what holds many back from what they want. I have lived with enough of my own masks to easily recognize them in front of me. Far too many are living behind masks and their denial of even having them. Whether willing to admit or not, we all hold masks of sadness and tragedy, dis-ease and discomfort, settling and survival. Behind the mask of Divine comedy is the false facade of happiness. I am not saying some of that is not real for many, but true joy embraces the opposite of itself. In the quiet spaces when we are alone, masks fall to the side to reveal the face we do not want to see. But there is beauty in that face, too. We create self-imposed prisons and can't see the door is actually wide open.

Why? I wrote this book because I Love you *enough* to share all of me so you may be willing to honor and acknowledge all of you. I am willing to be the example so that you have the permission to fully feel the depths of your longing and heights of belonging. I thought I could Love "anybody" when I chose to have an arranged marriage. What I discovered is my heart was too big to just Love "any body." I am here to Love everybody—all of humanity. That could only happen in Loving all of myself and reconnecting to my own humanity. This recognition opens the ability to hold the tragedy, hate, and pain on the planet as battered, wounded being-ness. In facing and embracing our humanity, US, the Ultimate Soul Mate expands into the entire collective body of humanity—mine, yours, theirs, ours. If I can let you see that every step of your life was your "why?", an all-important One, then maybe you will willingly leap into your "why not?" That is the place of freedom, courage, enthusiasm—*aliveness*!

I am not shameless, and I have no shame. I stand tall and proud in every step. We do the best we can with what we have until we can do better. We slip and slide and fall, but I guarantee we always rise. There are no wrong turns and no mistakes—never have been—but there is the ever-deepening manner of having more conscious action in place. We can never go back to who we were; we can only more forward into who we have always been. The only way to make a step in front of you is by always holding close the ones who stand behind you. It is all held in our true nature.

The forces of nature surge through each one of us. We are earth, wind, water, fire, and ether—in form and formation. As energy, we move from dust to form, to tears, to fire, to dust, and again and again. *From ashes to ashes*. This is our eternal reincarnation, our cremation. *From dust to dust*; we rise again and again and again. We are simply moving through cycles: experience continually experiencing itself, so that it can know itself, admire itself, see itself, feel itself, and be in awe of itself. It is Spirit, here to inspire, be inspired, and be the inspiration for itself.

I am often asked who inspires me. One would think the names Gandhi, Martin Luther King, Mother Teresa, Maya Angelou, Beethoven, Picasso, and many others would come to mind. They do not inspire me; these are the ones I celebrate. What inspire me are who they were and the walk they partook before they became so known. They are inspirational in how they handled what they had to live through, how they persevered, how they sustained their passions, how they stepped with courage to gain the pearls of wisdom and actions of service shared with the world. Their everyday selves are what inspire me.

Simran is to be celebrated, but Simmi is inspiring. Simran appears as the Light, but Simmi is the darkness that bore the Light. Simmi walked the path from hell's gate to heaven's halls, with the ember safely tucked inside her heart until time to shine. It was the imperfect me, the average me, the boring me, and the wounded me that took great steps and leapt with courage.

This is what must be recognized in each one of us. The average person willing to get up every single day is inspiring. It takes courage to do that. Facing everything known and unknown, mustering up the will, breath, and strength to keep prevailing—that is inspirational.

You are inspiring. You are strong. You just have not seen it from the perspective of truth. That illusion you bought into is sinfully sweet. But the truth, all of the truth, and nothing but the truth is delicious and leaves no cavities to be filled, because you will finally be full of yourself!

While surviving, we are thriving. We create the duality by the way we look at everything, judge, and separate. It is all Oneness. This is the chaos of creative capacity—the big bang of the Universe. From nothing comes something. From darkness there is Light. It is spacious and expansive. It is brilliant and beautiful. And when it knows itself, it will dive back into the w(hole) of nothingness only to come out on the other side as pure white Light.

Stop following, stop idolizing, stop placing people on pedestals as if they know more than you, because you think they have more than you. We are all the same, endowed with equal parts of Divinity and uniqueness. Ninety-nine percent of you is the Divine perfection that every other also possesses. So, we all have the same capacity to create. You are the God code. It is in the 1 percent that is unique. Individuality perceives *what* is possible, regardless of what is infinitely possible. Uniqueness creates the *how.* Our imperfection, as the shadow, determines *who, why, when,* and *where*. Everything else is experience witnessing and experiencing itself.

Go back and read the Lord's Prayer, but now read from the stance of speaking to yourself as if from the self within the shadows. There is only One in the room: you and God. They are ONE in the same. In fact, read every sacred text this way. Listen to every song and see every piece of art in this manner. Creation creates itself in honor of itself. Every word, stroke, step, and breath is simply the Divine in communion with itself, Lover and BeLoved. Would you really hold back this most Divine romance from its greatest experience of Love, Loving, and Being Loved? I can see you in this way because I willingly see myself as the same.

Thank you. Thank you. Thank *you*! You have held my heart with utmost care, and I hold yours sacredly always. You are embedded within me; your being is a blessing. There is no time and space between us. No difference or distance ever divides us. Be with me—in mind, in heart, in essence. In Love. As Love.

Whether we meet personally or not, I embrace you and feel bonded in a way that words cannot express. The dark night of the soul is an intimately personal journey that we never realize is shared by so many others. This writing has been the greatest catharsis for me—to know that I was never alone, that I was not uniquely and especially appointed the cross to bear, that somehow my life had not been specifically targeted or destined in a certain way. May you receive that in truth for you as well.

To reach a place of unity, we must find community. That begins with two, and within; only then can it expand beyond. We have now found that in each other—in our experiences and stories. You are my community, my family: my sister, my brother. Thank you for that. I Love you, and I am willing to be Loved by you. I Love you unconditionally because I Love myself in this way. We are one, always connected, knowing life in, through, and beyond the illusions upon illusions that exist.

I sit in awe and gratitude as I dive more deeply into the unknown. The magic and miracles are in the mundane, appearing exactly as what I could have created out of my limited mind—and beyond. It is clear that the unknown is one's own steeping into the vastness of self. That is the larger, grander experience of Divinity. There is no going back—not even forward; there is no outward—only more deeply into the ever-expanding presence that resides in the Universe within. We are In Love, Of Love, With Love, As Love. We are One.

My heart Loves you. My mind adores you. My soul cherishes you. My spirit holds you. My Being knows you. When I am not with you, I am. When I am with you, we are. What more could we ask for than this Presence? In this ever-expanding hologram, there is nothing between us, because we are One Love. Yet, there is everything between us because we are Unified Essence. I don't know what it is to be without you—or to be with you, because I am you. And it simply is. I am in Love. I am the Lover. You are the BeLoved.

My soul is a fertile garden, only and always experiencing the ever-increasing depths of this feeling, simply in Love all the time that I cannot separate, whether it is Love that I feel—and for whom, or simply just a more expansive greater experience of the Love I have for myself. There is only one here after all. So who is it that makes me rise in such a profound way? Is it simply myself, my mind, my heart, and my being? Do you even exist? Because we don't know, I might as well Love you. Is it too much? Too gushy? Too mushy? How much Love can you stand?

So, I am thankful you are here—and for what you reveal to me about me. Thank you for showing me my darkness and my Light, my shadows and clarity. Thank you for reflecting my weakness and my power. Thank you for all the ways I am able to see my Love and my calls for Love. Giving thanks for you/me/we/us, we are One.

Forever grateful. Loving and Being Love(d).

~Simran

43

Bare Naked

I sit before you, bare naked—proud, humble, and celebrating the allness of me. In the midst of everything harsh, dark, wounded: soft, Light, whole. In its beauty and its brilliance. Through its murkiness and the grit. Demon. Fallen angel. Animal. Human. Soul nature. Angel rising and god goddess. In the mist of what appears to be reality and the fine threads of illusion, draped in the tapestry of story and time. Through the valleys of death, climbing the mountains of longing. Above and beyond the world to belonging. I have crossed through oceans of tears and walked the desert into Death's Valley. I have risen again and again as a Phoenix from ashes to ashes and laid to rest in the winds of change as dust to dust revealed the crystalline nature of an ever rising staircase into the high heart of the Most High place.

I can speak of it glibly now. I have no shame. I literally have no shame. After getting up on stage across the nation, not knowing how to sing, attempting to be funny, and sharing stories of how my deepest pain led to the Light, I would have to have no shame. After doing a two-hour show in front of audiences, from one person to 500 people, what did I have to lose? I was baring my soul, and now it was time to be willing to stand bare naked, merging the dark and the Light, the deepest fear and the greatest Love, the shame and the glory.

I am free—truly free of all my secrets and skeletons, deceit and despair, mania and manipulation—in this unconditionally loving embrace of the dark guardian who sacredly escorted my every action to the careful courtship from the Light side of my being. Why would I condemn any piece, part, action, circumstance, or experience?

I certainly have coached plenty of people who have engaged in far more than I. Vast numbers of people have had far more horrific experiences as well. There are a lot of people in therapy—and even more that probably belong in counseling or coaching. But the bottom line is: Pain is pain. There is no difference in intensity when you are in pain. At that point, it's not about the story; it's about the feeling. And the deepest pain in our lives is derived from the deepest shame we have buried inside. What if we lifted the skirt on shame, so to speak? Might it be ashamed? Maybe it has not about healing anything, but more so about embracing, loving, and recognizing it all. It is really about midwifing—being birthed, and being born again, and again.

The greatest illusion of all was that it appeared to many as if I was fulfilling my life purpose, with the notion that for any of us that is a career. I never did any of this for a career. I did it for me. I did it on purpose because I wanted to heal, grow, discover, and get to know me. Do not do anything for an outcome or an agenda; do it because it fills your heart and soul, and gives you what you need in that moment. The byproduct of this experience has been that it has touched many others in the process.

What is my true purpose? The same as yours and everyone else's on the planet. Life purpose is to live each moment completely present, fully attentive to the feelings and desire that it holds, with complete commitment and openness. Approach every experience neutral and engaged.

The greatest act of service I can give is in being an example. It is the only true way of teaching. It goes beyond the words. The more one is willing to stand in his or her truth, integrity, authenticity, Love, Light, and expression while in full celebration of that nature, the deeper degree of permission others have to do the same. What example are you being? Willing to be and giving yourself permission to allow? Don't you know you are the blessing?

Breathe. Listen. Relax. Have gratitude. Love. This is the only real practice—the only real path. This engages, integrates, and unifies. It occurs within and ripples exponentially. This is power, grace, and truth for living, being and knowing. In the illusion, you need nothing else. In reality, it is all there is. Breathe. Listen. Relax. Have gratitude. Love.

To meet the soul's true mate, the ultimate courtship must take place. The Lover and the BeLoved are a union of this world and beyond. A true soul mate bridges all the gaps between time and space, wounding and healing, and the distorted experience of Love and sacredly being Loved. We are here to dismantle beliefs. This requires a journey through the inner landscape, which can appear like a battlefield, but at the same time has the makings for a beautiful stroll along Lover's lane. Integration of the opposite spectrums of life is how the "Ultimate Soul Mate" will be revealed; that means both dark and Light. This Love that births only grows, never disappoints, and never leaves.

Closure is not in having the relationship; it is in facing the feelings that are there: Loving, forgiving, betraying, denying—creating all that came before and after. It's not that you have to say anything to anyone or do anything unless that feels appropriate, but the you of "now" has to meet the you of all those "thens" and speak, listen, heal, and forgive. The truth is, they exist anyway until you marry them—one or the other running your life behind the new scenes of experience. People are reflections, meant to bring us back home. We are to go into reflection. Which part to "reflect-i-on"? They bring you back to the small *i* so that you may rise to meet the big *I*. The smaller *i* is the doorway to the larger *I*, the larger *I*, the doorway to the smaller—a path of infinite Love.

Let's play all the day long In Love, Of Love, With Love, As Love in the world of ever-ever land through endless days and countless nights forever more. It just makes me happy, giddy, enchanted—and takes me to the place of Lover and BeLoved: the Oneness of meeting the Self in such deep admiration, awe, Love, excitement. Bliss. The heights of floating above the skies in the most passionate and compassionate sensation. A Love affair of soul to soul. Heartbreak to heartbreak, and 'knowing' the river of sacredness that runs through all of it—the river that far too few ever let themselves see, feel, touch. Even to delight in the glimmer of it in the far-off distance is s gift. That is what this is: a full meeting upon the river that IS.

Open my heart that I find myself within the sacred chamber of each beat, that my soul song plays symphonically throughout every sphere of my world. Allow me to develop the tonality and rhythm that is in harmony with the Universe. And may I orchestrate a profound melody that is the ambiance of my peace/piece of the great cosmos.

May I be an instrument of your peace. May I be an advocate of your Love. May I be a sacred activator of your compassion. May I be a voice of your truth. May I be an example of your holiness/ wholeness. May my will align fully and completely in your will. I am the Lover. You are my BeLoved. We are One. Life is a magical tapestry that continues to be woven as it unweaves.

Being one with all things takes place in the heart. Even the earth is part of who we are. See within the word "heart" and "earth" are the same letters; simply a different placement exists, but perspective lets us see one and the other. If you allow earth and heart to stream one after the other as heart beats, a new union is formed—a common perspective: *heart-hearthhearthhearthhearth*. Won't you come to the hearth now and forever more?

There is only one thing that each one of us wants: recognition. It appears to be recognition from the outside: family, friends, partner, and public. But in actuality, it is our own recognition. The need for external validation would decrease if we simply saw ourselves, listened to the self, and celebrated and embraced the self. What would decrease? The struggle. The more you see you, the less you will see struggle.

How can we know ourselves when we are not listening, hearing, speaking, stilling, resting, opening, and believing? What we focus on is outside of us, so how can we possibly know all that is inside? Herein is the path, but either way all roads lead back home. And where do you think home is?

You can have what you want; there is no question or denial of that, but have what is good for you. The question is: How do you want it? Is the subconscious choice "struggle, work, and frenzied chaos," or "joy, fun and ease"? The outside will be where you *see* it; the inside is where you *be* it. In the land of all possibility is where you decree it.

It is not control you seek; it is presence. It is not help you need; it is unconditional Love. It is not saving you are looking for; it is time. It is not material things you want but the space to be together. It is nowhere in the words you think are necessary, but in the depths of your own gaze. Make continuous Love until there no longer is any separation.

There will come moments where your presence is required and you will not know why. You will be taken somewhere in your life where you are the grounding, the healing, and the blessing needed. You will be the answer to prayers. You need do nothing but show up. Your representation is the presentation of remembrance. A leap of faith only requires a step; any size will do. You can never go back to being who you were, but you can bring who you are to those you left behind.

The day appears for you, as does the night. This landscape is designed for you, as every valley, mountain, and desert. The flow is brought to you, as every river, stream, and waterfall. This is life; these are the mirrors of life. What can you give in return? Simply the expression of Love, gratitude, and presence. That is your aliveness and the reflection of your aliveness.

In this moment, you are not being asked to walk through the fire; life is inviting you to *be* the fire that cleanses long-imprinted patterns and tendencies in the world. It's asking you to be the fire of passion-warmth-expression. It's asking you to be the flame of Light that sets off a blaze of change. Stand in the fire and radiate all that you are.

Who knows what tomorrow holds when we are not even aware of what we hold? Who knows what others bring when we will not fully allow what we bring? Who knows the power of community and connection when we are not present in our own continuous communing or connection? There is nothing "out there"; the real Universe lay within.

It is all yours for the making. What in your world is not reflective of the highest Essence in you? What is the greatest beauty—the boldest expression of Love and self-Love that you will open to and allow in your experience of home, relationships, career, finance, sacred space, service, and social activity? It is here for you to invite, invoke, initiate, and illuminate because you are Creative Essence. Now integrate!

If I told you, "I Love you," could you receive it? In its full bounty, would you open to it? Would the words pass through you, or would you hear it? Would you hold it and truly feel it? Can you carry this with you, that you find yourself being carried by it instead? I Love you. These are more than words.

When I say, "I Love you," I am giving all of me to all of you. Cherish it. Don't deny it; don't take it for granted or think these are flimsy words to be easily discarded. This is not a game; it is not a passing fancy. This is everything; I am giving you everything. Can you truly sit in the depths of what I speak of and rise to the heights of what this is offering up and handing over?

Come into the space. There need be no agenda. Come into the quiet to just be with the self, into the sacredness because presence is enough, into the moment because that is all there is, into silence because that is pure Love, into meditation because you are worth your own time. Nothing is required. Nothing need happen. Because it all is.

There is a sacred YOU that rests beneath the skin, bones, muscles, mind, and personality. This YOU has Loved you more than any other. This YOU desires to live, Love, and become. This YOU is powerful. Let this YOU come into view. Allow the silhouette to form. You are beginning to know YOU. Be open to the discovery.

Write a Love letter to your BeLoved in your own words.

Become the Divine Trinity. Create life being fully connected to the loving presence of the Divine Child, Divine Father, and Divine Mother. Know that you are completely with your Higher Self and Holy Self. You are the Father, the Son/Daughter, and the Holy Spirit. You are Divine and Divinity. You are Love and Loving and Unconditional in your Loving. Invite it. Embrace it. Live it. Be it. Know it.

Hello, BeLoved Soul Mate,
I have so much to share with you....

Inhale IX: Attention to One

May I be an instrument of your peace. May I be an advocate of your Love. May I be a sacred activator of your compassion. May I be a voice of your truth. May I be an example of your holiness/wholeness. May my will align fully and completely in your will. I am the Lover. You are my Beloved. We are One. My Oneness accepts all that exists as extensions of my one Self.

In Devotion to One:

1. I AM devotion.

2. I AM Divine will.

3. I AM exquisiteness.

4. I AM rebirth, renewal, and rest.

5. I AM communion.

6. I AM transfiguration.

7. I AM awakening, ecstatic rapture, and ecstasy.

8. I AM sacrifice in bounteousness and truth.

9. I AM "synarchy"* in its harmony and sovereignty.

10. I AM grace full.

11. I AM Invisibility.

*"Synarchy" is defined here as the joint rulership of the two sides: The Light and the dark of Oneself.

Exhale IX: Communion in Oneness

Dearest Ultimate Soul Mate,

In the experience of Oneness...

There is nothing to say...

There is everything to say...

But, the silence says it best.

The Blessing

I decree and declare
my highest commitment to US…
"Ultimate Soul Mate"—Universal Source—Unending Synchronicity
as the great journey that I AM.

May the fire rise,
the wind provide the breath,
the air bring forth life,
the water quench any thirst,
and the ethers energetically protect,
as I awaken to a Divine Union within that Be….

ANNOINTED WITH THE BLESSING OF UNITY!
GRANTED THE GIFT OF GENEROSITY!
ATTUNED TO THE SONG OF SPIRIT!
CALIBARATED TO THE FREQUENCY OF
UNCONDITIONAL LOVE!
ENERGIZED WITH THE ESSENCE OF CREATION
BECOMETH!
LET IT BE SO...AND SO IT IS!

In Love, As Love

I hold sincere Love and appreciation for every person that has crossed my path, known and unknown, because you were a clue, a symbol, a message, an angel, a teacher, and a guide for me.
You, too, are a chapter in the Master-full creation of life.
I am a composite of all those whom I have met and have touched, and every experience that I have engaged.
Thank you for honoring me with your Presence.
I am in Love with you...

I AM

I am forever grateful to those who have Loved and supported me, especially in this last year, with special mention of Tuck Self, Kristi Reagor, Beth Hawkins, Pat Garvey, Lorraine White, Celeste Merek, Beth Parojcic, Radhika Hicks, Shanel Barney, Scotti Holloway, Martha O'Regan, Ann Seelye, NiSco, Stephen Derrick, Chelsea Kellis, Brigitte Bartley, Larry, Chad and Tiffany Reed, and Pammi and Indirjit Singh. There are countless others whom could I could name and fill a book with, who are equally special and mentionable. My sincere Love and gratitude to all of you.

Deep gratitude to Patricia Cotes-Robles, Maureen Moss, Sandra Sedgebeer, Aleya Dao, Juliet Doty, Richard Rudd, Nicholas David Ngan, Calvin Styles, Ken Kizer, Renee Kizer, the sisters of Infinite Love, and the beautiful souls I met on The Rebel Road.

Deep eternal gratitude to you, Iyanla, and all those who surround you, for having been a place of soft Love and tough Love; and for taking me in and pushing me out when I needed it.

Mom, Dad, Mitti, Nikki, and Gogi—you each amaze me. I hold tremendous respect for your lives. I cherish you and appreciate all that we have experienced together. I Love you.

Rick, Harvinder, Punjab, Bob, Jennifer, Dave, Danielle, Rene, Jacqueline, Matt, Maggie, Naomi, Krystal, Mark A., and Mark T.—thank you for being the darkness that birthed my power and voice. Without you, I would never have delved as deeply to discover the well of peace. You deserve Academy Awards.

Docs, angels in the darkness that picked up the pieces of my heart, thank you for mending me, tending me, and administering the medicine my body and soul needed to keep going. I Love you. Thank you for Loving me in the ways you did.

Laurie Kelly-Pye, Michael Pye, and my family at New Page Books/Career Press—thank you for being the purveyors of my sacred text.

My precious Sage and Krish—you are always in my heart. I Love you unconditionally for all eternity. Thank you for being my teachers, guides, and lanterns of Light through the dark. Your faces helped me remember my own.

My Dearest One, without you there would be no Love. We Loved each other before we even knew it. I will continue to meet you in the shadows, as you continue to meet me in the Light. Thank you for engaging in Love and loving, as we dance between the roles of Lover and BeLoved, married in mystical divine union for all time, in all spaces, backward and forward, in all directions, inside and out, infinitely circling the design of the holy heart. May we continue our devotion into the void, remembering and creating, unknowing and knowing, the all-ness and nothingness, in ecstatic rapture and beyond measure for all eternity. I Love you.

In Love, Of Love, With Love,
As Love—with you always, in ALL ways,
Simran

**Who shall you choose to be in gratitude for
your darkness and your Light?**

Honor them.

Cherish them.

Love them.

Forgive them.

Thank them.

They are Divine.

Resources

Websites
Simran Singh's main Website: *www.iamsimran.com*
Simran's books: *www.SimransBooks.com*
Conversations With the Universe: www.ConversationsWithTheUniverse.com
Your Journey to Enlightenment: www.YourJourneyToEnlightenment.com
Blog: *http://simransingh1111.wordpress.com*

Additional Websites
TedX Talk, May 2013: *http://youtu.be/8afTTFIwFrY*

Social Media Links
www.facebook.com/1111Magazine
www.facebook.com/simransingh1111
https://twitter.com/1111Magazine
https://twitter.com/simransingh1111
www.linkedin.com/in/simransingh1111
www.pinterest.com/simransingh1111/
www.youtube.com/simransingh1111

Electronic Media Kit, Images, and Longer Bios
http://simran-singh.instantmediakit.com
For Speaking Inquiries, Interviews, and Presentations, contact:
Kristi Reagor
  kristi@iamsimran.com or *kristi@simran-singh.com*

About Simran

Creative Visionary, Love Catalyst, and Rebel Humanitarian

Simran Singh is Publisher of the award-winning *11:11 Magazine* and host of the number-one-rated *11:11 Talk Radio*. Simran invites people to stand as "Examples of a New World Paradigms" through creative capacity and authentic living.

She is the author of *Your Journey to Enlightenment* and *Conversations With the Universe*. Simran's passionate style takes individuals on a journey into courage, fearless authenticity, and presence.

After spending 30 years in the fashion industry and the last decade as a voice of truth in the field of conscious humanitarianism, Simran's speaking and writings are real, heartfelt, and connecting because she knows where you are, where you have been, and where you have the possibility of going.

Visit www.iamsimran.com for more information.